VISIT US AT

www.syngress.com

Syngress is committed to publishing high-quality books for IT Professionals and delivering those books in media and formats that fit the demands of our customers. We are also committed to extending the utility of the book you purchase via additional materials available from our Web site.

SOLUTIONS WEB SITE

To register your book, visit www.syngress.com/solutions. Once registered, you can access our solutions@syngress.com Web pages. There you may find an assortment of value-added features such as free e-books related to the topic of this book, URLs of related Web site, FAQs from the book, corrections, and any updates from the author(s).

ULTIMATE CDs

Our Ultimate CD product line offers our readers budget-conscious compilations of some of our best-selling backlist titles in Adobe PDF form. These CDs are the perfect way to extend your reference library on key topics pertaining to your area of expertise, including Cisco Engineering, Microsoft Windows System Administration, CyberCrime Investigation, Open Source Security, and Firewall Configuration, to name a few.

DOWNLOADABLE E-BOOKS

For readers who can't wait for hard copy, we offer most of our titles in downloadable Adobe PDF form. These e-books are often available weeks before hard copies, and are priced affordably.

SYNGRESS OUTLET

Our outlet store at syngress.com features overstocked, out-of-print, or slightly hurt books at significant savings.

SITE LICENSING

Syngress has a well-established program for site licensing our e-books onto servers in corporations, educational institutions, and large organizations. Contact us at sales@syngress.com for more information.

CUSTOM PUBLISHING

Many organizations welcome the ability to combine parts of multiple Syngress books, as well as their own c   their own internal use. Contact us at sales@syngress

D1511311

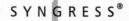

SYNGRESS®

Scripting VMware™

Power Tools for Automating Virtual Infrastructure Administration

Al Muller

Andy Jones Technical Editor

David E. Williams Technical Editor

Stephen Beaver

David A. Payne

Jeremy Pries

David E. Hart

KEY	SERIAL NUMBER
001	HJIRTCV764
002	PO9873D5FG
003	829KM8NJH2
004	BB298H54DS
005	CVPLQ6WQ23
006	VBP965T5T5
007	HJJJ863WD3E
008	2987GVTWMK
009	629MP5SDJT
010	IMWQ295T6T

PUBLISHED BY
Syngress Publishing, Inc.
800 Hingham Street
Rockland, MA 02370

Scripting VMware Power Tools: Automating Virtual Infrastructure Administration

Printed in Canada
1 2 3 4 5 6 7 8 9 0
ISBN-10: 1-59749-059-8
ISBN-13: 978-1-59749-059-7

Publisher: Andrew Williams   Page Layout and Art: Patricia Lupien
Acquisitions Editor: Gary Byrne   Copy Editor: Michael McGee
Technical Editor: Andy Jones and David E. Williams   Indexer: Nara Wood
Cover Designer: Michael Kavish

Distributed by O'Reilly Media, Inc. in the United States and Canada.
For information on rights, translations, and bulk sales, contact Matt Pedersen, Director of Sales and Rights, at Syngress Publishing; email matt@syngress.com or fax to 781-681-3585.

Acknowledgments

Syngress would like to acknowledge the following people for their kindness and support in making this book possible.

Syngress books are now distributed in the United States and Canada by O'Reilly Media, Inc. The enthusiasm and work ethic at O'Reilly are incredible, and we would like to thank everyone there for their time and efforts to bring Syngress books to market: Tim O'Reilly, Laura Baldwin, Mark Brokering, Mike Leonard, Donna Selenko, Bonnie Sheehan, Cindy Davis, Grant Kikkert, Opol Matsutaro, Steve Hazelwood, Mark Wilson, Rick Brown, Tim Hinton, Kyle Hart, Sara Winge, C. J. Rayhill, Peter Pardo, Leslie Crandell, Regina Aggio, Pascal Honscher, Preston Paull, Susan Thompson, Bruce Stewart, Laura Schmier, Sue Willing, Mark Jacobsen, Betsy Waliszewski, Kathryn Barrett, John Chodacki, Rob Bullington, Aileen Berg, and Wendy Patterson.

The incredibly hardworking team at Elsevier Science, including Jonathan Bunkell, Ian Seager, Duncan Enright, David Burton, Rosanna Ramacciotti, Robert Fairbrother, Miguel Sanchez, Klaus Beran, Emma Wyatt, Chris Hossack, Krista Leppiko, Marcel Koppes, Judy Chappell, Radek Janousek, and Chris Reinders for making certain that our vision remains worldwide in scope.

David Buckland, Marie Chieng, Lucy Chong, Leslie Lim, Audrey Gan, Pang Ai Hua, Joseph Chan, and Siti Zuraidah Ahmad of STP Distributors for the enthusiasm with which they receive our books.

David Scott, Tricia Wilden, Marilla Burgess, Annette Scott, Andrew Swaffer, Stephen O'Donoghue, Bec Lowe, Mark Langley, and Anyo Geddes of Woodslane for distributing our books throughout Australia, New Zealand, Papua New Guinea, Fiji, Tonga, Solomon Islands, and the Cook Islands.

Lead Author

Al Muller is a consultant for Callisma, a wholly owned subsidiary of AT&T. He has been in the IT field since 1995, getting his start as a database administrator in the Navy. In 2002 he began using VMware's GSX Server and within a year was involved in his first virtualization project. Since then, he has been an eager proponent of virtualization technology and has worked on a number of different server consolidation and virtualization projects. He holds a bachelor's degree in English.

A native Californian, he lives in San Diego with his wife, Sara, and their dog, Grace.

Al wrote Chapters 1 and 2.

Contributing Authors

Stephen Beaver (CCNA, MCSE, MCP+I, VCP), Technical Editor of *VMware ESX Server: Advanced Technical Design Guide.* He is currently a systems engineer with Florida Hospital in Orlando, FL. Stephen is the lead architect for all the virtual systems throughout the hospital. As such, he develops and touches every part of all things virtual through all the systems life cycle—from design, testing, integration, and deployment to operation management and strategic planning. Stephen's background includes positions as a senior engineer with Greenberg Traurig P.A, where he designed and deployed the company's virtual infrastructure worldwide. Stephen has over 10 years of experience in the industry with the last three years almost completely dedicated to virtualization. Stephen is also one of the most active participants in the VMware Technology

Network forums as well as being a presenter for VMWorld 2005 and the upcoming VMWorld 2006.

Stephen wrote Chapters 5 and 8.

David E. Hart (MCSE#300790, ASE #220919, VCP #4970) is a senior consultant with Callisma. He currently provides senior-level strategic and technical consulting to all Callisma clients in the south-central region of the U.S. His specialties include virtualization technologies, Microsoft Active Directory design and implementation, emerging technology planning, collaboration architecture and design, content delivery design and implementations, enterprise operating systems troubleshooting and optimization, and desktop architecture design and implementation. David's background spans over 15 years in the industry and includes positions at one of the top five consulting firms as the "South Central Microsoft Practice and VMware Lead" for seven years, Microsoft Practice Lead and Senior Microsoft Consultant at a top three telecommunication company for five years, and Desktop Enterprise Practice Lead for a nationwide consulting firm for two years.

I wish to thank my peers at Callisma for asking me to contribute to this book. I also wish to thank my biggest supporters: my wife, Nirma, for putting up with me and all the noise and heat coming from my office, and my two sons, Izzy and Corbin, for letting me work when they'd rather have daddy time. Lastly, I'd like to thank my parents, Don and Judy, for always encouraging me to follow my dreams.

David wrote Chapter 4.

David E. Payne is an IT enthusiast with a decade of real-world experience in the data center. David is currently CTO of Xcedex, the only U.S.-based professional services firm solely focused on virtualization solutions. David has been key in developing the virtualization practice for Xcedex Professional Services. Specifically over the last four years, David has been engaged in dozens of virtualization initiatives, providing architecture guidance and hands-on services for organizations of all sizes across the United States. His practical approach has taken some of the largest U.S. companies in finance, retail, and manufacturing beyond the marketing spin and into real results with today's virtualization technologies. David is a VMware Authorized Consultant (VAC) and a VMware Certified Professional (VCP).

Xcedex is a VMware Premier Partner, joining this invitation-only program as one of the first 10 partners in 2004. Xcedex is recognized nationwide for its professionalism, deep knowledge of virtual infrastructure, and experience in real-world implementations. With a laser focus on virtualization consulting, Xcedex has become one of the top go-to service delivery partners for VMware, Dell, and EMC.

David cowrote Chapter 7.

Jeremy Pries is a virtualization architect at Xcedex. He has an extensive background in computing infrastructure dating back 10 years, with experience ranging from networking and storage to security and Intel-based operating systems. Jeremy's current focus is 100 percent on virtualization technologies, gaining valuable experience on some of the largest ESX implementations. Jeremy's specialty is filling gaps in management tools to speed project timelines and increase accuracy. His expertise has made him one of the most sought after Xcedex architects. Jeremy is a VMware Authorized Consultant (VAC) and a VMware Certified Professional (VCP).

Xcedex is a VMware Premier Partner, joining this invitation-only program as one of the first 10 partners in 2004. Xcedex is recognized nationwide for its professionalism, deep knowledge of virtual infrastructure, and experience in real-world implementations. With a laser focus on virtualization consulting, Xcedex has become one of the top go-to service delivery partners for VMware, Dell, and EMC.

Jeremy cowrote Chapter 7.

Paul Summitt (MCSE, CCNA, MCP+I, MCP) holds a master's degree in mass communication. Paul has served as a network, an Exchange, and a database administrator, as well as a Web and application developer. Paul has written on virtual reality and Web development and has served as technical editor for several books on Microsoft technologies. Paul lives in Columbia, MO, with his life and writing partner, Mary.

Paul cowrote Chapter 6.

Technical Editors

Andy Jones (MCSE+I, MCT, CCIA, CCEA, CCI, CCNA, CCDA, MCIW, Network+, A+) is the Services Director for MTM Technologies, previously known as Vector ESP. He provides comprehensive solutions focused on Citrix and Microsoft technologies for clients ranging from 50 to 50,000 users, focusing mainly on architecting and deploying Access Infrastructure solutions for enterprise customers. One of Andy's primary focuses is in developing best practices, processes, and methodologies surrounding Access Infrastructure that take into consideration and integrate with virtually every part of a customer's infrastructure.

In addition to field work and business development, Andy regularly instructs Microsoft and Citrix courses. Andy holds a master's degree from Morehead State University.

David E. Williams works as an Infrastructure Manager for the
John H. Harland Company in Atlanta, GA. Harland is one of the
leading software companies focused on financial institutions, one of
the largest check printers in the country, and the leader in testing
and assessment solutions for the education market. In addition to
managing IT resources, he is also a senior architect and an advisory
engineer, providing technical direction and advice to Harland's management team in long-range planning for new or projected areas of
enterprise projects.

He is also a principal at Williams & Garcia, LLC, a consulting
practice specializing in delivering effective enterprise infrastructure
solutions. He specializes in the development of advanced solutions
based on Microsoft technologies and strategic infrastructure designs.

David studied Music Engineering Technology at the University
of Miami, and he holds MCSE, MCDBA, VCP, and CCNA certifi-
cations.

When not re-architecting corporate infrastructures, he spends his
time with his wife and three children.

David wrote Chapter 3.

Companion Web Site

Some of the code presented throughout this book is available for
download from www.syngress.com/solutions. Look for the Syngress
icon in the margins indicating which examples are available from
the companion Web site.

Contents

Chapter 1

Scripted Installation

Topics in this chapter:

- Setting Up the Scripted Installation
- Reviewing the Kickstart File
- Remote Network Installation

Introduction

If you are setting up your virtual infrastructure or plan on scaling it out and will be building ESX host servers, this chapter is a must for you. The scripted installation method is a fast, efficient, and sure way to provision ESX hosts, and you'll be amazed at how simple it is to set up. We'll also review the Kickstart file so you fully understand how this install method works, and touch on the remote network install procedure as well.

Setting Up the Scripted Installation

Setting up the scripted installation correctly will make the process run smoothly and provide you with a very satisfactory experience. As a result, you'll likely choose this method over any other for setting up ESX hosts that have similar configurations. You'll set up the script—a Kickstart configuration file—based on parameters you would normally select during an ESX server install. If you want the exact configuration of the ESX server where you are setting up the Kickstart file, then make the same choices you made when you built it originally. (You did document that, right?)

After you have set up the Kickstart file, you have two options for building new ESX servers: 1) From the new ESX server, insert the ESX Server installation CD in the local CD-ROM; or 2) install ESX Server across the network from installation files hosted on another ESX server. This second option is convenient if your data center or server room is geographically remote or just a pain to get to.

Additionally, the scripted installation method can run unattended. However, like any unattended install of software, if something goes wrong, you'll be prompted to respond, and the install will hang until you do so.

Creating the Script

So to begin, as a prerequisite for the scripted installation method, you need to have an ESX server built and ready to perform the setup for the scripted installation. Some of the unique parameters you will be setting include the following:

- **Installation Type** Two types are available: 1) *Initial Installation* (for a new install), and 2) *Upgrade* (if you are upgrading an existing ESX server such as an ESX Server 2.5 host).

- **Root Password**

- **Time Zone**

- **IP Address Information** It is recommended you statically set your ESX server IP address.

- **Disk Partition Information**

- **Licensing Data** This is a new "feature" in ESX 3.0.

You can choose DHCP if you want, but it is a good idea to have the IP information at hand, and it's recommended that your ESX server have static IP addresses.

To create the script, log on to the prebuilt ESX Server via a Web browser. You will be presented with the Web page shown in Figure 1.1.

Figure 1.1 The VMware ESX Server 3.0 Welcome Web Page

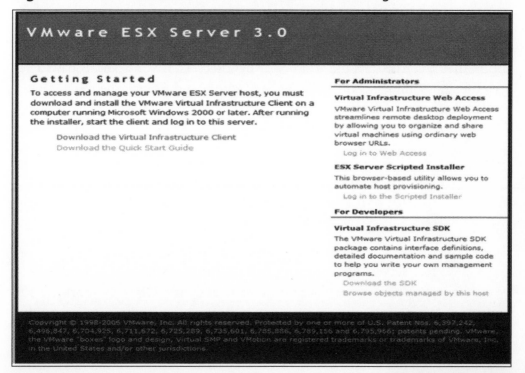

From this page, click the **Log In To The Scripted Installer** link under the ESX Server Scripted Installer heading. You will then be presented with the Scripted Install Web page, as shown in Figure 1.2.

Figure 1.2 The Scripted Install Web Page

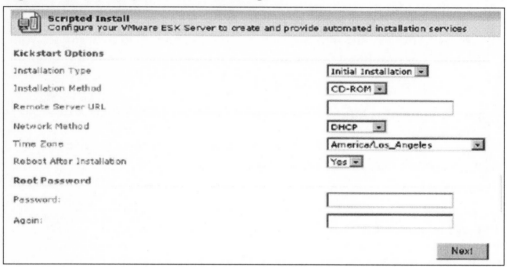

You must now input the information you want for the Kickstart script. In this example, the Installation Type field is set to Initial Installation, which means that this Kickstart file will be for new servers. If you want to have a script for upgrading existing ESX servers, you would change the install type to **Upgrade**.

In the Installation Method box, you can select one of the following three methods:

- **CD-ROM** This method allows you to install ESX Server from the CD-ROM of the new server itself. This method may require physical access to the server itself.

- **Remote** This method allows you to install ESX Server from a remote server that contains the ESX Installation files. If you choose this method, you will also need to include the URL and port number of the remote server.

- **NFS** This method allows you to use an NFS mount point. In the **Remote Server URL**, you would input the hostname of the NFS server and the mount point. For example, **esx01:loadesx**, where **esx01** is the server name and **loadesx** is the mount point.

In the **Network Method** section, you can choose **DHCP** if you want to give your ESX server a dynamic IP address. Alternatively, you can select **Static IP** if you want to set your ESX server with a static IP.

Swiss Army Knife...

Modifying IP Information

As mentioned earlier in this chapter, it's recommended that you give your ESX server a static IP address, although you can use DHCP to provision new ESX servers from the same Kickstart file. If you choose this method, it's a good idea to go back and statically set the IP information and change the hostname, or to create multiple Kickstart files with different hostnames and statically set the IP information. Changing the host name is a little complicated because you will need to regenerate the certificates for the ESX server once the name of the host has been changed.

In the **Time Zone** section, choose the time zone you would like your ESX server to be in. In the **Reboot After Installation** field, select **Yes** so your ESX server will reboot itself after the installation is complete.

Make sure you give the Root account a strong password and click **Next**.

If you chose to give your ESX server a static IP address, the next window you'll see will concern networking options (see Figure 1.3).

Next, input all of the IP information needed. Enter the specific information for your new ESX server, including the hostname and IP address, the subnet mask in the Netmask field, the gateway, and the nameserver (DNS). Use fully qualified domain names if you are running domains such as esx-host01.domian-name.net. Select which network device you would like the service console to run on and click **Next**.

Figure 1.3 The Networking Options Page

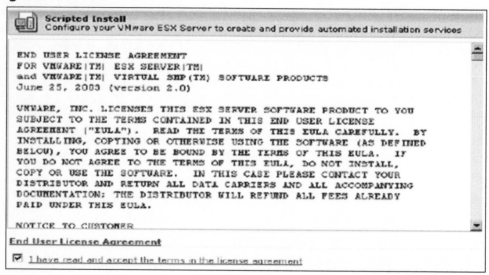

The End User License Agreement (EULA) windows will appear (see Figure 1.4).

Figure 1.4 EULA

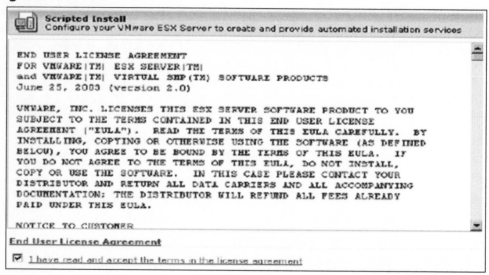

Of course, read the EULA, check the **I Have Read And Accept The Terms In The License Agreement** checkbox, and then click **Next**.

The Partition Configuration page should appear. It's here that you select how your ESX server's disk will be partitioned. A basic example can be seen in Figure 1.5.

Figure 1.5 The Partition Configuration Page

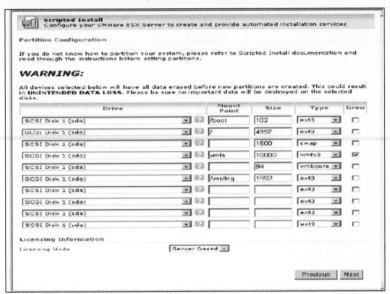

If you modify this, which surely you will, make sure you give it at least the minimum required space to do so. Also, be aware that some SCSI card manufacturers do not use SDA, employing instead other devices, such as Compaq (HP)'s CCISS.

From the Drive list, choose a drive such as SDA, IDE (use /dev/hda), CCISS, or one of many others. In the next column, choose the mount point, such as root (/), boot (/boot), vmfs (vmfs3), swap (swap), and so on. Give each mount point a size in the Size column (in megabytes, but do not use MB as a suffix, such as in 102MB; use only the number 102, as shown in Figure 1.5). Lastly, provide the type in the Type column, which offers four choices: ext3, swap, vmkcore, and vmfs3.

New to ESX 3.0 is the Licensing Mode. Thus, you must select the appropriate mode for your installation:

- **Server Based** This mode allows you to obtain a license automatically from your license server, which may have been set up on your VirtualCenter server.

- **File Based** This mode allows you to upload a license file

- **Post Install** This mode allows you to configure your licensing after the install is complete.

Once you have completed the partitioning information and licensing mode, click **Next**.

In the preceding example, Server-Based Licensing was chosen, so the next page that appears is that for Server-Based Licensing Information, as shown in Figure 1.6. You will add your license server information on this page.

Figure 1.6 The Server-Based Licensing Information Page

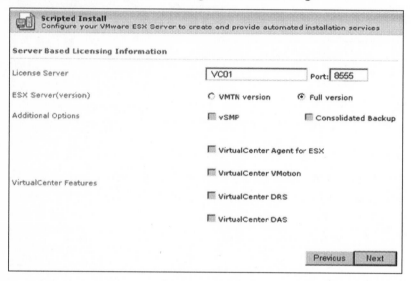

Fill in the License Server information, including its port number—for example, 8555. In the **Additional Options** section, you may select **vSMP** (virtual symmetric multi-processing) and/or **Consolidated Backup**.

Additionally, you can select any VirtualCenter options as well. Click **Next** when you have finished.

If you chose File-Based licensing, you'll be presented with the page shown in Figure 1.7.

Figure 1.7 The File-Based Licensing Information Page

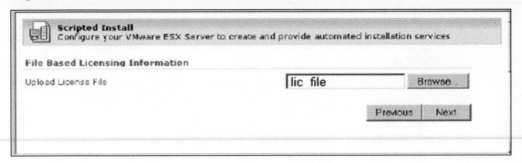

Input the license file, or click the **Browse** button to browse and select the license file. Once you've done so, click **Next**.

Now you can choose **Download Floppy Image** or **Download Kickstart Image**. The differences between these two include the following:

- **Floppy Image** This provides you with a disk image of a VMware ESX Server boot disk which can be used for unattended, scripted installations of ESX Server.

- **Kickstart Image** This provides the kickstart image that can be used by third-party deployment tools.

If you selected **Download Floppy Image**, save the image with an .img file extension. If you did not select DHCP in the preceding step because you want to create multiple images for multiple ESX hosts, go back and change the hostname and static IP information and save the floppy images with unique names.

VMware has modified the handling of partition tables so that ESX Server automatically clears only the LUNs you specifically designate in the Management Interface.

NOTE

If you are considering booting from your SAN, you should adhere to the following recommendations and work closely with your SAN Administrator:

- Only present the LUN used for the operating system of the ESX Server installation (known as the boot LUN) to the ESX host you are building. Do not present the boot LUN to any other ESX host or server. Do not share boot LUNs between servers.
- During the installation, ensure that you mask off all additional LUNs—like for your vmfs partitions—other than the boot LUN during the installation.

Remote Network Installation

Using a remote network installation to install ESX Server, create a boot floppy image to run the installation instead of scripting the installation. During the installation, you are asked to specify the location of the ESX Server CD-ROM.

To perform a remote network installation with a boot floppy, you need to follow three steps. First, use **dd**, **rawwritewin**, or **rawrite** to create a floppy image called bootnet.img. This file is located on the ESX Server CD-ROM in the /images directory. The second step is to put the boot floppy in your ESX host, and then boot the server. When the installation starts, you will be prompted to choose one of the following selections:

- **HTTP** This is the preferred installation method. Specify the name of the remote machine where the ESX Server CD-ROM is located, the root directory (/), and HTTP port 8555.

- **NFS** You must have an NFS server set up. Copy the ESX Server CD-ROM to the NFS server and point the new system to the NFS server.

- **FTP** You must have an FTP server set up. Copy the ESX Server CD-ROM to the FTP server and point the new system to the FTP server.

The third step is to complete the installation, which is very similar to installing ESX Server normally.

Summary

This chapter should have given you a good understanding of how to quickly scale out your virtual infrastructure using scripted installation methods. You should now be able to create an installation script that is customized for either one specific ESX host or many.

## Chapter 2

An Introduction to ESX Native Tools and How to Use Them

Topics in this chapter:

- Esxtop
- Vmkfstools
- Vmware-cmd
- Vmkusage

Introduction

This chapter is going to review the tools that come native to all ESX servers. It is important that, one, you understand these tools exist, and, two, you know how to use them from the command line and how you can incorporate them into scripts. VMware provides some very powerful tools that are built on native Linux functionality and that are expanded for use within the ESX host and the virtual machines residing on them.

Esxtop

Esxtop is a very simple yet powerful tool that can be used for diagnosing performance issues of the ESX host as well as the virtual machines. In Linux, there exists a comparable command-line tool, called *Top*, which can be used similarly for Linux OSes to gather performance metrics. VMware has expanded Esxtop to provide metrics specific to virtualization. Esxtop provides real-time monitoring of virtual machine processes (also known as *worlds*). Worlds are simply virtual machine processes run by the VMkernel. VMware has identified three types of worlds, or virtual machine processes, which exist in ESX Server. These are

- Virtual Machine
- System
- Service Console

But before delving too deep into specific processes or the worlds that Esxtop monitors, let's take a quick look at Esxtop when you run it.

Esxtop Overview

Esxtop comes installed natively when you install ESX Server, so there is nothing you need to load. To run Esxtop, you need to access the service console of your ESX host. Once at the service console, type **[root@esx01 root]#** *esxtop*.

The output displayed will be similar to that shown in Figure 2.1.

Figure 2.1 Esxtop Output

```
 9:37am  up 15 days,  4:31, 20 worlds,  load average: 0.05, 0.05, 0.01, 0.00
PCPU:   3.36%,   4.58% :   3.97% used total
LCPU:   2.80%,   0.56%,   1.09%,   3.50%
MEM: 3914752 managed(KB), 1482752 free(KB) :  62.12% used total
SWAP: 4193280 av(KB), 0 used(KB), 4151348 free(KB) :    0.00 MBr/s,    0.00 MBw/s
DISK vmhba0:0:0:   0.00 r/s,    8.35 w/s,    0.00 MBr/s,    0.05 MBw/s
NIC vmnic0:   29.63 pTx/s,   31.82 pRx/s,    0.05 MbTx/s,    0.16 MbRx/s
NIC vmnic2:    0.00 pTx/s,    0.20 pRx/s,    0.00 MbTx/s,    0.00 MbRx/s
NIC vmnic1:    0.00 pTx/s,    0.20 pRx/s,    0.00 MbTx/s,    0.00 MbRx/s

VCPUID  WID  WTYPE      %USED  %READY  %EUSED  %MEM
  128   128  idle       54.69   0.00   54.69   0.00
  130   130  idle       52.21   0.00   52.21   0.00
  131   131  idle       42.26   0.00   42.26   0.00
  129   129  idle       42.26   0.00   42.26   0.00
  142   142  vmm         2.41   0.33    2.41  22.00
  127   127  console     1.86   0.00    1.86   0.00
  146   146  vmm         0.97   0.14    0.97   5.00
  148   148  vmm         0.84   0.56    0.84  11.00
  144   144  vmm         0.60   0.40    0.60   8.00
  143   143  vmm         0.47   0.02    0.47   8.00
  147   147  vmm         0.43   0.02    0.43   1.00
  140   140  driver      0.00   0.00    0.00   0.00
  139   139  reset       0.00   0.00    0.00   0.00
  138   138  reset       0.00   0.00    0.00   0.00
  137   137  helper      0.00   0.00    0.00   0.00
  136   136  helper      0.00   0.00    0.00   0.00
  135   135  helper      0.00   0.00    0.00   0.00
  134   134  helper      0.00   0.00    0.00   0.00
  133   133  helper      0.00   0.00    0.00   0.00
  132   132  helper      0.00   0.28    0.00   0.00
```

Quickly going through the output, note on the top line the time, which in this example is 9:37 A.M. This server has been up 15 days, 4 hours, and 31 minutes and is running 20 worlds. These worlds are not all virtual machines (we will explain each of the different worlds further in the chapter). The load average shows the load the ESX host's CPUs are under. A load average of 1.0 means that the CPU is being fully utilized; thus, an average of 0.5 would mean that the CPU is only being utilized at approximately 50 percent. You can see from the example in Figure 2.1 that the CPUs are hardly being touched on this ESX host, the highest running at 5-percent utilization. However, if you run Esxtop and find that your CPUs are running consistently at 1.0 or above, you may need to adjust the load of virtual machines on that host or increase the number of CPUs on the host itself. The four load averages are collected every five seconds at one-, five-, and fifteen-minute intervals, which give you a snapshot of the overall CPU load of your ESX host during those time slices. The load averages can be used to quickly identify CPU-bound hosts.

The PCPU line and the LCPU line show the number of physical processors, and if hyperthreading is enabled, the number of logical processors and the utilization of each physical and logical processor as well as their averages.

CCPU displays the percentage of toatl CPU time as reported by the Service Console.

The MEM line shows the total amount of physical memory on the ESX host, the amount of free or nonutilized memory, and the percentage of used memory—in this example, 62.12 percent.

The SWAP line displays a metric you want to pay attention to. The first number shows the amount of swap given to the ESX host, which in the preceding example is 4193280 (KB). Swapping is not necessarily a bad thing. However, excessive swapping can indicate a memory issue and can cause performance degradation. If you see persistently high levels of swapping, which would be shown in the used section, you may need to add physical memory to the ESX host, adjust the amount of memory allocated to your virtual machines, or increase your swap space on the ESX host.

The next section is the disk which will give you the performance data for your disks on the ESX host. If you are experiencing issues related to disk read/write performance or simply want to monitor disk performance, you can review this data. There will be an entry for each LUN per Target per HBA.

The NIC section will give you statistics on the performance of all of your NICs dedicated to virtual machines (Vmnic0 on up). As shown in Figure 2.1, there will be one line per NIC.

Now let's take a look at the different types of worlds or processes Esxtop monitors.

The Virtual Machine World

A virtual machine world is the process under which a specific virtual machine's virtual processor is run. If you are experiencing an issue with a specific virtual machine, this is one place you will want to check out. So what processes are virtual machine world processes? In Figure 2.2, see the highlighted processes from an Esxtop readout from ESX 2.X.

Figure 2.2 Virtual Machine Processes

```
 9:22am  up 15 days,  4:16, 20 worlds,  load average: 0.04, 0.07, 0.02, 0.01
PCPU:   4.22%,   2.26% :   3.24% used total
LCPU:   3.73%,   0.49%,   1.17%,   1.09%
MEM: 3914752 managed(KB), 1481728 free(KB) :  62.15% used total
SWAP: 4193280 av(KB), 0 used(KB), 4151348 free(KB) :    0.00 MBr/s,    0.00 MBw/s
DISK vmhba0:0:0:   0.00 r/s,    9.36 w/s,    0.00 MBr/s,    0.05 MBw/s
NIC vmnic0:    2.19 pTx/s,    3.58 pRx/s,    0.00 MbTx/s,    0.00 MbRx/s
NIC vmnic2:    0.00 pTx/s,    0.20 pRx/s,    0.00 MbTx/s,    0.00 MbRx/s
NIC vmnic1:    0.00 pTx/s,    0.20 pRx/s,    0.00 MbTx/s,    0.00 MbRx/s

VCPUID  WID  WTYPE     %USED  %READY  %EUSED    %MEM
 131    131  idle      58.50   0.00    58.50    0.00
 129    129  idle      58.50   0.00    58.50    0.00
 130    130  idle      38.58   0.00    38.58    0.00
 128    128  idle      37.34   0.00    37.34    0.00
 127    127  console    2.02   0.00     2.02    0.00
 148    148  vmm        0.89   0.30     0.89   14.00
 146    146  vmm        0.86   0.50     0.86    7.00
 142    142  vmm        0.86   1.03     0.86   26.00
 144    144  vmm        0.68   0.26     0.68   10.00
 143    143  vmm        0.62   0.02     0.62   10.00
 147    147  vmm        0.41   0.02     0.41    3.00
 140    140  driver     0.00   0.00     0.00    0.00
```

For quick identification of the type of world each of these processes are, see the WTYPE column. The virtual machine world is denoted by *vmm*. What is not readily evident is which vmm world relates to the specific virtual machine name. However, by examining the VCPUID you can map that number to the VMID found in the MUI. This is shown in Figure 2.3

Figure 2.3 VMID in MUI

NOTE

The PID number shown in Figure 2.3 is the Process ID, which can be seen if you run Top from the service console. You can perform functions such as *kill* using the PID, which is like pulling the plug on your virtual machine. Be careful with this. In ESX 3.0 we are given the name of the VM, so there is no longer any question about which ID goes with which VM.

System World

System worlds are created to run a number of system services. *Idle worlds* are created for each processor on your ESX host. Idle worlds run an idle loop process, consuming free CPU cycles when the CPUs have nothing else to run. Additionally, *helper worlds* are run for specific system tasks and *driver worlds* are specific drivers within your ESX host. This value is no longer listed in ESX 3.0

The Service Console World

The *service console* is itself a world which runs by default on cpu0.

Some Other Helpful Esxtop Metrics

In this section, we discuss other Esxtop metrics that are useful for monitoring the performance of virtual machines.

%USED

The %USED metric identifies how much of a physical processor's utilization is being used by the virtual machine's virtual processor.

%Ready/%Wait

The %READY/%Wait metric shows the percentage of time a virtual machine was waiting but could not get scheduled on a physical processor. VMware recommends this number be under 5 percent.

%EUSED

The %EUSED metric shows how much of the maximum physical processor utilization a virtual machine is currently using.

%MEM

The %MEM metric shows how much physical memory is utilized by each virtual machine and world.

vmkfstools

vmkfstools is a powerful command-line tool that comes native to ESX Server. The tool can create and manipulate VMDK files, performing such tasks as importing and exporting disk files, growing and shrinking existing disk files, and committing REDO or snapshot files. The tool can also create VMFS partitions and has a host of other capabilities. To see the full range and power of the vmkfstools command, from your service console type **man vmkfstools**.

We will next examine some common and very helpful ways to use vmkfstools and its associated arguments.

Viewing Contents VMFS Partition

Similar to the Linux command *ls*, if you want to view the contents of a VMFS volume on your ESX host, type **vmkfstools –l vmfs_label**. This command works only on ESX 2.X

You may specify the HBA number, SCSI target, LUN number, and partition number. For example, from the service console, type **vmkfstools –l vmhba0:0:0:11**.

Figure 2.4 displays the output from running *vmkfstools –l*. By adding an **h** after the **–l**, the size of the files on the VMFS partition are displayed in a more human-readable format. So the command in the preceding example would look like **vmkfstools –lh vmhba0:0:0:11**.

Figure 2.4 Vmkfstools–l Output

```
[root@esx-server01 root]# vmkfstools -l vmhba0:0:0:11
Name: local       (public)
Capacity 50610115584 (48258 file blocks * 1048576), 10501488640 (10015 blocks) avail
Permission  Uid  Gid     Attr    Bytes (Blocks) Last Modified Filename
rw--------   0    0       swap 2146435072 ( 2047)  May 27 19:49 SwapFile.vswp
rw--------   0    0       disk 4194304000 ( 4000)  Jun  1 20:03 cluster-01.vmdk
rw--------   0    0       disk 4194304000 ( 4000)  Jun  1 19:54 server-02.vmdk
rw--------   0    0       disk 4194304000 ( 4000)  Jun  1 20:03 server-03.vmdk
rw--------   0    0       disk 4194304000 ( 4000)  Jun  1 20:03 srv-node1.vmdk
rw--------   0    0       disk 4194304000 ( 4000)  Jun  1 20:03 srv-node2.vmdk
rw--------   0    0       disk 4294967296 ( 4096)  Jun  1 20:03 nt4.vmdk
rw--------   0    0       disk  104857600 (  100)  Jun  1 20:03 quorum1.vmdk
rw--------   0    0       disk 2097152000 ( 2000)  Mar  6 21:30 server2k01.vmdk
rw--------   0    0       disk 2097152000 ( 2000)  Jun  1 20:03 server-20.vmdk
rw--------   0    0       disk 4194304000 ( 4000)  Jun  1 20:03 server-05.vmdk
rw--------   0    0       disk 4194304000 ( 4000)  Jun  1 12:29 webserver-01.vmdk
```

Import/Export Files

As mentioned earlier, if you need to import or export .vmdk files onto your VMFS partition, you can use the vmkfstools command. VMware recommends using vmkfstools rather than the Linux command cp to do this. For example, if you need to export a virtual disk from a VMFS partition to a different location on your ESX Server, type

```
vmkfstools -e /targetdirectory/filename.vmdk
/vmfs/volume_label/sourcefile.vmdk
```

One reason you would want to do this is to move a virtual machine template from the VMFS volume to a directory that contains your template images on your server.

If you need to import a virtual disk file from VMware Server or Workstation, you will first need to scp or ftp the .vmdk file(s) onto a directory of your ESX host (not the VMFS partition) and then run the following command in ESX 2.X:

```
vmkfstools -i source_directory_name /vmfs/volume_label/targetfile.vmdk
```

In ESX 3.x the command has changed because the vmkfstools export command is deprecated. In ESX 3.X the command is as follows

```
'vmkfstools -i srcDisk -d 2gbsparse dstDisk'
```

Adding a New Virtual Disk, Blank Virtual Disk, and Extending Existing Virtual Disks

A very cool use of vmkfstools is its capability to create and modify existing .vmdk files. For example, if you need to create a new blank virtual disk type from the service console, use the following syntax:

```
vmkfstools -c size vmfs-name:vmdk-name
```

Example:

```
vmkfstools -c 2024m SanRaid1:data01.vmdk
```

What this allows you to do is add a new 2GB hard disk which can then be added to existing virtual machines and formatted at the OS level within the VM.

But what if you need to extend or grow an existing virtual disk? For this, you would type the following syntax:

```
vmkfstools -X new-size vmfs-name:vmdk-name
```

Example:

```
vmkfstools -X 12288m SanRaid1:database.vmdk
```

The preceding command extends the existing database.vmdk from its existing size to 12288 megabytes.

NOTE

The virtual machine will need to be powered off prior to extending the virtual disk. VMware recommends that you make a full backup on the VMDK file prior to completing this task. If you want to extend the partition within the virtual machine itself, you may need to use a utility like Partition Magic for the VM to recognize the additional space added to the disk file. Or you will need to create an additional partition within the virtual machine itself.

Swiss Army Knife…

man vmkfstools

Become familiar with vmkfstools command. To obtain a full list of the arguments associated with vmkfstools, from the service console, type
man vmkfstools

vmware-cmd

The *vmware-cmd* command allows you to perform many different tasks related to virtual machines. If you type **vmware-cmd** from the service console, you will see that vmware-cmd has both Server Operations and VM Operations. Figure 2.5 shows the Server Operations that can be performed on the service console using vmware-cmd. As you can see from the list, you can register and unregister virtual machines and get/set resource variables.

Figure 2.5 Vmware-cmd Server Operations

```
Server Operations:
  /usr/bin/vmware-cmd -l
  /usr/bin/vmware-cmd -s register <config_file_path>
  /usr/bin/vmware-cmd -s unregister <config_file_path>
  /usr/bin/vmware-cmd -s getresource <variable>
  /usr/bin/vmware-cmd -s setresource <variable> <value>
```

For example, if you type

```
vmware-cmd -l
```

from the service console, a list of registered virtual machines and the path to the .vmx configuration file will be displayed.

Figure 2.6 shows the VM Operations that can be performed from the service console using the vmware-cmd utility. You can stop, start, reset, and suspend virtual machines, add and commit .redo files (very powerful; especially for backups which will be discussed later in the book), as well as get information about the virtual machine.

Figure 2.6 Vmware-cmd VM Operations

```
VM Operations:
  /usr/bin/vmware-cmd <cfg> getconnectedusers
  /usr/bin/vmware-cmd <cfg> getstate
  /usr/bin/vmware-cmd <cfg> start <powerop_mode>
  /usr/bin/vmware-cmd <cfg> stop <powerop_mode>
  /usr/bin/vmware-cmd <cfg> reset <powerop_mode>
  /usr/bin/vmware-cmd <cfg> suspend <powerop_mode>
  /usr/bin/vmware-cmd <cfg> setconfig <variable> <value>
  /usr/bin/vmware-cmd <cfg> getconfig <variable>
  /usr/bin/vmware-cmd <cfg> setguestinfo <variable> <value>
  /usr/bin/vmware-cmd <cfg> getguestinfo <variable>
  /usr/bin/vmware-cmd <cfg> getid
  /usr/bin/vmware-cmd <cfg> getpid
  /usr/bin/vmware-cmd <cfg> getproductinfo <prodinfo>
  /usr/bin/vmware-cmd <cfg> connectdevice <device_name>
  /usr/bin/vmware-cmd <cfg> disconnectdevice <device_name>
  /usr/bin/vmware-cmd <cfg> getconfigfile
  /usr/bin/vmware-cmd <cfg> getheartbeat
  /usr/bin/vmware-cmd <cfg> getuptime
  /usr/bin/vmware-cmd <cfg> getremoteconnections
  /usr/bin/vmware-cmd <cfg> gettoolslastactive
  /usr/bin/vmware-cmd <cfg> getresource <variable>
  /usr/bin/vmware-cmd <cfg> setresource <variable> <value>
  /usr/bin/vmware-cmd <cfg> addredo <disk_device_name>
  /usr/bin/vmware-cmd <cfg> commit <disk_device_name> <level> <freeze> <wait>
  /usr/bin/vmware-cmd <cfg> answer
```

For example, to add a .redo file to a virtual machine, type the following syntax from the service console:

```
vmware-cmd <cfg> addredo scsi0:0
```

NOTE

The scsi0:0 in the preceding command is the actual scsi device name of the virtual machine. This command works only with ESX 2.X. With 3.X the use of snapshots has replaced redo files

If the command runs successfully, the resultant output would look something like:

```
Addredo (scsi0:0) = 1
```

To commit the redo you just added, type

```
Vmware-cmd <cfg> commit scsi0:0 001
```

vmkusage

Although not a command-line tool, vmkusage is a great tool for troubleshooting and one you should be aware of. Monitoring the utilization of servers in the past was not the most exciting work. In the past, a server maxed could mean a lot of work for an administrator. Now, allocating more memory, an additional CPU, hard drive, or NIC is a process of minutes not days or weeks. Monitor the performance of your virtual machines to ensure you meet your service level agreements. Use the excellent VirtualCenter for this. You can also use vmkusage, which provides the utilization of your ESX Server as well as all running virtual machines.

NOTE

Vmkusage is not included with ESX 3.x. The next section applies only to ESX 2.x

To start vmkusage, from the command line of your ESX Server's service console, type

```
vmkusagectl install
```

This will create the utilization reports in the /var/log/vmkusage directory. These reports will be updated every five minutes by default. You view the reports with a Web browser by typing

```
https://esxservername.corp.com/vmkusage.
```

Substitute the URL with the appropriate information in your environment. You will see a window similar to that shown in Figure 2.7.

Figure 2.7 Vmkusage

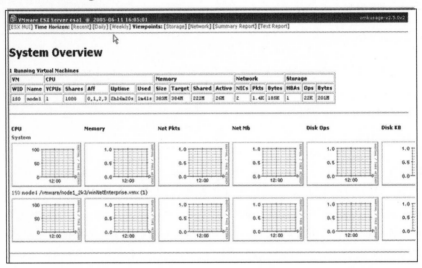

You can pull very specific utilization reports that you will find important for capacity planning, future demand availability, server sizing, and hardware purchasing. The HTML files and vmkusage graphs are located in /usr/lib/vmware-mui/apache/htdocs/vmkusage.

Summary

These native tools are powerful and you can create many different scripts calling these commands. It is recommended that you become thoroughly familiar with these tools and use them to unlock the power and flexibility of your virtual infrastructure. Of course, be sure to thoroughly test all of your scripts and commands in a test environment prior to using them in production.

## Chapter 3

Scripting and Programming for the Virtual Infrastructure

Topics in this chapter:

- VMware Scripting APIs
- VMware Virtual Infrastructure SDK
- Other VMware SDKs

Introduction

Simplification of administration and its related overhead is a strategic impera-
tive that most companies are mandating. Although programmatic automation
has existed in the Windows and Linux operating systems for some time now,
getting a complete solution for system management and automation often
requires purchasing expensive third-party, proprietary software that was difficult to learn and sometimes suffered from compatibility issues. Fortunately,
VMware has incorporated a variety of interfaces that you can take advantage
of to simplify the management of your virtual infrastructure. In this chapter,
we will discuss the available APIs and SDKs as they apply to the following
VMware products and versions:

- VMware ESX Server 3.0 and 2.5.x
- VMware Server and VMware GSX Server 2.x or later
- VMware VirtualCenter 2.0 and 1.x

So, without further ado, let's jump into scripting and programming techniques for VMware ESX, VMware Server, and VMware VirtualCenter. To
help you establish a firm foundation in writing code for VMware products,
we will discuss several techniques and technologies in this chapter, specifically:

- VMware scripting APIs
- VMware VirtualCenter SDK
- Other VMware SDKs

VMware Scripting APIs

With the release of the VMware scripting application programming interfaces
(APIs), VMware has been offering two components that you can use to
develop custom code to manage your VMware ESX, VMware GSX, and
VMware Server hosts directly: VmCOM and VmPerl. These APIs have no
dependency on any other VMware product, such as VirtualCenter, and are
available for use as quickly as you can download them from VMware's site.

VmCOM is a Component Object Model (COM) interface you can use with any language that supports the instantiation of COM objects, such as VB.NET, VBScript, C++, C#, Python, Delphi, and Java, just to mention a few. You must install this interface on a machine with a supported version of the Microsoft Windows operating system. VmCOM is not supported on the Linux platform.

VmPerl is an API that can be utilized through the Perl scripting language. You can install this component on either a Windows-based or a Linux-based admin client.

Master Craftsman

Choosing an IDE

To efficiently develop, edit, debug, and test your code, you should standardize on an integrated development environment (IDE) that supports the language(s) you plan to write in. Several commercial and open-source products are available, so your decision will really be based on preference. When choosing an IDE, you should look for products that offer file management, integrated building/debugging/testing, deployment, source control, and reference tools to assist with rapid, yet accurate, coding. The following IDEs are good choices when developing against any of the APIs and SDKs discussed in this chapter:

■ **Microsoft Visual Studio (commercial)** For example, most COM developers opt for Microsoft Visual Studio as the preferred IDE since it supports all of the Microsoft languages. With Visual Studio 2005, you get a powerful IDE, code snippets, mobile device support, source control, and code profiling tools. To make coding even easier and faster, you get great features like Intellisense, which helps you with code against methods and properties for objects that you instantiate and provides an "auto-complete" function (Visual Studio only runs on Windows). For those on a budget, a free version is available, called Visual Studio Express, which provides more than enough features to support development against the Scripting APIs. For more information, see http://msdn.microsoft.com.

Continued

- **NetBeans IDE (open source)** A fast and feature-rich tool for developing Java software. It includes support for AWT/Swing, Servlets and JSP, and J2EE (EJB and Web services). It also includes a database engine and a J2EE-compliant application server. For more information, visit www.netbeans.org.

- **Eclipse (open source)** Available as a complete SDK, Eclipse is a leading open-source IDE, as well as a suite of tools for building applications based on the Eclipse platform. By adding development components, you can customize the Eclipse platform as an IDE for Java (using JDT), C/C++ (using CDT), or both. It runs on a wide range of operating systems, including Windows, Linux, Mac OS, Solaris, AIX, and HP-UX. For more information, visit www.eclipse.org.

- **ActiveState Komodo (commercial)** For Perl development, the Komodo IDE from ActiveState is a good choice. Not only does it support Perl, but you can use it for Python, Tcl, and Ruby development as well. Komodo is available for Windows, MacOS, and Linux. For more information, visit www.activestate.com.

- **Sapien Technology's PrimalScript (commercial)** This is one of the more cost-effective, yet powerful, commercial IDEs available. It provides the same scripting language support as Komodo, but also adds support for VBScript, Actionscript, and KiXtart. It also supports Web development efforts in ASP, ColdFusion, JSP, and PHP...a plus if your code is going to have a browser-based UI. For more information, visit www.sapien.com.

Both components are supported by VMware ESX Server as well as VMware Server/GSX. There are some differences when targeting operations against the different VMware server products, so we'll indicate any discrepancies as we discuss the APIs further in this chapter.

What Are the VMware Scripting APIs?

The interfaces for VmCOM and VmPerl are functionally the same. Both interfaces allow developers and savvy administrators to tap into the power of VMware ESX or VMware Server/GSX hosts programmatically. Even more important, they support a wide range of object-oriented languages, allowing just about anyone to immediately write code to simplify the administration and management of their virtual infrastructure. Although the two interfaces are technically different, both provide task automation functionality, such as virtual machine registration, performing power operations on virtual machines, and information gathering and sending to and from the virtual machine's guest operating system. All sessions between the API and the VMware ESX or VMware Server host are secured and use a single TCP port for communication (TCP port 902 is the default), as shown in Figure 3.1.

Figure 3.1 The VMware Scripting API Architecture

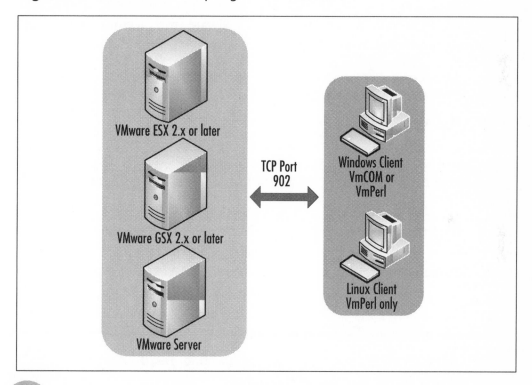

TIP

For Windows installations, you'll also need to install Perl support, such as ActivePerl from ActiveState, to use the VmPerl API. Additional Perl modules may also be required to support certain features needed to work with the API.

VmCOM support is built into Windows by default if you plan on using an interpreted language based on Microsoft's scripting technology (VBScript or JScript). However, if you plan on using a language that requires you to compile your code, such as VB.NET, C#, Java, or Delphi, you will need to install some additional development tools.

Installing the VMware Scripting APIs

Before you can create your own custom scripts to manage your ESX servers, you must install the VMware Scripting APIs on the workstation or server where your scripts will run. The APIs are available at no cost from VMware at www.vmware.com/support/developer/scripting_download.html.

You must log in to the site with your VMware store account and accept the license agreement. You will then be presented with the download links for:

- COM API for Windows
- Perl API for Windows
- Perl API for Linux

To install the scripting API on a Windows client machine, follow these steps:

1. Run the installer package with an account that has administrator rights on the Windows client machine. The naming convention for the installer package is **VMware-VmCOMAPI-x.x.x-yyyyy.exe** (for the VmCOM API) or **VMware-VmPerl-x.x.x-yyyyy.exe** (for the VmPerl API), where "x.x.x" is the ESX Server version the API is for, and "yyyyy" is the build number.

2. Agree to the license agreement by selecting **Yes, I accept the terms in the license agreement.**

3. Click **Next**.

4. Choose the install location by either accepting the default directory or clicking **Change** and browsing to your preferred location.

5. Click **Next**.

6. Click **Install** to begin the copying of files.

7. Click **Finish** when prompted after the install is complete.

To install the scripting API on a Linux client machine, follow these steps:

1. Copy the VmPerl package to the Linux client machine where the scripts will be run.

2. Log on to the machine as root.

3. Untar the installation package. The naming convention for the package is **VMware-VmPerl-x.x.x-yyyyy.tar.gz**, where "x.x.x" is the specific ESX version number and "yyyyy" is the build number.

4. Change to the directory where the extracted files are found, and run the install script **./vmware-install.pl**.

5. Agree to the license agreement by pressing **Enter** when prompted.

6. Enter the installation path for the VmPerl binaries or accept the default destination directory.

7. Enter the installation path for the VmPerl libraries or accept the default destination directory.

Putting the VMware Scripting APIs to Work for You

Once the VMware Scripting APIs have been installed on your management client or server, the next step is to dive in and develop some code to become familiar with the capabilities of the APIs. In this section, we will review the various components for both VmCOM and VmPerl. If you are only familiar with Windows administration, you may feel more comfortable with the VmCOM methods and properties using a scripting language such as Microsoft's VBScript or JScript. If you have a Linux or UNIX background, you should feel right at home with the modules or packages exposed by the VmPerl API using the Perl scripting language. You will find the following examples helpful in either case since the functionality of both VmCOM and VmPerl is the same.

Working with the VmCOM API

The VmCOM API exposes five objects that are used to establish, maintain communication, and interact with a VMware ESX server or virtual machine. Two of these objects will serve as primary objects that expose the methods and properties you will use in your scripts to interact with, or gather information from, your hosts and virtual machines. In function, these objects are similar to the VMware::VmPerl::Server and VMware::VmPerl::VM modules provided by the VmPerl API, discussed later in this chapter. They are

- **VmServerCtl** Used to create a session with an ESX host and expose the services and functionality of the API's server interfaces.
- **VmCtl** Used to manage and perform operations against a virtual machine on a particular ESX host.

Supporting these primary objects are three other objects that provide a secondary, supporting role. These support objects provide the input or output resources needed to pass to the primary object's properties and methods. They are

- **VmConnectParams** Provides host information and authentication credentials used when establishing a connection to an ESX host.
- **VmCollection** Provides a collection or array of properties or other interfaces to be passed to the primary objects.
- **VmQuestion** Provides an interactive interface to respond to questions or error conditions for a virtual machine running on an ESX host.

The process begins by establishing a connection with an ESX or GSX host, or a virtual machine on a particular host using the *Connect()* method of either an instantiated *VmServerCtl* or *VmCtl* object. *VmServerCtl.Connect()* method uses the *VmConnectParams* object to set the target host information and credentials to establish the connection. The *VmCtl.Connect()* method also uses the *VmConnectParams* object, just as the *VmServerCtl* does, in addition to the configuration file name for the target virtual machine. After you have connected to an ESX server host or a virtual machine on that host, you can then call the other methods and properties of the VmCOM component.

As with any COM API, you must expose the VmCOM objects first by either creating an instance of those objects or retrieving an instance of the objects as a returned value for a property. We will discuss this in further detail shortly.

Depending on what your script does, you work with instances of one or more of the following objects:

- VmConnectParams

- *VmCollection*

- *VmServerCtl*

- VmCtl

Before we jump deeper into these topics, we should discuss the development environment within which you will be writing your code. Commonly, VmCOM development is done in a Microsoft development language, be it VBScript or one of the .NET languages (VB.NET, C++, or C#). If you opt to write code in the latter, the IDE best suited for the job is Microsoft Visual Studio.

Although every IDE provides its own set of strengths and benefits, development efforts surrounding COM objects find themselves at home with Microsoft Visual Studio 2005. Two key things that I would like to call out are the ease of including VmCOM in your code and using Intellisense to speed up your development and reduce time spent debugging your code.

If you opt to use Visual Studio 2005 as your IDE, you need to reference the VmCOM Type Library, as shown in Figure 3.2, after creating a new project or solution.

If the library was successfully referenced and included in the project, you should see it listed in the References tree in the Solution Explorer, as portrayed in Figure 3.3. You will also be able to browse the API with VS 2005's Object Browser, as shown in Figure 3.4. Not enough can be said about coding with the appropriate tool for your language. The more feature-rich the tool is, the easier and faster your coding will go.

Figure 3.2 Referencing the VMware VmCOM 1.0 Type Library

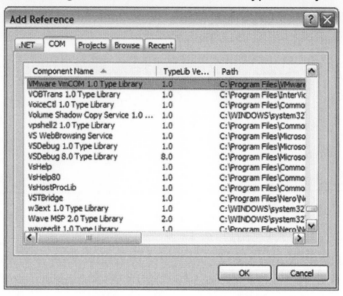

Figure 3.3 The VMCOMLib Reference in Solution Explorer

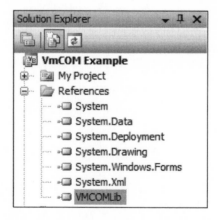

But enough of the formalities…let's move on and take a look at the VmCOM objects.

Figure 3.4 Using the Object Browser to View the Methods and Properties of the *VmCtl* Object

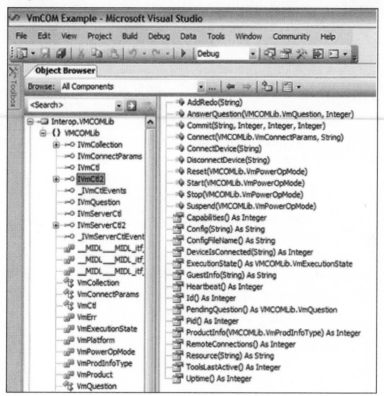

VmConnectParams

The *VmConnectParams* provides the host information and user credentials required by the *Connect()* method for either the *VMServerCtl* or *VmCtl* object, and exposes properties whose values you can set, as shown in Table 3.1. You can use these properties for data retrieval or modification through your script or application.

Table 3.1 *VmConnectParams* Properties

Property Name	Description
Hostname	A string value that represents the DNS host name of the VMware ESX or GSX host or its IP address.
Port	An integer value representing the TCP port that should be used to establish a connection with the VMware ESX or GSX host. This property is optional. If omitted, the default value of 0 (zero) will be used, telling the *Connect()* method to use the standard management TCP port 902.
Username	A string value containing the username to pass as credentials for the connection.
Password	A string value containing the password for the user set in the *Username* property.

The following demonstrates the instantiation of the *VmConnectParams* object in VBScript and how to set the properties listed earlier.

```
Set objConnParams = CreateObject("VmCOM.VmConnectParams")

objConnParams.hostname = "esxserver1"

objConnParams.username = "adminuser1"

objConnParams.password = "password1"
```

VmCollection

This is a good point to introduce the next object in our discussion, the *VmCollection* object. Although you will never instantiate it directly, there are a couple of properties in the other objects we will discuss that return a *VmCollection*. The *RegisteredVmNames* property of the *VmServerCtl* object and the *Choices* property of the *VmQuestion* object both return a range of elements, or values, as a *VmCollection* object.

A *VmCollection* object has two properties: Count, which is an integer value for the number of elements in the collection; and *Item(index)*, which is a string value that returns the specific element represented by the index value you pass. You can navigate the elements returned by stepping through them as you would an array, or access a specific element by referencing its index. You will see examples of this later in the chapter as we work with those properties that return *VmCollection* objects.

VmServerCtl

The *VmServerCtl* object is used to interact with a specific VMware ESX or GSX host. This object exposes two properties and three methods, as shown in Table 3.2. One particular property, *RegisteredVmNames*, returns a *VmCollection* object that contains a complete list of virtual machines registered on the host. This property will prove particularly useful as you query for the host's inventory.

Table 3.2 *VmServerCtl* Properties and Methods

Item	Type	Description
RegisteredVmNames	Property	Returns a listing of all registered VMs on the VMware ESX or GSX host as a *VmCollection* object.
Resource	Property	Used syntactically with a particular system resource variable, this property returns the value as a string variant.
Connect	Method	Used to establish a connection with a VMware ESX or GSX host. You must reference a *VmConnectParams* object when calling the method.
RegisterVm	Method	Used to register a VM on a host. You must reference the configuration file name of the VM being targeted.
UnregisterVm	Method	User to unregister a VM on a host. You must reference the configuration file name of the VM being targeted.

NOTE

The VmCOM API limits the total number of concurrent connections supported by the API. Connections established by the *VmCtl* object and the *VmServerCtl* object cannot exceed 62 when using the API. Keep this in mind when you run scripts concurrently to manage VMs and hosts. If you need to perform multiple tasks against a particular virtual machine or host, and you cannot do so in the same connection, try chaining the tasks synchronously, thus freeing connections by destroying instantiated *VmCtl* and *VMServerCtl* objects before establishing new ones.

The following continues from our last code example, adding the instantiation of the *VmServerCtl* object and connecting to the host using the previously defined *VmConnectParams* object.

```
Set objVMServer = CreateObject("VmCOM.VmServerCtl")

objVMServer.Connect objConnParams

objVMList = objVMServer.RegisteredVmNames

for vmIndex = 1 to objVMList.Count

    WScript.Echo VM.objVMList(vmCounter)

    vmCounter = vmCounter + 1

next
```

In this example, we connect to the host according to the property values set in the *VmConnectParams* object earlier, retrieve the collection of registered VMs, and enumerate them, writing their configuration file path as output.

NOTE

Like most methods of the VmCOM component objects, *Connect()* runs synchronously. The script will not continue until the connection attempt has finished successfully, failed, or timed out after two minutes of waiting to connect.

VmCtl

Similar to the *VmServerCtl* object, the *VmCtl* object is used to gather information from or control a virtual machine running on a VMware ESX or GSX host. *VmCtl* exposes quite a few properties and methods, making this object quite powerful. What makes it even more unique than the other VmCOM objects we have discussed so far is that several of the properties and methods use symbolic constant enumerations (SCE) which must be inter-preted. As this can get quite complicated, we will review the various proper-ties and methods along with their relationship and dependency on SCEs. You can also reference the VMware Scripting API User's Manual which provides additional information about each method and property we briefly mention in this chapter.

Tables 3.3 and 3.4 outline the properties and methods exposed by *VmCtl*, including the references to the SCEs, and Table 3.5 lists the symbolic constant enumerations and their interpreted values.

Table 3.3 *VmCtl* Properties

Property Name	Description
ExecutionState	Returns the current state of the VM. Returns the SCE *VmExecutionState*.
PendingQuestion	Returns a *VmQuestion* object (a *VmCollection*) with the details of the question if the VM is in a stuck state.
GuestInfo(key)	Accesses the shared variables (discussed later in this chapter).
Config (key)	Accesses the configuration variables defined in the con-figuration files of the VM.
ConfigFileName	Returns just the name of the configuration file, not the path.
Heartbeat	Returns the heartbeat count generated by the VMware Tools in the guest OS.
ToolsLastActive	Returns an integer representing the number of seconds since the last heartbeat was detected.
DeviceIsConnected (dev)	Returns a Boolean value concerning the state of the specified device.
ProductInfo(type)	Returns information concerning the VMware product. Returns the SCEs *VmProductInfoType*, *VmProduct*, or *VmPlatform*.
Uptime	Returns the uptime of the Guest OS running in the VM.
PID	Returns the process ID of a running VM.
Resource(name)	Accesses the VM resource variable passed as "name".
ID	Returns the UUID for a running VM.

Continued

Table 3.3 continued *VmCtl* Properties

Property Name	Description
Capabilities	Returns the access permissions for the current user.
RemoteConnections	Returns the number of users connected to the VM remotely.

Note that *Resource*, *ID*, *Capabilities*, and *RemoteConnections* only apply to virtual machines running on a VMware ESX host. These properties will return an error when attempting to retrieve values from a virtual machine running on a VMware GSX host.

Table 3.4 *VmCtl* Methods

Method Name	Description
Connect(params,name)	Establishes a connection to a VM. You must pass a *VmConnectParams* object and the configuration file name of the VM you are connecting to.
Start(mode)	Powers on or resumes a VM. Utilizes the SCE *VmPowerOpMode* to control the behavior of the operation.
Stop(mode)	Shuts down and powers of a VM. Utilizes the SCE *VmPowerOpMode* to control the behavior of the operation.
Reset(mode)	Shuts down and reboots a VM. Utilizes the SCE *VmPowerOpMode* to control the behavior of the operation.
Suspend (mode)	Suspends a VM. Utilizes the SCE *VmPowerOpMode* to control the behavior of the operation.
AddRedo(diskName)	Adds a redo log to a running VM's virtual disk.
Commit(diskName,level, freeze,wait)	Commits changes in redo logs for a running VM's virtual disk.
AnswerQuestion(question, choice)	Replies to a question for a stuck VM with a specific answer.

Continued

Table 3.4 continued *VmCtl* Methods

Method Name	Description
ConnectDevice(dev)	Connects a specific device to a running VM.
DisconnectDevice(dev)	Disconnects a specific device from a running VM.
SetRunAsUser(uname,pwd)	Runs the VM as a specified user under the credentials passed by the method.
RunAsUser	Returns the name of the user running the VM. Does not return the password.

Note that *AddRedo()* and *Commit()* only apply to virtual machines running on a VMware ESX host. These properties will return an error when attempting to retrieve values from a virtual machine running on a VMware GSX host. Likewise, *SetRunAsUser()* and *RunAsUser()* only apply to virtual machines running on a VMware GSX host, and will return errors if invoked against a VMware ESX host.

> **NOTE**
>
> Similar to *VmServerCtl*, the total number of concurrent connections per VM is limited and cannot exceed two when using the API. To establish new connections to the VM, free up a connection by destroying instantiated *VmCtl* objects first.

Table 3.5 *VmCtl* Symbolic Constant Enumerations (SCE)

SCE Name	Value	Description
VmExecutionState	VmExecutionState_On	VM is powered on.
	VmExecutionState_Off	VM is powered off.
	VmExecutionState_ Suspended	VM is suspended.
	VmExecutionState_ Stuck	VM is awaiting input from user.

Continued

Table 3.5 continued *VmCtl* Symbolic Constant Enumerations (SCE)

SCE Name	Value	Description
	VmExecutionState_ Unknown	VM is in an unknown state.
VmPowerOpMode	VmPowerOpMode_Soft	Runs predefined scripts via the VMware Tools in the Guest OS and attempts to gracefully perform the operation.
	VmPowerOpMode_Hard	No scripts are run. Immediately and unconditionally performs the operation.
	VmPowerOpMode_TrySoft	Attempts to perform the operation with the *VmPowerOpMode_Soft* behavior. If it fails to do so, the operation will then be performed as a *VmPowerOpMode_Hard*.
VmProdInfoType	vmProdInfo_Product	Returned as *VmProduct*.
	vmProdInfo_Platform	Returned as *VmPlatform*.
	vmProdInfo_Build	Product's build number.
	vmProdInfo_Version_ Major	Product's major version number.
	vmProdInfo_Version_ Minor	Product's minor version number.
	vmProdInfo_Version_ Revision	Product's revision number.
VmProduct	vmProduct_WS	Product is VMware Workstation.
	vmProduct_GSX	Product is VMware GSX Server.
	vmProduct_ESX	Product is VMware ESX Server.
	vmProduct_UNKNOWN	Product is unknown.
VmPlatform	vmPlatform_WINDOWS	Host platform is an MS Windows OS.

Continued

Table 3.5 continued *VmCtl* Symbolic Constant Enumerations (SCE)

SCE Name	Value	Description
	vmPlatform_LINUX	Host platform is a Linux OS.
	vmPlatform_VMNIX	Host platform is the ESX Server service console.
	vmPlatform_UNKNOWN	Host platform is unknown.

Using our previous example, we can utilize the established connection via *VmServerCtl* and the *VmCollection* of virtual machines on our host to query the uptime for each of the registered VMs using *VmCtl*. The following retrieves the configuration file name for each VM, connects to the VM, and gets the value from the *uptime* property. The results are then echoed as output.

```
For each ConfigFile in objVMList

      Set objVM = CreateObject("VmCOM.VmCtl")

      objVM.Connect objConnParams, ConfigFile

      vmUptime = objVM.Resource("cpu.uptime")

      WScript.Echo "Uptime for VM " & ConfigFile & " is " & VMUptime

Next
```

With VmCOM, you can also write scripts that perform configuration management activities on your hosts and VMs. Focusing on establishing configuration standards, you can ensure that optimal and approved configurations are always maintained without having to use the VMware ESX/GSX MUI to do so. For example, a sample script may ensure that no floppy drives are left connected to the VM. On a host running many VMs, leaving physical devices, such as floppy and optical drives, places unnecessary load on the service console (ESX) or host OS (GSX).

The following demonstrates how you can accomplish this via a simple script. After connecting to the ESX host and retrieving a *VmCollection* of all registered VMs, the script connects to each VM individually, checks the connection status of the floppy device, and disconnects it accordingly.

```
' Set parameters used to connect to the ESX Server.

Set objConnParams = CreateObject("VmCOM.VmConnectParams")

objConnParams.hostname = "esxserver1 "
```

```
objConnParams.username = "adminuser1"
objConnParams.password = "password1"


' Establish connection with ESX host
Set objVMServer = CreateObject("VmCOM.VmServerCtl")
objVMServer.Connect objConnParams


' Obtain list of registered VMs on host
Set objVMList = objVMServer.RegisteredVmNames


' Step through list of VMs and connect to each one
' individually. Disconnect floppy drive, if connected
For each ConfigFile in objVMList
    Set objVM = CreateObject("VmCOM.VmCtl")
    objVM.Connect objConnParams, ConfigFile
    vmDevice = "floppy0"
    if objVM.DeviceIsConnected(vmDevice) Then
        objVM.DisconnectDevice(vmDevice)
        vmDeviceStatus = "Now Disconnected"
    Else
        vmDeviceStatus = "Was already disconnected"
    End If
    WScript.Echo "Floppy for VM " & ConfigFile & ":"
    WScript.Echo vbTab & "Status: " & vmDeviceStatus
    WScript.Echo
Next


objVM = Nothing
objVMServer = Nothing
objConnParams = Nothing
```

Managing Guests with User-Defined Variables

As mentioned earlier, another unique feature within the VMware Scripting API is the ability to pass data between a script and a running virtual machine. This can be accomplished in any direction—either passing information from the script to a running virtual machine or passing information from inside a running virtual machine to a script. The VMware Tools service facilitates the interaction between the script and the virtual machine.

To pass information to or from the running virtual machine, you must set the *GuestInfo* class of variable using the *VmCtl* object. You can define any number of key names and assign any string value to them. The following example assumes that you have already established a connection to a specific VM using the *VmCtl* object. Here we pass specific values to be retrieved later inside the Guest OS.

```
Set objVM = CreateObject("VmCOM.VmCtl")

objVM.Connect objConnParams, "/home/vmware/server1/server1.vmx"


objVM.GuestInfo("Department") = "Accounting"

objVM.GuestInfo("CostCenter") = "5008620"

objVM.GuestInfo("Priority") = "Low"
```

Once these values have been set, the information can be retrieved using the *VMwareService.exe* command for Windows guests or the *vmware-guestd* command for Linux guests. In a similar fashion, you can use those commands to set rather than get values to user-defined variables and retrieve them via VmCOM scripts.

NOTE

When passing information using *GuestInfo*, the data is not persistent. If the virtual machine is powered off and all sessions connected to the virtual machine are closed, the information originally shared with the VM is lost. When the VM is powered on again, all *GuestInfo* variables are again undefined.

Working with the VmPerl API

The VmPerl API provides four Perl modules that are used to establish, maintain communication, and interact with a VMware ESX or GSX server or virtual machine. Two of the modules are functionally equivalent to the *VmServerCtl* and *VmCtl* objects exposed by the VmCOM API, as discussed earlier in this chapter. Both of these modules will serve as the primary modules for your Perl scripts. They are

- **VMware::VmPerl::Server** Used to create a session with an ESX or GSX host and expose the services and functionality of the API's server interfaces.

- **VMware::VmPerl::VM** Used to manage and perform operations against a virtual machine on a specific ESX or GSX host.

Also, similar to the supporting objects in the VmCOM API, there are two supporting modules provided by the VmPerl API. These modules are used as the inputs or outputs to the properties and methods exposed by the primary modules. They are

- **VMware::VmPerl::ConnectParams** Provides host information and authentication credentials used when establishing a connection to an ESX or GSX host.

- **VMware::VmPerl::Question** Provides an interactive interface to respond to questions or error conditions for a virtual machine running on an ESX or GSX host.

The process begins by establishing a connection with an ESX or GSX host or a virtual machine on a particular host using the *Connect()* method of either the *VMware::VmPerl::Server* or *VMware::VmPerl::VM* objects. The parameter *$connectparams* provides the appropriate input for the *Connect()* method when establishing the connection to a host or virtual machine.

VMware::VmPerl::ConnectParams

The *VMware::VmPerl::ConnectParams* module provides the host information and user credentials required by either the *$server->connect()* or *$vm->connect()*, as well as the methods listed in Table 3.6.

Table 3.6 *VMware::VmPerl::ConnectParams* Methods

Method	Description
$connectparams->get_hostname()	A string value that represents the DNS host name of the VMware ESX or GSX host or its IP address.
$connectparams->get_port()	An integer value representing the TCP port that should be used to establish a connection with the VMware ESX or GSX host. This property is optional.
$connectparams->get_username()	A string value containing the username to pass as credentials for the connection.
$connectparams->get_password()	A string value containing the password for the user set in the *Username* property.

The following demonstrates the instantiation of the *VMware::VmPerl::ConnectParams* object:

```
use VMware::VmPerl;

use VMware::VmPerl::ConnectParams;

use strict;


my $sName = "esxserver1";

my $port = 902;

my $user = "adminuser1";

my $passwd = "password1";


my $connectParams =
VMware::VmPerl::ConnectParams::new($sName,$port,$user,$passwd);
```

VMware::VmPerl::Server

The *VMware::VmPerl::Server* module is used for programmatic interaction with, and manipulation of, VMware ESX or GSX hosts running virtual machines. Table 3.7 lists the methods associated with this module. With these methods, you can

- Connect to a server.

- List the virtual machines on that server.

- Register and unregister configuration files for virtual machines.

- Create virtual machine objects

- Disconnect from the server

Table 3.7 *VMware::VmPerl::Server* Methods

Method	Description
$server->connect()	Used to establish a connection with a VMware ESX or GSX host. You must pass *$connectParams* that specifies host information and authentication credentials.
$server->is_connected()	Used to determine if a connection exists.
$server->get_last_error()	Returns an array with information about the last error.
$server->registered_vm_ names()	Returns an array with the configuration file name of each virtual machine registered with the host.
$server->register_vm()	Registers a virtual machine with the host. You must pass the configuration file name for the virtual machine.
$server->unregister_vm()	Unregisters a virtual machine from the host. You must pass the configuration file name for the virtual machine.
$server->get_resource()	Gets the value of a particular ESX Server system resource variable. You must pass the variable name. This method applies to ESX Servers only.
$server->set_resource()	Sets the value of a particular ESX Server system resource variable. You must pass the variable name. This method applies to ESX Servers only.

VMware::VmPerl::VM

The *VMware::VmPerl::VM* module is used for controlling interaction with virtual machines on VMware ESX or GSX hosts. Table 3.8 lists the methods associated with this module. Examples of operations provided by this module are

- Connect to a virtual machine.

- Check a virtual machine's state.

- Start, stop, suspend, and resume virtual machines.

- Query and modify configuration file settings.

- Answer status questions from virtual machines.

- Get a basic heartbeat from a virtual machine.

- Pass parameters to and from VMware tools in each virtual machine.

Table 3.8 *VMware::VmPerl::VM* Methods

Method	Description
$vm->connect()	Used to establish a connection with virtual machines running on a VMware ESX or GSX host. You must pass *$connectParams* and the configuration file name for the desired virtual machine.
$vm->is_connected()	Used to determine if a connection exists.
$vm->get_last_error()	Returns an array with information about the last error.
$vm->start()	Powers on a virtual machine. You must pass VM_POWEROP_MODE for the appropriate behavior for this operation.
$vm->stop()	Powers off a virtual machine. You must pass VM_POWEROP_MODE for the appropriate behavior for this operation.
$vm->reset()	Powers off and then powers on a virtual machine as a single operation. You must pass VM_POWEROP_MODE for the appropriate behavior.

Continued

Table 3.8 continued *VMware::VmPerl::VM* Methods

Method	Description
$vm->suspend()	Suspends a virtual machine. You must pass VM_POWEROP_MODE for the appropriate behavior for this operation.
$vm->add_redo()	Used to add a redo log to a virtual SCSI disk. You must pass a reference to the target disk for this operation. This method applies to ESX Servers only.
$vm->commit()	Commits all changes in a redo log to a virtual SCSI disk. You must pass a reference to the target disk for this operation along with the LEVEL, FREEZE, and WAIT parameters. This method applies to ESX Servers only.
$vm->get_connected_users()	Returns a list of users connected to the host. The list includes connections via a VmCOM or VmPerl API session, MUI, and remote console sessions.
$vm->get_execution_state()	Returns the virtual machine's current state.
$vm->get_guest_info()	Returns the value of a shared variable of the VMware Tools running in a virtual machine, as referenced by the passed key index.
$vm->set_guest_info()	Sets the value of a shared variable of the VMware Tools running in a virtual machine, as referenced by the passed key index.
$vm->get_heartbeat()	Returns the current count for a virtual machine's heartbeat as generated by the VMware Tools.
$vm->get_tools_last_active()	Returns the number of seconds since the last heartbeat was detected by the VMware Tools running inside a virtual machine.
$vm->get_config_file_name()	Returns the name of the configuration file.
$vm->get_config()	Returns the value of a variable from the configuration file of a virtual machine. You must pass the name of the variable to retrieve.

Continued

Table 3.8 continued *VMware::VmPerl::VM* Methods

Method	Description
$vm->set_config ()	Sets the value of a variable from the configuration file of a virtual machine. You must pass the name of the variable to set. Note that some variables cannot be changed while a virtual machine is powered on, such as memory size or CPU count.
$vm->get_product_info()	Returns information about the VMware product.
$vm->get_pending_question()	Returns a *VMware::VmPerl::Question* object with information regarding any pending questions.
$vm->answer_pending_ question()	Used to answer a pending question with an available selection, as indicated by the *VMware::VmPerl::Question* object.
$vm->device_is_connected()	Used to determine if a virtual device is currently connected. You must pass a reference to the device to target for this operation.
$vm->connect_device()	Connects a currently disconnected virtual device. You must pass a reference to the device to target for this operation.
$vm->disconnect_device()	Disconnects a currently connected virtual device. You must pass a reference to the device to target for this operation.
$vm->get_resource()	Returns the value of a virtual machine resource variable. You must pass a reference of the variable to target for this operation. This method applies to ESX Servers only.
$vm->set_resource()	Sets the value of a virtual machine resource variable. You must pass a reference of the variable to target for this operation. This method applies to ESX Servers only.
$vm->get_uptime()	Returns the uptime of the guest OS in a virtual machine.
$vm->get_id()	Returns the UUID of a virtual machine.
$vm->get_pid()	Returns the process ID of a virtual machine.

Continued

Table 3.8 continued *VMware::VmPerl::VM* Methods

Method	Description
$vm->get_capabilities()	Returns the permission of the user used to establish the connection. This method applies to ESX Servers only.
$vm->get_runas_user()	Returns the name of the user running the virtual machine. This method applies to GSX Servers only.
$vm->set_runas_user()	Sets the user credentials for the virtual machine to run under the next time a power-on operation is performed. You must pass the username and password as parameters for this method. This applies to GSX Servers only.

In addition to these methods, the *VMware::VmPerl::VM* module exposes symbolic constants that also provide inputs and outputs to methods in Table 3.8. They are

- **VM_EXECUTION_STATE** Specifies the state or condition of the virtual machine.

- **VM_POWEROP_MODE** Specifies the behavior of a power transition operation.

- **VM_PRODINFO_PRODUCT** Specifies the name of the VMware product.

- **VM_PRODINFO_PLATFORM** Specifies the host's platform.

VMware::VmPerl::Question

The *VMware::VmPerl::Question* module provides an interface to answer pending questions or error conditions that leave virtual machines in a stuck execution state. As a sub-object to the *VMware::VmPerl::VM* module, you instantiate the *Question* object by calling the *get_pending_question()* method. Table 3.9 lists the methods associated with this module.

Table 3.9 *VMware::VmPerl::Question* Methods

Method	Description
$question->get_id()	Returns an integer value to identify the question.
$question->get_text()	Returns the text of the question as a string value.
$question->get_choices ()	Returns an array of string values that represent all of the possible answers to the question.

Putting It All Together

With the objects that we have reviewed, you can build simple yet powerful scripts and applications to manage your VMware ESX and GSX Servers and the virtual machines that run on them. Similar to how scripting with WSH and WMI has revolutionized Windows administration similar to what Unix administrators have always enjoyed, you can automate many VMware administration tasks, ensuring that each host and VM has a consistent and managed configuration.

You will really reap the benefits of the VmCOM and VmPerl API as you write scripts and applications to address tasks that were either too complex to perform manually (and subsequently never performed) or too difficult to manage in an infrastructure that frequently changes. In this section, we will review some examples of how the APIs can solve some common problems.

NOTE

For all these examples, and for all of your own development efforts, be sure to have the appropriate Scripting API installed on your development machine, as well as on your test machine, if not the same.

Example 1: Disconnecting Devices from Every Registered VM

Often, VMware administrators put excessive loads on the Service Console by leaving devices that are seldom used connected to the hosted VMs. In particular, administrators should try to disconnect virtual CD/DVD–ROM drives, especially in Windows-based VMs, as well as floppy drives (probably the most unused device), to minimize the overhead these devices place on the Service Console. For our first example, we will demonstrate a simple administration script using VmPerl to perform this administration task easily, regardless of how many VMs are running on the VMware host.

First, we begin by ensuring that the Perl modules are located and can be used by the script. This is only a consideration that needs to be addressed in Perl scripts running on a Windows-based machine.

```
# This script will disconnect the following devices from the

# running VMs on the target ESX or GSX server:

#       * floppy0

#       * ide1:0


# Add paths when running script on a Windows machine
BEGIN {

    if ($^O eq "MSWin32") {

        @INC = (

            # Set the path to your VmPerl Scripting directory if different

            'C:\Program Files\VMware\VMware VmPerl Scripting
API\perl5\site_perl\5.005',

            'C:\Program Files\VMware\VMware VmPerl Scripting
API\perl5\site_perl\5.005\MSWin32-x86');

    }

}
```

Next, we begin instantiating our Perl modules. In this example, we will only need *VMware::VmPerl::ConnectParams*, *VMware::VmPerl::Server*, and *VMware::VmPerl::VM*.

```
use VMware::VmPerl;

use VMware::VmPerl::ConnectParams;

use VMware::VmPerl::Server;

use VMware::VmPerl::VM;

use strict;
```

Then we define our connection parameters and establish a connection with our VMware host. It is always a good practice to code error handling each time you invoke a method. The most basic way to handle any exception is to simply stop the execution of the script with the die directive.

```
# Create a Connect_Params object; no params to new() connects to local
machine
my $sName = "esxserver1";

my $port = 902;

my $user = "adminuser1";

my $passwd = "password1";


my $connectParams =
 VMware::VmPerl::ConnectParams::new($sName,$port,$user,$passwd);


# Create a Server object
my $server = VMware::VmPerl::Server::new();


# Connect to the server using the connect_params
if(!$server->connect($connect_params)) {
        die "Could not connect to local server\n";
}
```

Next, we enumerate the VMs registered with the VMware host and attempt to disconnect the floppy drive and CD-ROM drive from each VM. In this example, we are assuming that only one floppy drive exists as floppy0 and that only one CD/DVD-ROM exists on the IDE bus as ide1:0.

```
# Get a list of registered vmxs
my @list=$server->registered_vm_names();
foreach my $vmx (@list) {
        my $vm = VMware::VmPerl::VM::new();
        if($vm->connect($connect_params, $vmx)) {
                print "\n" . $vm->get_config("displayName");
                if($vm->disconnect_device("floppy0")) {
```

```
                        print "\n\tFloppy disconnected.";

              } else {

                        print "\n\tFloppy not disconnected.";

              }

              if($vm->disconnect_device("ide1:0")) {

                        print "\n\tCD-ROM disconnected.";

              } else {

                        print "\n\tCD-ROM not disconnected.";

              }

      } else {

              print "\nCould not connect to VM.";

      }

}
```

This script can be easily modified to perform other operations against each VM, such as initiating a snapshot, suspending them, or simply gathering information about each VM as part of a documentation process.

Example 2: Simple GUI to List All Virtual Machines

This example follows a simple workflow, demonstrated in Figure 3.5. First, you capture the basic information as required by the VmConnectParams object in one form. Then you will pass that information to another form that will connect the VMware host and retrieve the list of VMs using the *VmCollection* object. Finally, you will display the configuration file information for each registered VM.

The first step is to create two forms, one called *frmConnect* and the other called *frmVMList*. An example of *frmConnect* is shown in Figure 3.6. This form is composed of three labels, three text boxes (*vHostName*, *vUserName*, and *vPassword*), and one button (*btnConnect*).

Figure 3.5 Process Diagram for Simple GUI Application

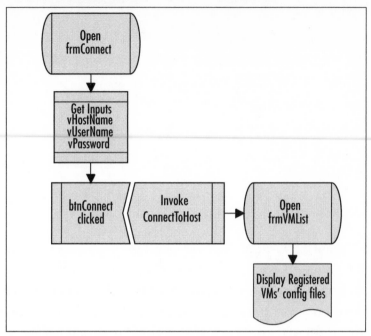

Figure 3.6 The Connection Form in Design Mode

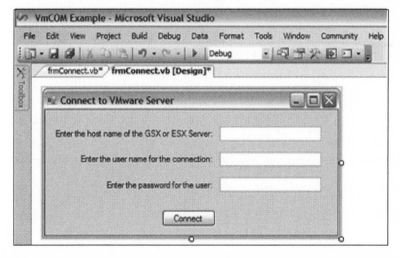

The *btnConnect* control is then used to pass this data to *frmVMList*. This is accomplished by creating a new instance of *frmVMList* and assigning the

ConnectToHost method to the click event of the control, as shown in the following code fragment.

```
Public Class frmConnect

    Private Sub btnConnect_Click(ByVal sender As Object, ByVal e As _

    System.EventArgs) Handles btnConnect.Click

        Dim VMListForm As New frmVMList

        VMListForm.ConnectToHost(vHostName.Text, vUserName.Text, _

            vPassword.Text)

        VMListForm.Show()

    End Sub

End Class
```

The logic in *frmVMList* captures the value for the host name, username, and password to build to connection parameters. After establishing the connection to the host, we then enumerate all of the VMs registered with the VMware host and retrieve the configuration file for each one, afterward adding that string value to a *listbox* control visible in the form. The following code shows how this is done.

```
Public Class frmVMList

    Dim objConnParams As New VMCOMLib.VmConnectParams

    Dim objVMServer As New VMCOMLib.VmServerCtl

    Dim objVMList As New VMCOMLib.VmCollection

    Dim ConfigFile As String


    Friend Sub ConnectToHost(ByVal HostName As String, ByVal UserName As _

    String, ByVal Password As String)

        objConnParams.Hostname = HostName

        objConnParams.Username = UserName

        objConnParams.Password = Password

        objVMServer.Connect(objConnParams)

        objVMList = objVMServer.RegisteredVmNames

        For Each ConfigFile In objVMList

            lbxVMs.Items.Add(ConfigFile)
```

```
        Next

    End Sub


    Private Sub btnClose_Click(ByVal sender As Object, ByVal e As _
      System.EventArgs) Handles btnClose.Click
        Me.Close()
    End Sub
```

```
End Class
```

Figure 3.7 shows a sample output from running our VmCOM sample application. Although this example is basic, you can easily expand on its code base and create your own management application.

Figure 3.7 A Sample Listing Showing the Configuration Files for Each Registered VM

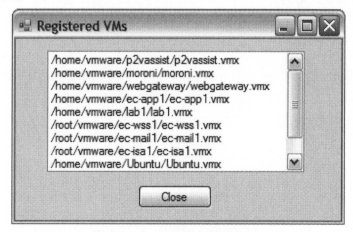

Example 3: Test Automation with VMware

Quality management departments are regularly challenged by the difficulties and expense of configuration testing. To truly certify that software products will run on the wide variety of hardware and software that exists in the field, they must run tests against a daunting variety of configurations. Virtual machines provide a great way to cost-effectively provision the various config-urations which the test application runs, including hardware differences (for example, amount of memory, network speed, graphics display resolution, and so on) and software differences (such as OS version, service packs, browsers and their versions, shared libraries, and so forth). However, managing a large library of virtual machines can itself present challenges to the testing process.

You can help realize great benefits by enhancing quality and functional testing further with virtual machines by including automation in the test cycle. By identifying and documenting the testing process and workflow, you can then create automation scripts that quality analysts and managers can run to "initialize" their test environment prior to running a battery of tests, and then release those resources when the test is complete.

The diagram shown in Figure 3.8 demonstrates a process diagram outlining the steps that the automation scripts must take, easily built on Perl or an ActiveX–compatible scripting language. This workflow can involve interaction with other interfaces, such as ADO, WSH, and WMI; however, the Scripting APIs play a big role in the design and execution of this testing process. Although we do not show any script samples here, the operations to be performed are well-documented in the programming and reference guides provided by VMware.

Figure 3.8 Sample Process Diagram for Test Automation with VMware

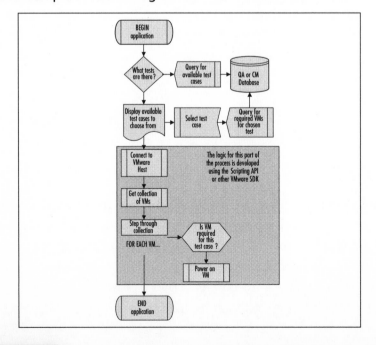

VMware Virtual Infrastructure SDK

Even more powerful than the VMware Scripting APIs, VMware has released Virtual Infrastructure (VI) SDK to give developers a standards-based avenue to manage their VMware investment. Today, there are two versions of the VI SDK tied to the two predominant releases of the VMware ESX Server and VirtualCenter products. In this section, we will review the architecture of the VI SDK 2.0 (for managing ESX 3.0 and VirtualCenter 2.0), as well as the VI SDK 1.1 (for managing ESX Server 2.5.x and VirtualCenter 1.x).

Why continue to discuss the original VI SDK release 1.1? With the release of the Virtual Infrastructure 3 and VI SDK 2.0 in June 2006, VMware is banking on lots of customers upgrading to the latest release to take advantage of the additional benefits and features available. However, the conversion to this major upgrade will take some time, as customer test their upgrade strategies, gain acceptance from the user and business community, and actually perform the upgrades in accordance with their internal change management processes. In addition, VI SDK 1.1 scripts can still be run against the new version if configured for backwards-compatibility.

In the following sections, we will review the architecture and composition of the VI SDK, developing with the SDK 1.1, and developing with the SDK 2.0. Each version of the SDK is discussed separately because of the substantial differences between them; however, the concepts discussed can be incorporated in your development activities regardless of which version you are coding for.

What Is the VMware Virtual Infrastructure SDK?

About the time that VMware released ESX Server 2.x, VMware VirtualCenter started to really become the central tool for managing the virtual infrastructure. Although the Management User Interface, or MUI, continued to be available, it was primarily used for host configuration while administrators chose to manage the virtual machines themselves with the VirtualCenter client. As the virtual infrastructure continued to grow, the MUI also showed its weakness in managing larger farms or arrays of VMware hosts, since each MUI instance can manage one and only one VMware host.

The paradigm change of VI, management shifting its focus to managing in groups in a hierarchal manner rather than managing individual resources was further heightened by the introduction of new infrastructure features such as virtual machine migration, new provisioning techniques and options, and managing virtual machines independently of what VMware host they are running on. Such an extensive and complex management scope provided opportunities to ISVs and savvy administrators and developers to create custom tools to increase the efficiency of managing VI; however, they needed internal hooks into the products to be able to do so in an open manner.

VMware responded to this need by releasing and continuing to enhance the Virtual Infrastructure SDK. With the VI SDK, developers can integrate the management of VMware's server products into their existing data center management solutions or develop a new solution from the ground up. With the release of VI SDK 2.0, VMware has expanded the capability of the SDK to include managed objects and a robust, yet less complex, object model that supports all the previous operations, as well as new ones, such as host configuration, DRS, and HA feature set.

The VI SDK Architecture

The VMware VI SDK is made up of two important elements, the VMware VirtualCenter Web Service and the actual SDK package itself, which contains the supporting binaries needed, samples, and reference and programming guide documentation.

Before starting to develop with the SDK, you must understand its architecture. As shown in Figure 3.9, the VI SDK 1.1 interfaces with the Web service component of VirtualCenter via SOAP calls over HTTP or HTTPS. This interface is the only available Web service for managing virtual machines running VMware ESX hosts. Without VirtualCenter, administrators and developers must utilize the VMware Scripting APIs discussed earlier in this chapter to perform a more limited set of operations against virtual machines.

Figure 3.9 The Virtual Infrastructure SDK 1.1 Architecture

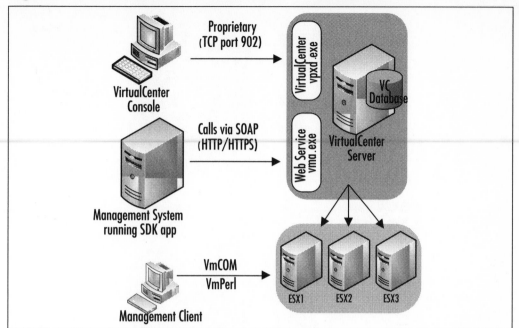

In contrast, Figure 3.10 shows the updated architecture of the VI SDK 2.0, both with and without VirtualCenter implemented. Beginning with the VI SDK 2.0, VMware has standardized the SDK for both ESX hosts and VirtualCenter. In addition, VMware has overhauled the object model and hierarchy of the SDK and included robust host management operations as well. As a result, management applications built on VI SDK 2.0 are more powerful and no longer have a dependency on VirtualCenter. That does not mean that the SDK replaces VirtualCenter, though, as enterprises should still implement VirtualCenter to maximize their management capabilities and potential.

The VirtualCenter console, or client, still connects to VirtualCenter using the proprietary VMware communication protocol over TCP port 902, the same as the communication between the VirtualCenter server and the registered ESX hosts. Although the two communication interfaces are different, they both expose the same operations that administrators can use to accomplish the same set of tasks.

Figure 3.10 The Virtual Infrastructure SDK 2.0 Architecture

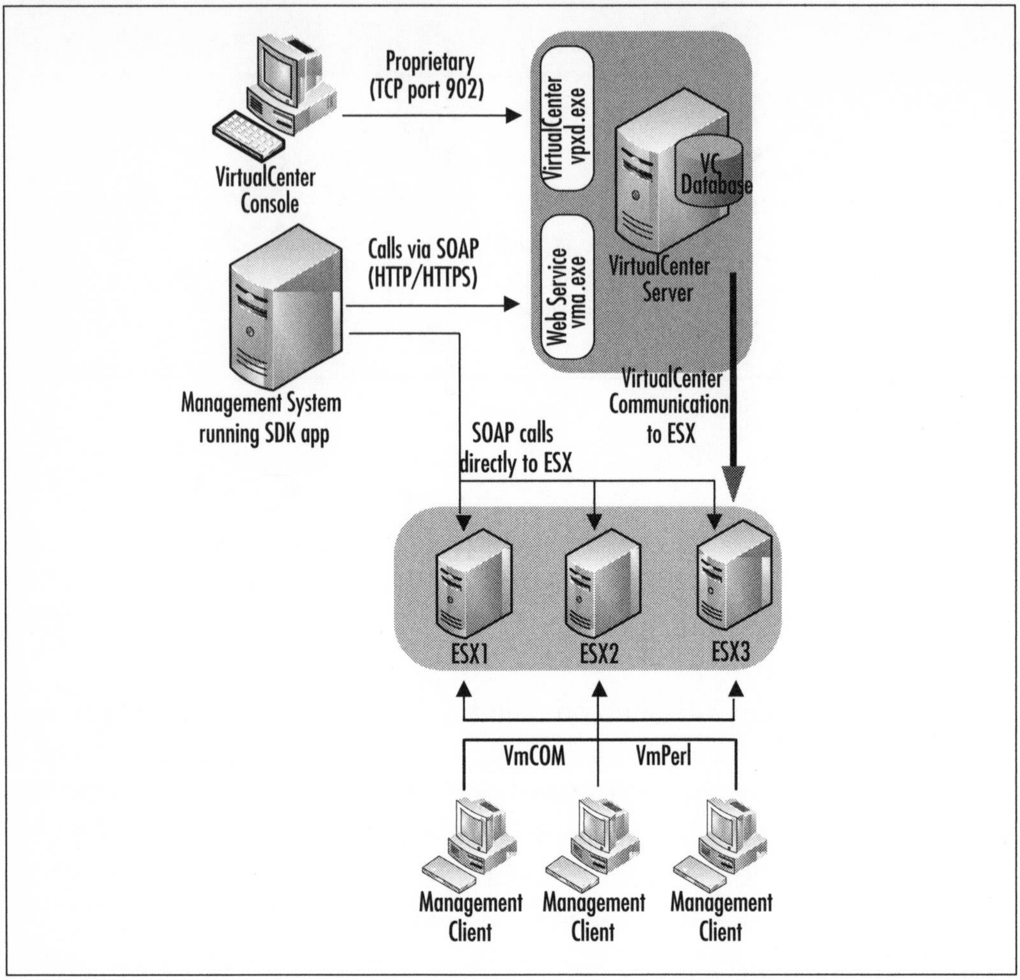

Overview of the VMware
Virtual Infrastructure Web Service

As previously mentioned, there are two components to the VMware SDK, the Web Service and the SDK package itself. The web service installs as part of the VirtualCenter installation, and as part of the ESX installation (version 3.0 only), and serves as the gateway to all of the advanced management operations that can be performed against VirtualCenter, ESX Server, and virtual machines.

What Are Web Services?

According to the W3C, a Web service is a software system designed to support interoperable machine-to-machine interaction over a network. It has an interface that is described in a format called a Web Service Description Language (WSDL), which is an Extensible Markup Language (XML)–based description on how to communicate with the Web service. Other systems interact with the Web service in a manner prescribed by its interface, or WSDL, by exchanging XML messages that are enclosed in a Simple Object Access Protocol (SOAP) envelope. These messages are typically conveyed using HTTP, and normally comprise XML in conjunction with other Web-related standards. Software applications written in various programming languages and running on various platforms can use Web services to exchange data over computer networks like the Internet in a manner similar to interprocess communication on a single computer.

This interoperability is due to the use of open standards. These standards are defined and maintained by several committees and organizations responsible for the architecture and standardization of Web services, such as:

- Organization for the Advancement of Structured Information Standards (OASIS)
- World Wide Web Consortium (W3C)
- Web Services Interoperability Organization (WS-I)

The latter organization, WS-I, is a charter that promotes interoperability across platforms, applications, and programming languages. Its goal is to be a standards integrator to help Web services advance in a structured, coherent manner. There are so many standards that need to be coordinated to address basic Web service interoperability issues, and the standards are all being developed in parallel and independently. To overcome these issues, the WS-I has developed the concept of a profile, defined as a set of named Web services specifications at specific revision levels, together with a set of implementation and interoperability guidelines recommending how the specifications may be used to develop interoperable Web services.

VMware VI SDK Conformance and Web Service Standards

Both the VMware Infrastructure SDK 1.1 and 2.0 conform to the WS-I Basic Profile 1.0, which expresses a set of assertions about the format and interoperation of the SOAP messages and the WSDL document exchanged between clients and the Web service itself. This profile covers and ensures compliance with the following:

- XML Schema 1.0
- SOAP 1.1
- WSDL 1.1
- UDDI 2.0

One of the advantages of Web services is that they are language-agnostic; any programming language may be used to access the interface. In practice, an adequate Web services toolkit must be available and supported by the chosen language; however, administrators and developers can design management applications based on the SDK with any language and toolkit they choose thanks to the high level of testing and compliance to the above standards.

Operations Available Using the Virtual Infrastructure SDK

The API exposed by the VI Web service provides a powerful set of operations that can be performed when managing your virtual infrastructure. These operations can be categorized into three areas—basic, element management, and virtual computing. The exact set of operations available to you will depend on which version of the VI SDK you are developing against, and what VMware products you are using.

Operations for Basic Web Service Client Interaction

Each version of the VI SDK has standard functionality to facilitate establishing and maintaining connections with the VI Web service. These operations are used regardless of what function or role your applications will have. These basic operations include

- Logging in to the Web service

- Logging off from the Web service

- Traversing up and down the object hierarchy

- Grabbing a handle of objects and items exposed by the Web service

Operations for Element Management

Element management consists of the operations used to manage the physical host machine running the VMware ESX Server software. All versions of the VI SDK expose APIs for the following element management operations:

- Virtual machine creation

- Virtual machine deletion

- Virtual machine configuration, including all attributes found in the corresponding VMX file

- Virtual machine power operations, including power on, power off, reset, suspend, and resume

- Virtual machines inventory in a flat namespace

- Virtual disk configuration and management

- Virtual machine guest OS customization

- Physical host and virtual machine performance data collection

- Event and alert management

In addition to these, VI SDK 2.0 also adds the following element management operations that facilitate additional management capabilities for the physical components in the virtual infrastructure:

- Virtual machine inventory with a nested folder hierarchy

- Filtered property collection using the Property Collector

- Host connection and disconnection from VirtualCenter

- Host reboots or shuts down

- Datastore creation and removal from a specific host

- Internet service and firewall configuration for a specific host

- Detection and configuration of storage attached to a host
- Configuration of network interfaces and virtual switches, and configuration for a specific host

Operations for Virtual Computing

Virtual computing consists of the operations used to manage the virtual infrastructure as a whole without targeting any specific host. These operations are more geared towards the virtual machines themselves, providing an API to the features that make VMware VI such a powerful platform. All versions of the VI SDK expose the following virtual computing operations:

- Direct virtual machine management, regardless of which physical host the virtual machines are running on
- Virtual machine migration via VMotion
- Virtual machine provisioning using templates and cloning

The VI SDK 2.0 also adds operations that take advantage of the new features release with VirtualCenter 2.0 and ESX 3.0. These new virtual computing operations are

- Distributed Availability Services (DAS), allowing virtual machines to failover to another host in the event of a host failure
- Distributed Resource Scheduling (DRS), supporting the migration of virtual machines from one host to another based on resource requirements and desired load-balancing results.

Developing with the Virtual Infrastructure SDK 1.1

The first step to developing with either SDK is to download the appropriate SDK package. The latest package for VI SDK 1.1 when this book was published was build 19058 for VirtualCenter 1.3. The SDK package is distributed as a Zip file that contains two primary directory paths. The first path contains the wsdlProxyGen.exe tool, and the second path contains code samples and automation scripts for building the samples, documentation, and sample vma.wsdl and autoprep-types.xda files.

TIP

It is recommended that you always download and use the latest version of the SDK, available on VMware's site at www.vmware.com/support/developer. Although code that you write against the SDK released alongside a previous release of VirtualCenter may work, it is a good practice to make sure that the SDK is the same version as your VirtualCenter installation or newer.

Central to any interaction or development with a Web service is the consumption of that Web service by the client application. In order to consume the Web service, we must follow three basic steps:

1. Prepare the VI Web service by modifying the configuration file as needed.

2. Generate the proxy class of the VI Web service and consume the Web service source file.

3. Write the code for your management application.

As we walk through these steps, we will demonstrate them in both C# and VB using Microsoft Visual Studio 2005. Even so, this example and walk-through can easily be modified for Java or Perl development. For additional examples of using VI SDK 1.1 in those languages, see the samples included with the SDK Package.

Preparing the Virtual Infrastructure Web Service

Out of the gates, the VMware VI Web service has an initial configuration based on the configuration options selected during the VirtualCenter installation. However, you may find it necessary to modify those configuration settings in order to support your custom management applications. Since the Web service is only used by custom applications with this release of the SDK, any configuration changes made will not impact the functionality of the VirtualCenter client or its interaction with the ESX hosts that are managed by VirtualCenter.

The recommended approach is to test your changes, and then commit them. To do both, you use vma.exe. But first, let's review the configuration options and discuss the syntax for the *vma.exe* command. Code Listing 3.1 is a sample of a vmaConfig.xml file.

Code Listing 3.1 A vmaConfig.xml File

```
<vma>

    <service>

        <wsdl>vma.wsdl</wsdl>

        <eventlog rollover="true" file="vma" level="info"
    console="true"/>

        <sslport>8443</sslport>

        <externalSchemas>

            <schema>autoprep-types.xsd</schema>

        </externalSchemas>

        <sslCert>C:\Documents and Settings\All Users\Application
    Data\VMware\VMware VirtualCenter\VMA\server.pem</sslCert>

        <sslCAChain>C:\Documents and Settings\All Users\Application
    Data\VMware\VMware VirtualCenter\VMA\root.pem</sslCAChain>

    </service>


    <subjects>

        <subject>

            <implementation>VCenter 1.1</implementation>

            <path>/vcenter</path>

            <hostname>localhost</hostname>

            <port>905</port>

            <eventlog level="info"/>

            <ssl>true</ssl>

            <preload>true</preload>

            <index>

                <defaultFarm>Default Farm</defaultFarm>
```

```
            </index>
        </subject>
    </subjects>
</vma>
```

Three elements, or sections, make up the Web service configuration: *service*, *externalSchemas*, and *subjects*. The *service* element, a top-level element, is used to configure the Web service itself. The *externalSchemas* element, a child element of the service, contains a list of all the XSD files that should be included and exposed in addition to the vma.wsdl file. These files are used to customize the VI Web service's schema, and should not be modified. Currently, the only XSD listed is autoprep-types.xsd, which is used to perform customization operations against the guest operating system running in a virtual machine. The *subjects* element, another top-level element, contains child elements, or individual subject elements, that hold configuration attributes used to support connections to other data sources. Only one subject is currently supported, and represents the connection the Web service established with the VirtualCenter Server. Table 3.10 and Table 3.11 describe the configuration attributes for the two top-level elements, service and subjects.

Table 3.10 Service Configuration Attributes

Element	Description
Eventlog	Configures the event logging of the Web service.
Sslport	The port the HTTPS listener is configured to listen on.
sslCert	The certificate file and path.
sslCAChain	The certificate CA chain file and path.

Table 3.11 Subjects Configuration Attributes

Element	Description
Path	Beginning of the VirtualCenter hierarchy.
Hostname	The host name of the VirtualCenter server. Default is "localhost".

Continued

Table 3.11 continued Subjects Configuration Attributes

Element	Description
Port	TPC port for the proprietary VMware communication with the VirtualCenter server. This is not the same port used for SOAP HTTP-based communication.
Ssl	Boolean parameter for whether the VirtualCenter connection should be secured with SSL.
defaultFarm	The server farm in VirtualCenter that connections will default to.
periodicPerfRefresh Enable	Boolean parameter for performance counters. This attribute is not documented in any of the SDK documentation and does not exist by default. It should only be added if this functionality is needed and will be used.
authorizationEnable	Boolean parameter for the state of managing security with object ACLs. By default, this attribute is not declared in vmaConfig.xml and is enabled. To disable the use of ACLs, add this attribute with the value of false.

Once you have determined what parameters need to be adjusted, you should test those new parameters. You can do this by manually running the VI Web service from a command line. The following steps demonstrate a sample testing process for validating your changes.

1. Make a copy of the vmaConfig.xml file from c:\Documents and Settings\All Users\Application Data\VMware\VMware VirtualCenter\VMA

2. Edit the copy of vmaConfig.xml with the updated parameters. Among your changes, set eventlog to verbose and console to true.

3. From a command line, change to the directory where the copy of vmaConfig.xml exists.

4. From that directory, run the Web service manually using the following vma.exe statement: <InstallDrive>:\Program Files\VMware\VMware VirtualCenter\vma.exe –config vmaConfig.xml

5. To commit your changes, either copy your modified vmaConfig.xml file to the directory mentioned in step 1 or use the vma.exe command with –update and the appropriate option switches.

6. Restart the VMware VirtualCenter Web Service using the Services MMC snap-in.

Working with the VMware WSDL

With the Web service configured and ready to use, you can now generate a proxy class, or stub, for the VI Web service. This is done by consuming the service source file, or WSDL. You can view the WSDL by browsing the appropriate URL, such as https://esx1.sample.com:8443/?wsdl. The server name and port number will vary, depending on how you have configured your VI Web service.

You can choose to create a proxy using any method. However, you should ensure that any declarations to types defined by the WSDL that conflict with .NET classes are escaped. For example, a stub in the proxy source code for the type CPUPerf (WSDL-defined) with a field called system would normally look like the following snippet:

```
Public System as SystemInfo
```

Since this field will conflict with the .NET predefined class System, it should be escaped by explicitly declaring the field as an XML element attribute and using a name other than "System" in the class declaration, as follows:

```
<System.Xml.Serialization.XmlElementAttribute("System")> _
    Public VMSystem As SystemInfo
```

NOTE

Since our examples here will be based on .NET languages in the Microsoft Visual Studio 2005 IDE, most developers will opt for using the build in a WSDL.exe proxy generator from the command line or including a Web Reference in the project. However, due to misclassifications when running WSDL.exe, these are not valid methods for generating the proxy. For more information, see http://support.microsoft.com/default.aspx?scid=kb;en-us;326790.

The sample application included with the SDK Package demonstrate this workaround, and can be directly included in your projects.

Alternately, VMware provides a proxy generator tool, wsdlProxyGen.exe, which you can use to create the appropriate proxy class for either C# or VB.NET. This tool is a simple GUI that will parse the vma.wsdl file as well as any external schemas referenced, such as autoprep-types.xsd, to create a proper reference source code file. Figure 3.11 demonstrated sample input when using this tool to create a reference file for your project. Using the following steps, you can create your own WSDL proxy to use in your project.

1. Run *wsdlProxyGen.exe* on any Microsoft Windows 2000, XP, or 2003 system.

2. In the Input section, enter or browse to the location of the vma.wsdl file that is included in the SDK Package. For example, the file may be located at C:\VMware-sdk-e.x.p-19058\SDK\WebService\wsdl\vma.wsdl.

3. In the Output section, enter or browse to the location where you want the resulting output source code file to be located. To reduce steps, you should enter the path to your existing Visual Studio project, if you have created one already. This file should be named appropriately for the language that it will be compiled in, such as *reference.vb* for VB.NET projects, or *reference.cs* for C# projects.

4. Select the appropriate *output language* you want the resulting source code to be in. This, of course, should match the language your project is in.

5. Click **Generate**.

Figure 3.11 VMware's wsdlProxyGen Tool

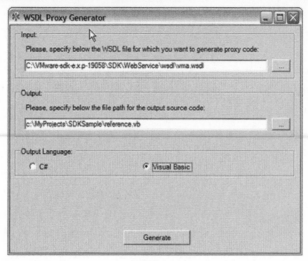

Looking at the resulting file, you will notice important .NET 2.0 namespaces included (if you are developing in Visual Studio .NET 2003, you will see .NET 1.1 namespaces). It is possible that one of the required namespaces, such as System.Web.Services, may not exist as a reference in the project, and will need to be manually added to avoid compilation errors. If you do receive any errors when compiling that state a particular type "is not defined" or that a type "is not a member" in the proxy file you created (as shown in Figure 3.12), add the appropriate reference to the project and attempt to compile again.

Figure 3.12 Compilation Errors Received When System.Web.Services Is Not Imported

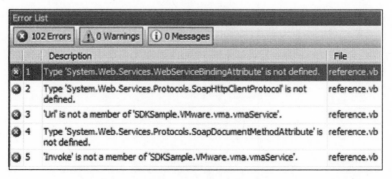

Virtual Infrastructure SDK 1.1 Concepts and Terminology

With all of that preparation out of the way, you are probably ready to jump in and start writing some code. An understanding of the data model and datatypes will allow you to perform the element management and virtual computing operations programmatically. This logical structure of the VI Web service is critical to your success in developing effective and functional applications.

Path Hierarchy

There are several key concepts that must be understood prior to diving into code development against the SDK. The logical presentation of Web service's data and methods is in the structure of a path hierarchy, similar to a file system's hierarchy of directories and files. In this comparison, files are the target of most file system operations, although some operations can be performed against directories as well. Also, directories can contain file or other directories, forming a type of hierarchy that can be traversed. Similarly, the objects exposed by the VI Web service are arranged in a hierarchical structure, as shown in Figure 3.13. This structure can be traversed to accomplish VI management tasks in your applications.

Figure 3.13 The Virtual Infrastructure SDK 1.1 Path Hierarchy

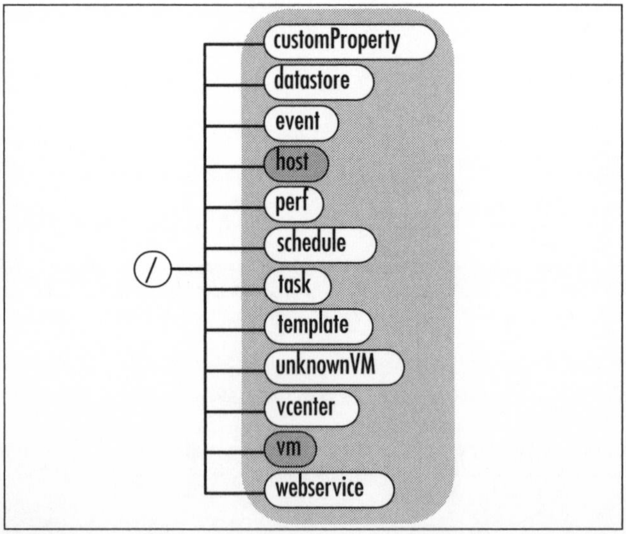

One particular path, /vcenter, can be a particularly large hierarchy. It represents the hierarchy that administrators see using the VirtualCenter client. It can also be one that changes regularly, as administrators reorganize virtual resources into farms and groups. This can cause challenges to your application since targeting a particular host or virtual machine using this path requires that you know its complete path in VirtualCenter. For example, you may have two virtual machines located at the following path:

```
/vcenter/FarmGroup1/VirtualMachineGroup1/VirtualMachineA
/vcenter/FarmGroup1/VirtualMachineGroup2/VirtualMachineB
```

An administrator may choose to relocate VirtualMachineB to a new Virtual Machine Group, VirtualMachineGroup3, resulting in a path as follows:

```
/vcenter/FarmGroup1/VirtualMachineGroup3/VirtualMachineB
```

Without any knowledge of this change, operations that targeted VirtualMachineB would now fail unless the referenced path was altered to reflect the virtual machine's new location. Although it is possible to keep track or identify paths by recursively traversing the entire /vcenter hierarchy to seek out a host or virtual machine, you may choose to use the /host or /vm paths instead. Both /host and /vm are a flat namespace, shortcuts if you will, that contain every host and virtual in the /vcenter hierarchy. Because of its flat nature, you don't have to know its exact path to target it in your application. This can be particularly useful if the only input you have is the host or virtual machine name.

Terminology

While traversing the hierarchy, you will deal with objects and items. Objects are described by an XML document and are the central focus of the VI Web service. This XML document describes the type associated with the object as well as its value. Some objects have child objects that are referenced as nodes in the XML document, and subsequently have their own structure as well. Continuing with our file system analogy, the following is a list of objects exposed by the VI Web service that compare with directories:

- Container

- Farm

- VirtualMachineGroup

All of these objects are containers by nature; however, *Farms* and *VirtualMachineGroups* are special containers with limitations and boundaries imposed on them. Containers are logical assemblies, or arrays, of items.

A container object is the most general and highest-level object type. The *Farm* and *VirtualMachineGroup* objects are also containers, but contain a limited subset of item types. Farms represent the farms in VirtualCenter and are located in the /vcenter path. They can only contain the *VirtualMachineGroup*, *Host*, and *VirtualMachine* objects. The *VirtualMachineGroup* object is also a representation of the same in VirtualCenter and located in /venter. It can only contain the other *VirtualMachineGroup* and *VirtualMachine* objects.

The items, again comparable to files in a file system, are only found within these three object types. They are secured using an ACL, the same security definition you configure in the VirtualCenter client. Each item is identified by a key, which is a unique handle assigned to the item during the session.

The remaining objects, shown in continuation, are all comparable with files in a file system, and are handled similarly:

- Host

- VirtualMachine

- Task

- TaskSchedule

- EventDeclList

- EventCollection

- PerfFilter

- PerfCollection

- Template

In order to work with all of these objects, you will need to get their Handle or vHandle. A handle is a pointer or token that is associated with each object during your connection session. Handles uniquely reference each object; so consequently there can only be one handle per object and only one object per handle. These handles are needed to invoke any operations against the object. Handles are retrieved using the *GetContents* method.

vHandles are similar to handles, but refer to the state of the object at a particular point in time. As objects can change over time, vHandles can be used to determine if any changes have occurred since the last time information was retrieved. vHandles are updated with the *GetUpdates* method and are very efficient since only XML diff documents are sent with the changes, if any, rather than the entire XML document describing the object.

Programming Logic for the SDK

Interaction between your management applications and the Web service will involve certain activities. Which activities you will need to perform will be based on what task you are trying to accomplish. Your application needs to obtain handles to each object that you will perform operations against as referenced by their path. You can then read information about the object through the returned XML document, request updated information about the object, modify and commit any changes (using the *PutUpdates* method), and perform any operations exposed by the Web service.

Your programming logic should also factor in all of the concepts we have discussed so far. For example, if you need to make sure you have the latest information about an object, use the *GetUpdates* method rather than calling *GetContents*. The XML diff document that is returned tends to be much smaller, reducing overall network bandwidth. However, you must have a valid vHandle to be able to call the *GetContents* method.

You should also take the Web service's security model into consideration, as well as how the VM and Host objects are identified. Hosts are referenced using their host name, fully qualified DNS name (FQDN), or IP address, all of which are ways to identify network resources that administrators are familiar with. VMs, however, are not referenced by name or IP, but rather by their universally unique identifier, or UUID. The UUID is a 128-bit hexadecimal number, sometimes called a GUID, and may look something like:

```
564d71c5-d04d-b62e-748a-9020f0ee481e.
```

Data Models and Datatypes

Several data models are presented by the Web service, each one focusing on a particular part of VI management. Table 3.12 lists each of these data models exposed by the Web service. Each data model represents a logic structure of datatypes in a hierarchical organization, providing information about ESX hosts, virtual machines, and VirtualCenter-specific items as well.

Table 3.12 Data Models Exposed by the Virtual Infrastructure Web Service

Model	Description
Core Data Model	Describes the hierarchy of the Web service, including the *Container*, *ViewContents*, and *Update* datatypes.
Host Machine Data Model	Describes the ESX host and its configuration. One particular configuration item is whether the host supports the Non-Uniform Memory Architecture, or NUMA. This data model includes the *HostInfo*, *CPUInfo*, *MemoryInfo*, *NetworkInfo*, and *VolumeInfo* datatypes.
Virtual Machine Data Model	Describes the configuration of a virtual machine and its "shares" on the host it is running on. This data model includes the *VirtualMachineInfo*, *GuestInfo*, and *VirtualHardware* datatypes.
Performance Metric Data Model	Describes the performance metrics and counters exposed by the Web service. This model is dependent on the *periodicPerfRefreshEnable* attribute being set in the vmaConfig.xml file. The primary datatype for this data model is *PerfCollector*.
Event Data Model	Describes both ESX host and virtual machine events that are generated and received by VirtualCenter. This data model includes the *EventDeclList* and *EventCollection* datatypes.

Continued

Table 3.12 continued Data Models Exposed by the Virtual Infrastructure Web Service

Model	Description
Task Data Model	Describes the various tasks that have been created or can be created, as well as those that can be started programmatically. This data model includes the *Task* and *TaskSchedule* datatypes.
Template Data Model	Describes the templates found in the VirtualCenter template repository used to create new virtual machines. This data model only contains a single datatype, *Template*.
Guest Customization Data Model	Describes the configuration items that can be customized when creating new virtual machines from templates. The primary datatype for this data model is *autoprep*. This data model is directly linked to auto-prep-types.xsd referenced as an external schema in vmaConfig.xml.

As described earlier, the data models contain information that can be retrieved by your management application. This information is accessed as a datatype that is presented in a hierarchical organization and retrieved as a response to certain methods, such as *GetContents*, *GetUpdates*, *QueryPerfData*, and others.

Datatypes contain one or more fields that further describe the datatype. These fields can be retrieved, modified using the *PutUpdates* method if supported, or linked to other datatypes within the data model's hierarchy. The field values can either be one of the common types, *xsd:int*, *xsd:string*, *xsd:long*, and *xsd:Boolean*, or references to another datatype through a special field, or key.

There are too many datatypes to list in this chapter. However, you can get a complete listing by referencing pages 37–112 of the *Virtual Infrastructure SDK Reference Guide* available for download at www.vmware.com/support/developer/vc-sdk.

Developing Your Management Application

We are now ready to dive into coding management applications. Your applications can perform several functions, such as:

- Systems management
- Performance management
- Provisioning
- Utility computing
- Disaster recovery
- Clustering
- Niche vertical applications

In the previous sections, we discussed all of the core concepts, terminology, and data models. Using that information, we will look at several code examples in both Visual Basic and C#, and we will discuss the process of connecting to the Web service, obtaining the handle for objects, and working with those objects.

The Connection Process

Your application must first connect to the Web service using methods exposed by the stub you created. At this point, you have already created a new project in Visual Studio and have generated the stub, of proxy class, and included it in your project. Code Listings 3.2 and 3.3 demonstrate how to connect to the VI Web service.

Code Listing 3.2 C# Script for Connecting to VI Web Service

```csharp
using System;
using VMware.vma;


protected vmaService vma_;


string url = "https://esx1.sample.com:8443";
string username = "adminuser1";
string password = "password1";


public void Connect(string url, string username, string password) {
    vma_ = new vmaService();
```

```
    vma_.Url = url;

    vma_.CookieContainer = new System.Net.CookieContainer();

    vma_.Login(username, password);

}
```

Code Listing 3.3 VB.NET Script for Connecting to VI Web Service

```
Imports System

Imports VMware.vma


Protected vma As VMware.vma.vmaService


Dim url As String = "https://esx1.sample.com:8443"

Dim username As String = "adminuser1"

Dim password As String = "password1"


Public Function Connect(url As string, username As string, password As _
   string)

    vma = New vmaService

    vma.Url = url

    vma.CookieContainer = New System.Net.CookieContainer

    vma.Login(username, password)

End Function
```

In the preceding example, we started with some declarations, including the required string variants for the URL for the Web service, the username to use in the connection, and its password. We also declared an instance of the class *VMware.vma.vmaService* as vma. This will be the base class that exposes the Web service.

The properties of the *vmaService* class needed to properly handle a connection to the Web service are *vma.Url* and *vma.CookieContainer*. The CookieContainer is a special system container that will host a collection of cookies collected during our session, a requirement if your application will need to maintain session state. With those properties set, we can then call the

Login method, passing the user credentials we established previously. Upon successfully logging in to the VI Web service, the following response is received.

```
<?xml version="1.0" encoding="UTF-8"?>

<env:Envelope xmlns:xsd="http://www.w3.org/2001/XMLSchema"
xmlns:env="http://schemas.xmlsoap.org/soap/envelope/"
xmlns:xsi="http://www.w3.org/2001/XMLSchema-instance">

  <env:Body>

    <LoginResponse xmlns="urn:vma1">

    </LoginResponse>

  </env:Body>

</env:Envelope>
```

Since this is a process that is required for any type of management application that you develop, the remaining examples in this section will assume that vma has already been declared and a session with the VI Web service has already been successfully established.

Handling SSL Certificates

In most cases, you will connect to the Web service through the HTTPS listener instead of HTTP. By default, every VirtualCenter installation comes with a certificate that is used to secure the VI Web service. However, as shown in Figure 3.14, the certificate is not a valid one for production use since it was not issued by a trusted root certificate authority (CA). You can choose to handle this condition one of two ways. First, you can replace the certificate with a valid one from a trusted CA and update the vmaConfig.xml accordingly, as discussed earlier in the chapter. Another option would be to handle the "bad" certificate programmatically in your application. Although the certificate cannot be trusted, it can still be used to encrypt the HTTP data payload transmitted between the management client and the Web service.

Figure 3.14 A Default VMware Test Certificate

The latter option is the most common and still provides adequate security for most situations. The examples found in the SDK package all include a sample workaround which we will discuss briefly. The key component is the CertPolicy.vb or CertPolicy.cs file, which can be copied from any sample and added to your project. Using the System.Security.Cryptography.X509Certificates .NET component and hashtables, the CheckValidationResult function is passed the certificate and assesses its validity. If the function detects any issues with the certificate, it will then display a message box stating any problems that were found, and presenting the management client user the option to continue regardless.

To take advantage of this certificate validation functionality, you can implement ICertificatePolicy. Then you must pass ICertificatePolicy to ServicePointManager.CertificatePolicy before any Web service method calls are made. Include the following code in the client code. Before you make the Web service method call from the client code, the following statement must be executed in C#:

```
System.Net.ServicePointManager.CertificatePolicy = new CertPolicy();
```

In VB.NET the code is as follows:

```
System.Net.ServicePointManager.CertificatePolicy = New CertPolicy
```

In addition to using the CertPolicy distributed in the SDK package, you can create you own CertPolicy that will validate, for example, all certificates. The script shown in Code Listings 3.4 and 3.5 implements ICertificatePolicy and then accepts every request under SSL.

Code Listing 3.4 C# Script for Implementing ICerfificatePolicy

```csharp
using System.Net;

using System.Security.Cryptography.X509Certificates;


public class CertPolicy : ICertificatePolicy {

    public bool CheckValidationResult(

            ServicePoint svcPnt

        , X509Certificate cert

        , WebRequest req

        , int certProblem) {

        return true;

    } // end CheckValidationResult

} // class CertPolicy
```

Code Listing 3.5 VB.NET Script for Implementing ICerfificatePolicy

```vbnet
Imports System.Net

Imports System.Security.Cryptography.X509Certificates

Public Class CertPolicy Implements ICertificatePolicy

  Public Function CheckValidationResult(ByVal _

    svcPnt As ServicePoint, ByVal cert As X509Certificate, _

    ByVal req As WebRequest, ByVal certProblem As Integer) _

    As Boolean Implements ICertificatePolicy.CheckValidationResult

    Return True

  End Function

End Class
```

Obtaining with Object Handles

Once connected, you can now target specific objects in order to get or modify their information or perform operations. The *ResolvePath* method is used to obtain the handle for the object represented by the path, and the *GetContents* method is used to retrieve the XML document that is the value of the object. Code Listings 3.6 and 3.7 continue our sample code:

Code Listing 3.6 C# Script for Obtaining Information with *ResolvePath* and *GetContents*

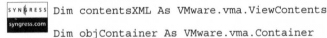

```
string path = "/vm";

string handle = vma_.ResolvePath(path);

ViewContents contentsXML = vma_.GetContents(handle);

Container objContainer = (Container) contentsXML.body;
```

Code Listing 3.7 VB.NET Script for Obtaining Information with *ResolvePath* and *GetContents*

```
Dim contentsXML As VMware.vma.ViewContents

Dim objContainer As VMware.vma.Container


Dim path As String = "/vm"

Dim handle As String = vma.ResolvePath(path)

contentsXML = = vma.GetContents(handle)

objContainer = CType(contentsXML.body, VMware.vma.Container)
```

In this example, we target /vm of the VI Web service hierarchy. We obtain its handle by invoking *ResolvePath* and passing it the string value of the path as set by vPath. The returned XML document from invoking *ResolvePath* is similar to Code Listing 3.8.

Code Listing 3.8 XML Document Returned by Invoking *ResolvePath*

```
<?xml version="1.0" encoding="UTF-8"?>

<env:Envelope xmlns:xsd="http://www.w3.org/2001/XMLSchema"
xmlns:env="http://schemas.xmlsoap.org/soap/envelope/"
xmlns:xsi="http://www.w3.org/2001/XMLSchema-instance">
```

```xml
<env:Body>

  <GetContentsResponse xmlns="urn:vma1">

    <returnval>

      <handle>vma-0000-0000-0008</handle>

      <vHandle>vma-0000-0000-0008@c2f53ca4e000003</vHandle>

      <body xsi:type="Container">

        <item>

          <key>vma-vm-00000000011</key>

          <name>564d0f8b-3bde-1003-fe19-0f77cc31a3dc</name>

          <type>VirtualMachine</type>

        </item>

        <item>

          <key>vma-vm-00000000012</key>

          <name>564d71c5-d04d-b62e-748a-9020f0ee481e</name>

          <type>VirtualMachine</type>

        </item>

        <item>

          <key>vma-vm-00000000014</key>

          <name>564d63db-9aaf-97af-4c47-8562e1dc65e0</name>

          <type>VirtualMachine</type>

        </item>

        <item>

          <key>vma-vm-00000000015</key>

          <name>564d71b4-d1fc-fdb9-9c4b-125b3ba0b32a</name>

          <type>VirtualMachine</type>

        </item>

      </body>

    </returnval>

  </GetContentsResponse>

</env:Body>

</env:Envelope>
```

With that handle, we then obtain the contents of the object located at the path using *GetContents*, retrieving its descriptive XML document as a ViewContents datatype, converting the body of the returned document to a collection of relevant items as a Container datatype. In some cases, you will want to retrieve updates from an object to process or evaluate items that have changed. Although you can request the full contents XML document again, doing so may generate a large amount of network traffic and impact application performance. Instead, utilize the *GetUpdates* method to retrieve just the items that have changed, passing with the vHandle of the object to update.

The vHandle is an item that is passed along with the handle in the results of calling the *GetContents* method. In fact, the vHandle consists of the handle plus a time stamp. For example, an object may have a handle of `vma-0000-0000-0008`. Consequently, the vHandle returned with a handle by *GetContents* is `vma-0000-0000-0008@c2f53ca4e000003`. Every time an item is updated, the vHandle will change, denoting that an update is available. The timestamp is used as a reference point and lets the Web service know if the information that the management client has is older than what is currently available. Code Listings 3.9 and 3.10 demonstrate the use of vHandles in C# and VB.NET, respectively.

Code Listing 3.9 C# Script for Using vHandles

```
while (
    myTask.currentState.Equals(TaskRunState.running) ||
    myTask.currentState.Equals(TaskRunState.scheduled) ||
    myTask.currentState.Equals(TaskRunState.starting)
) {
    VMware.vma.VHandleList vhlist = new VHandleList();
    vhlist.vHandle = new string[] { vc.vHandle };
    UpdateList ul = vma_.GetUpdates(vhlist, true);

    for (int u = 0; u < ul.update.Length; u++) {
        for (int c = 0; c < ul.update[u].change.Length; c++) {
            if (ul.update[u].change[c].target == "currentState") {
                myTask.currentState =
```

```
                    (TaskRunState)ul.update[u].change[c].val;
          } else if (ul.update[u].change[c].target ==
              "percentCompleted") {
            myTask.percentCompleted =
                (Single)ul.update[u].change[c].val;
            Console.Write("..." +
                myTask.percentCompleted.ToString());
          }
        }
      }
    }
```

Code Listing 3.10 VB.NET Script for Using VHandles

```vbnet
While migrateTask.currentState = VMware.vma.TaskRunState.running Or _
  migrateTask.currentState = VMware.vma.TaskRunState.scheduled Or _
  migrateTask.currentState = VMware.vma.TaskRunState.starting
    Dim vhlist As VMware.vma.VHandleList = New VMware.vma.VHandleList
    vhlist.vHandle = New String() {vc.vHandle}
    Dim ul As VMware.vma.UpdateList = vma.GetUpdates(vhlist, True)
    For u = 0 To ul.update.Length - 1
      For c = 0 To ul.update(u).change.Length - 1
        If (ul.update(u).change(c).target = "currentState") Then
          migrateTask.currentState = ul.update(u).change(c).val
        ElseIf (ul.update(u).change(c).target = "percentCompleted") Then
          migrateTask.percentCompleted = ul.update(u).change(c).val
          Console.Write("..." + migrateTask.percentCompleted.ToString())
        End If
      Next c
    Next u
End While
```

Here we pass the vHandleList (an array of vHandles to be updated) to the *GetUpdates* method. This method has a Boolean parameter that defines whether the Web service should wait to send a response until at least one of the vHandles in the vHandleList changes. This blocking action is less intensive than polling for updates on a regular interval and also a more real-time response for change notifications. The diff that returns as an XML document consists of change elements that describe the changes in the update.

Retrieving Items and Performing Operations

The containers consist of items that each have a key, name, type, and ACL. The key is also the handle for the item named. Issuing *GetContents* against an object that is not a container will return an XML document that contains information relevant to that object type, such as Hosts and virtual machines. In Code Listings 3.11 and 3.12, we demonstrate enumerating all virtual machines in a particular Virtual Machine Group and their CPU and memory performance configuration.

Code Listing 3.11 C# Script for Enumerating VMs in a Particular Group

```csharp
string path = "/vcenter/ESXFarm1/ProductionVMs-Fin";

string handle = vma_.ResolvePath(path);

ViewContents contentsXML = vma_.GetContents(handle);

Container objContainer = (Container) contentsXML.body;

Item[] listVMs = objContainer.item;


for (int i = 1; i <= listVMs.Length-1; i++)
{
    contentsXML = vma_.GetContents(listVMs(i).key);

    VirtualMachine vm = contentsXML.body;

    string Name = vm.info.name

    int cfgNumCPU = vm.hardware.cpu.count

    string cfgCPUShares = vm.hardware.cpu.controls.shares

    int cfgSizeMem = vm.hardware.memory.sizeMb

    string CfgMemShares = vm.hardware.memory.controls.shares

    string msg = vmName + "\t"+ cfgNumCPU + "\t" + cfgCPUShares +
```

```
            "\t" + cfgSizeMem + "\t" + CfgMemShares;

        System.Console.WriteLine(msg);

}
```

Code Listing 3.12 VB.NET Script for Enumerating VMs in a Particular Group

```
Dim path, handle, vmName, cfgCPUShares, CfgMemShares, msg As String

Dim i, cfgNumCPU, cfgSizeMem As Integer

Dim contentsXML As VMware.vma.ViewContents

Dim objContainer As VMware.vma.Container

Dim listVMs() As VMware.vma.Item

Dim vm As VMware.vma.VirtualMachine


path = "/vcenter/ESXFarm1/ProductionVMs-Fin"

handle = vma.ResolvePath(path)

contentsXML = vma.GetContents(handle)

objContainer = CType(contentsXML.body, VMware.vma.Container)

listVMs = objContainer.item


For i = 0 To listVMs.Length - 1

    contentsXML = vma.GetContents(listVMs(i).key)

    vm = contentsXML.body

    vmName = vm.info.name

    cfgNumCPU = vm.hardware.cpu.count

    cfgCPUShares = vm.hardware.cpu.controls.shares

    cfgSizeMem = vm.hardware.memory.sizeMb

    CfgMemShares = vm.hardware.memory.controls.shares

    msg = vmName & vbTab & cfgNumCPU & vbTab & cfgCPUShares & _

      vbTab & cfgSizeMem & vbTab & CfgMemShares

    System.Console.WriteLine(msg)

Next i
```

This example outputs the name, number of virtual CPUs, configured CPU shares, the amount of memory allocated, and the configured memory shares for each virtual machine in the ProductionVMs–Fin Virtual Machine Group. We also take advantage of the virtual machine data model, traversing the various data types in the data model's hierarchy.

We can use a similar set of logic to perform operations against a single object or a group of objects. Code Listings 3.13 and 3.14 demonstrate performing a virtual machine migration operation via VMotion.

Code Listing 3.13 C# Script for Migrating a VM via VMotion

```
string handleHost = vma_.ResolvePath(pathHost);

string handleVM = vma_.ResolvePath(pathVM);

ViewContents contentsXML = vma_.MigrateVM(handleVM, handleHost,
   Level.normal);
```

Code Listing 3.14 VB.NET Script for Migrating a VM via VMotion

```
Dim handleHost, handleVM As String

Dim contentsXML As VMware.vma.ViewContents


handleHost = vma.ResolvePath(pathHost)

handleVM = vma.ResolvePath(pathVM)

contentsXML = vma.MigrateVM(vm, host, VMware.vma.Level.normal)
```

In this example, the handles for both the virtual machine and the target host are retrieved using *ResolvePath*. The *MigrateVM* method is then invoked to initiate the migration process. The request to migrate the virtual machine is returned with a new handle for the task, as well as an XML document that describes the task's details. This particular operation, like many others, can be monitored by using the returned vHandle to retrieve updates on the task's progress. For example, Code Listing 3.15 is a sample result from a *StopVM* operation.

Code Listing 3.15 Results for a *StopVM* Operation

```
<?xml version="1.0" encoding="UTF-8"?>
```

```
<env:Envelope xmlns:xsd="http://www.w3.org/2001/XMLSchema"
xmlns:env="http://schemas.xmlsoap.org/soap/envelope/"
xmlns:xsi="http://www.w3.org/2001/XMLSchema-instance">

  <env:Body>

    <StopVMResponse xmlns="urn:vma1">

      <returnval>

        <handle>vma-task-active-0a810</handle>

        <vHandle>vma-task-active-0a810@c2f53ca4e000001</vHandle>

        <body xsi:type="Task">

          <cause>user</cause>

          <entity>vma-vm-00000000012</entity>

          <eventCollector>vma-0000-0000-009b</eventCollector>

          <operationName>Power off VM</operationName>

          <queueTime>2006-07-12T00:56:10-05:00</queueTime>

          <allowCancel>false</allowCancel>

          <currentState>starting</currentState>

        </body>

      </returnval>

    </StopVMResponse>

  </env:Body>

</env:Envelope>
```

Updating Interior Nodes

Just as you can use the *GetUpdates* method to retrieve a list of changes that are of the Change datatype, you can also work with changes using the *PutUpdates* method. Some of the data values, or interior nodes, returned by *GetContents* or *GetUpdates* can be edited, inserted into, deleted, moved, or replaced. By using the *PutUpdates* method, you can make on-the-fly configuration changes to effectively manage your virtual infrastructure. Code Listings 3.16 and 3.17 demonstrate how to change the priority of a virtual machine by adjusting the shares allocated to its vCPUs.

Code Listing 3.16 C# Script for Changing the Priority of a VM

```
ViewContents vc = vma_.GetContents(vm);
```

```
Change change = new Change();

change.target = "hardware/cpu/controls/shares";

change.val = "high";

change.op = ChangeOp.edit;

change.valSpecified = true;


ChangeReqList changeList = new ChangeReqList();

ChangeReq changeReq = new ChangeReq();

changeReq.handle = vc.handle;

changeReq.change = new Change[] { change };

ChangeReq[] changeReqs = new ChangeReq[] { changeReq };

changeList.req = changeReqs;

UpdateList updateList = vma_.PutUpdates(changeList);
```

Code Listing 3.17 VB.NET Script for Changing the Priority of a VM

```
Dim vc As VMware.vma.ViewContents = vma.GetContents(vm)

Dim change As New VMware.vma.Change

change.target = "hardware/cpu/controls/shares"

change.val = "high"

change.op = VMware.vma.ChangeOp.edit

change.valSpecified = True


Dim changeList As New VMware.vma.ChangeReqList

Dim changeReq As New VMware.vma.ChangeReq

changeReq.handle = vc.handle

changeReq.change = New VMware.vma.Change() {change}

Dim changeReqs() As VMware.vma.ChangeReq = {changeReq}

changeList.req = changeReqs

Dim updateList As VMware.vma.UpdateList = vma.PutUpdates(changeList)
```

In this example, we used several datatypes to perform the update operation. *PutUpdates* is passed a *ChangeReqList* as input. This datatype is an array of the *ChangeReq* datatypes containing the handles or vHandles of the objects to be updated. Each change in the set is of the *Change* datatype. This interface allows multiple changes to an object to be performed by using one *PutUpdates* call.

Developing with the Virtual Infrastructure SDK 2.0

With the release of Virtual Infrastructure (VI) 3, VMware has made a considerable departure from the architecture of the ESX Server and VirtualCenter products. Similarly, the latest VI SDK supporting this release has substantially changed. We will review the primary changes and key concepts that you need to know to effectively develop code against the new SDK, as well as introduce some of the new features available in VI 3 and exposed by the SDK.

Addressing each of the changes in detail is outside the scope of this book. However, VMware has made available guides to ease your introduction to the VI SDK 2.0. If you are a seasoned VI SDK developer, these guides will be instrumental in helping you transition to the new SDK. The code references in this chapter are Microsoft-centric, focused on VB.Net or C#. You can reference the programming and reference guides for additional information about developing against the VI SDK 2.0 in Java or Perl.

Features Added to Virtual Infrastructure 2.0

Let's dive in now with a discussion of the differences between the two versions of the SDK, principally regarding what new items or functionality have been added, as shown in Table 3.13. You can perform all of the same operations in VI SDK 2.0 that you could in VI SDK 1.x; however, VMware has made some substantial changes with the new releases. The following is a list of some of those new features.

Table 3.13 New Features Added to Virtual Infrastructure SDK 2.0

Category	Feature	Description
Virtual Infrastructure Management	Web service availability	The VI SDK 2.0 is now available through both the Virtual Infrastructure Web service hosted on the VirtualCenter Management Server as well as the Web service running on the ESX hosts themselves. The latter is provisioned by the *host agent*.
	Host configuration	ESX hosts can now be configured via the SDK.
	All ESX and VirtualCenter features available	All of the new features in ESX 3.0 and VirtualCenter 2.0 are available programmatically through the VI Web service.
Object Model	Consolidated inventory hierarchy	All manageable objects and data are now located within a single inventory hierarchy or tree, including hosts, virtual machines, data centers, networks, and datastores.
	Abstraction of resources	The new SDK offers a complete abstraction of VI resources, including physical computer resources, resource pools, and clusters.
	PropertyCollector	A new mechanism that supports filtering of complex resources.
	SearchIndex	A mechanism for searching the inventory hierarchy for a specific managed entity based on one of its properties, such as name, UUID, or IP address.

In addition to the new and enhanced features, VI SDK 2.0 has changed from the perspective of the Web service itself. Hosted by both the VirtualCenter Management Server as well as the ESX server's host agent, the definition of the Web service has also changed substantially.

Preparing the Virtual Infrastructure 2.0 Web Service

The VMware VI 2.0 Web service has an initial configuration based on the configuration options selected during the VirtualCenter installation. You can customize the Web service, just as you can the VI 1.0 Web service, if you find it necessary to modify those configuration settings in order to support your custom management applications. The Web service is available on both the VirtualCenter Management Server and the ESX Server, each with its own configuration location and parameters.

For the VirtualCenter Management Server, you can find the Web service configuration at *C:\Documents and Settings\All Users\Application Data\VMware\VMware VirtualCenter\vpxd.cfg*. On an ESX host, you must modify the */etc/vmware/hostd/config.xml* file. This file is the configuration file for all host agent functions, not just the VI Web service, so you should exercise caution modifying this file in particular. Code Listing 3.18 shows the port configuration for the HTTP/HTTPS proxy.

Code Listing 3.18 Port Configuration for the HTTP/HTTPS Proxy

```
<proxyDatabase>
    <server id="0">
        <namespace> / </namespace>
        <host> localhost </host>
        <port> -1 </port>
    </server>
    <server id="1">
        <namespace> /sdk </namespace>
        <host> localhost </host>
        <port> -2 </port>
    </server>
    <redirect id="2">/ui</redirect>
```

```
<server id="3">

    <namespace> /mob </namespace>

    <host> localhost </host>

    <port> 8087 </port>

</server>

</proxyDatabase>
```

Table 3.14 describes some of the properties you may want to consider changing to customize the VI Web service to support your management applications. You should create a backup copy of the configuration files, though, before making any changes. Once you have saved the updated version of the configuration file, you must restart the Web service. On a VirtualCenter Management Server, this can be done using the Services control panel applet. On an ESX host, you can restart the host agent with the command *service mgmt-vmware restart*.

Table 3.14 Configuration Information for the VirtualCenter Web Service

Element	Node/Item	Description
ws1x	Enabled	Boolean that defines whether the Web service should support the 1.x SDK calls. Notice that enabling this will disable some functionality in the SDK 2.0 realm. This only applies to the VirtualCenter Web service.
	Datafile	File path to the WS1X file needed to set up the VI SDK 1.x–compatible environment. This only applies to the VirtualCenter Web service.
vpxd	namespace (proxyDatabase)	Relative path of the site being configured, such as "/", "/sdk", or "/mob".

Continued

Table 3.14 continued Configuration Information for the VirtualCenter Web Service

Element	Node/Item	Description
	host (proxyDatabase)	The host that is being proxied. This value should always be the management server. You may want to change the value to the host name if your security policy requires that you remove the *localhost* reference from the local DNS cache.
	port (proxyDatabase)	The port that the HTTP/HTTPS process hosting the management site is listening on.
	Serializeadds	The DAS parameter. Boolean value for whether VirtualCenter should add proposed VMs in a serial manner or concurrently. The default value is *true*. This only applies to the VirtualCenter Web service.
vmacore	TaskMax	Maximum number of concurrently running threads for task-related operations. If you notice that your tasks queue up excessively, you can increase this number. *10* is the default. This only applies to the VirtualCenter Web service.

Working with the VMware VI SDK 2.0 WSDLs

The VMware VI SDK 2.0 Web Service is far more complex than its predecessor. As a result, the WSDLs that describe the interaction with the Web service are much larger in size compared to the WSDL for VI SDK 1.x. There are two options at your disposal for obtaining the necessary stubs to work in your VB.Net or C# code: user-generated stubs or pre-generated, VMware provided stubs.

If you choose to generate your own stubs, you can either run the *Build2003.cmd* or *Build2005.cmd* commands found in the SDK package or run wsdl.exe directly. The following example shows the portion of the build batch files for Visual Studio 2005 included in the SDK package that generates the .CS stubs and compiles them as VimService2005.dll.

```
wsdl /n:VimApi /out:stage\VimObjects.cs ..\..\vimService.wsdl ..\..\vim.wsdl
csc /t:library /out:VimService2005.dll stage\*.cs
```

This sample generates a stub file, **VimObjects.cs**, in the \stage directory. This stub is a merge of *vimService.wsdl* and *vim.wsdl*. You can choose to include VimObjects.cs directly in your source code for your project, or reference *VimService* in your project, being sure to include VimService.dll in your /bin directory. A similar approach would be used for VB.NET, which creates as output the VimObjects.vb stub that you can compile to create VimService2005.dll.

The simpler option would be to use the reference.vb or reference.cs files found in the \SDK directory of the SDK package and include that file in your project, or copy the VimService2005.dll found in the \SDK\samples_2_0\DotNet directory of the SDK package to the \bin directory and reference it in your project.

TIP

The performance of creating new objects from the VimService class when using .NET Framework 2.0 is slower than .NET Framework 1.1, mostly due to the way the .NET 2.0 generates XML serializer assemblies at runtime. One approach to work around this is to generate the assemblies in advance using the sgen.exe tool from Microsoft, as described in http://msdn2.microsoft.com/en-us/library/bk3w6240.aspx. However, this approach is complicated and renames the namespace and associated classes, requiring a deeper knowledge of .NET development.

Another approach would be to extract the functions needed from the generated class while still referencing the VimService DLL. This is particularly useful for simpler projects that do not require all of the methods and functions exposed by VimService. One way to perform this extract would be to execute the following steps:

1. Create a new class (in this example, *myClass*) that inherits from the *SoapHttpClientProtocol* class.

2. Open **\stage\VimObjects.cs**, included in the VI SDK 2.0 package.

3. Copy the class **XmlIncludeAttribute**, removing any items you do not need in your project.

4. Include a reference to VimService2005.dll and place "using Vim" in *myClass* for each method retained.

5. Locate each method and copy/paste the code to *myClass*.

Virtual Infrastructure SDK 2.0 Concepts and Terminology

The key to moving forward with your development efforts using VI SDK 2.0 is your understanding of the SDK's architecture. Whether you have experience developing with the previous VI SDK 1.x or you are new to programming against the VI SDK, you will find that the concepts and terminology are critical to the functionality you plan on incorporating into your next management application. In this section, we will discuss the object model and review a few of the critical management objects central to most development efforts.

Data and Managed Objects

Managed objects are composite objects that exist on ESX host and the VirtualCenter 2 management server. They do not exist in the WSDL schema, but are passed indirectly as references, called managed object references, in the WSDL data stream between the Web service and the management client. Data objects, in turn, are also composite objects that are passed by value between the management client and Web service.

Since data objects are actually passed between client and Web service, they are treated in an object-oriented manner. The WSDL schema is not object-oriented itself; however, the class hierarchy of the WSDL can be represented as a hierarchical chain of properties that are exposed by instantiated data objects. The key distinguishing factor for data objects is that they only have properties, or values, not methods. Those values are passed in SOAP messages compliant to the WSDL schema as XML elements serialized by the Web service and client. Operations, in contrast, are components of methods contained in managed objects.

Throughout your coding efforts, you must obtain managed object references. These references are derived from managed object methods, or operations, presented by the WSDL schema. You can learn more about the managed object associated with the reference by:

- Calling a method associated with the managed object that reports its properties.

- Calling a method associated with the managed object that returns a data object. The value defined in the data objects can tell you more about the managed object itself.

- Create a *property collector* filter that can be used to retrieve the properties from or monitor the managed object. Property collectors will be discussed in more detail later in the chapter.

Managed Entity Inventory

Using the VI SDK 2.0, you can manage your infrastructure's virtual machines and host resources using a hierarchical model that represents the inventory, as shown in Figure 3.15. This inventory, as found in VirtualCenter, contains managed entities of various types, including datacenters, resource pools, virtual machines, and hosts. The managed entities are organized and grouped into folders. This hierarchical inventory is in its most complete form when working with the VirtualCenter product. A more limited version of the inventory model is available on hosts.

Host Agent versus VirtualCenter Feature Set

VirtualCenter 2 has not changed in function from its predecessor, VirtualCenter 1.x. The product is still designed to help Virtual Infrastructure administrators design, deploy, and manage virtual machines and, new to this release, hosts. The hosts can either be the ESX 3, ESX 2.x, or VMware Server (formerly GSX Server).

Figure 3.15 Logical Representation of the Managed Entity Inventory from the VirtualCenter Hierarchy

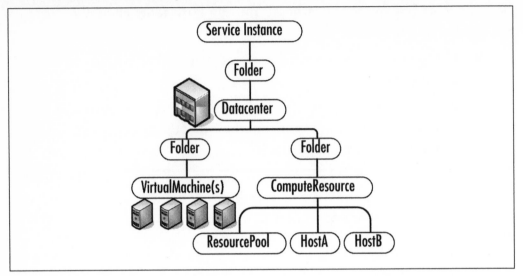

The major differences between using the SDK to manage through the Service Instance presented by VirtualCenter and the Service Instance presented by a stand–alone host are

- **Management of resources** Refined control of resource pools that scale across more than one host, treating resources as a collective whole rather than that offered by a single physical host. This is also supplemented by VMware DRS and VMware HA, features not available on standalone hosts.

- **Provisioning of new virtual machines** Deployment of new virtual machines from templates rather than clones. Template deployment also allows guest OS customization.

- **Migration** Using the VMotion technology that has made VMware ESX an enterprise-ready product, virtual machines can be relocated from one physical host to another. This action can be invoked manually or based on the automation logic facilitated by VMware DRS.

- **Clustering** A configuration item defining how virtual machines and associated storage failover to available resources on two or more physical hosts. This is the essence of VMware HA.

- **Monitoring** The ability to configure and report against the data center as a whole. Response to detected conditions can be invoked at a physical or virtual level.

The host agent basically exposes a subset of the VirtualCenter feature set, limited to those operations that can be implemented on a single host. If you mistakenly invoke an operation against a standalone host instead of a VirtualCenter management server, the SDK will throw a *NotSupported* exception. Although this is not a fatal exception, you will want to code for it accordingly while also preventing users of your client from targeting operations against invalid targets.

Data Models and Data Types

All management entities can be grouped into data models that represent the structure they stand for. For example, all power operations, virtual hardware definition, and guest OS information are found in the data model for virtual machines. Table 3.15 and Table 3.16 provide a summary of each data model. Additional information can be found in the documentation accompanying the VI SDK 2.0 package.

Table 3.15 Service Instance, Folder, and Datacenter Data Models

Data Model Name	SDK 1.x Equivalent	Description
Service Instance	Server Farm	This managed object type represents the central entry or access point for the management data and operations. It describes the virtual infrastructure's capabilities, licensing, and discovered host machines. The properties of the Service Instance include the root folder of the managed entity inventory, the session manager, and the property collector.

Continued

Table 3.15 continued Service Instance, Folder, and Datacenter Data Models

Data Model Name	SDK 1.x Equivalent	Description
Folder	Farm Group, Virtual Machine Group	This managed object type represents a folder. This object type is used to organize virtual machines, hosts, and host resources. Folders can be nested, but its contents must be consistent with the *childType* associated with the folder. The key features of the folder managed type
Datacenter	Farm	This managed object type groups virtual machines and hosts under a top-tier construct. The entire object represents a single management unit contained in the root folder of the associated Service Instance. The key features are virtual machine management methods, managed entity management methods, computer resource management for clusters, datacenter objects, and task information.

Table 3.16 Virtual Machine and Host Resource Data Models

Data Model Name	Sub-Objects	Description
VirtualMachine	VirtualMachine Summary VirtualMachine ConfigSpec CustomizationSpec Manager Task	Describes the data type used to model a virtual machine. This managed object type contains sub-objects which contain the majority of its properties. Use this object type to: Define or retrieve basic properties for a virtual machine

Continued

Table 3.16 continued Virtual Machine and Host Resource Data Models

Data Model Name	Sub-Objects	Description
		View or set virtual machine configuration parameters Customize the virtual machine during deployment from a template Perform power operations List or identify the resources available to, and used by, the virtual machine
HostSystem	HostCapability HostConfigInfo HostConnectInfo HostDatastore Browser HostRuntimeInfo HostHardwareInfo HostListSummary	Describes the host machine configuration. Use this data type to manage the physical hosts upon which your virtual machines are running. Use this object to: Define or retrieve basic properties for a particular host Retrieve information about the capability of the host's hardware and software View or set the host configuration properties View the host's hardware Connect to the interface to access files in the datacenter
Datastore	DatastoreSummary HostSystem VirtualMachine	Describes data types used to manage physical storage resources. Use this data type to gain access to the catalog of storage devices attached to the host systems in the datacenter. Some of the information available includes the total capacity and free space, as well as the path of the physical storage.

Continued

Table 3.16 continued Virtual Machine and Host Resource Data Models

Data Model Name	Sub-Objects	Description
ComputeResource	ComputeResource Summary EnvironmentBrowser ResourcePool	Describes the model used to hosts as resources with which to run virtual machines. The compute resource exported by the Web service can represent a single host or a cluster of hosts available to run virtual machines. Each ComputeResource contains the following: List of hosts List of datastores List of network objects Summary information, including resource usage and availability An environment browser that facilitates access to hardware information, configuration objects, and files stored on the associated datastores.
ResourcePool	ResourceConfigSpec ResourcePool Summary ComputerResource VirtualMachine	Describes the division of available host resources, whether individual or aggregated, available to run virtual machines. Use this datatype to create divisions of CPU and memory resources that are presented to virtual machines. Those resources can be configured with upper and lower limits as well as with shares, similar to ESX 2.x.

Continued

Table 3.16 continued Virtual Machine and Host Resource Data Models

Data Model Name	Sub-Objects	Description
ClusterComput Resource	ClusterConfigInfo ClusterDrs Recommendation ClusterDrsMigration HostSystem Task	Describes additional components not exposed by the ComputeResource data type used by VMware HA and VMware DRS features. The operations and properties available to support DRS and HA include *AddHost_Task* and *MoveInto_Task*, *RecommendHostsforVm* and *ApplyRecommendation*, *ReconfigureCluster_Task*, and many others.

It is recommended that you keep the Web-based Reference Guide that is included in the SDK package to reference additional information on the previously mentioned datatypes and sub-objects covered in the preceding tables. There are a few datatypes worth mentioning briefly, though, since they support monitoring and managing the virtual infrastructure as a whole. Those datatypes are as follows:

- **SessionManager** Provides control of sessions, including login and log off operations

- **AuthorizationManager** Controls access to objects. The access control is defined in a permission object that includes the managed entity reference, user or group name, and role.

- **PropertyCollector** Used to create property filters that only exist during the user's session. Once the session is destroyed, so are the filters. These filters expose efficient methods that management clients can use to obtain values for properties or target-specific managed objects. In function, the *PropertyCollector* is similar to the *GetContents* and *GetUpdates* methods of VI SDK 1.x.

- **EventManager** Provides historical information about changes that have taken placed with managed entities.

- **TaskManager** Similar to *EventManager*, this datatype provides real-time information about tasks in progress, queued, or recently completed.

- **ScheduledTaskManager** Used to manage scheduled tasks that are not already in progress or queued.

- **AlarmManager** Used to manage alarms that resulted from defined conditions or situations.

- **PerformanceManager** Provides an interface that can be used to collect performance statistics for hosts and virtual machines.

Programming Logic for the VI SDK 2.0

Similar to the VI SDK 1.x logic, your management application will follow a standard logical flow regardless of the functionality you have coded it for. You should take into consideration the managed entity inventory hierarchy as previously discussed in this chapter and make good use of property collector filters to minimize traversal times spent traversing through what may be a rather extensive hierarchical structure.

As mentioned before, you will be working with either managed objects or data objects. As input, most operations require a reference to a managed object (called a managed object reference) and possibly a few additional string, integer, or Boolean values. In some cases, you may need to pass a data object in its entirety, usually called a *spec* object. Those operations will either return a data object which contains values for you to work with, or another managed object reference for additional operations invocations.

In most cases, you will code the following steps in the workflow of your application. While reviewing these steps, notice some of the objects referenced and the relationships they have with other objects.

- Establish a session with the Web service. This clearly is the first step for you application. You must obtain a session token by successfully logging into the Web service. This token is used to invoke operations from your client throughout the duration of each user's session.

- Instantiate the *ServiceInstance* managed object. This is a core action that must take place to gain access to the underlying managed and data objects.

- Retrieve the *ServiceContent* data object. This is a very common action that you will perform, and it is accomplished by invoking the *RetrieveServiceContent* operation. This is a prerequisite to instantiating a *PropertyCollector* managed object.

- Once you have made it this far, you can now work with specific managed objects within your inventory. You can target those objects by constructing a *PropertyFilterSpec*. This data object type defines the managed object you wish to target, the properties of that object, and the manner within which you traverse the inventory.

- With a managed object reference for the *PropertyCollector* and the *PropertyFilterSpec* that you constructed, you can then retrieve the properties of the targeted managed object. This is accomplished by invoking the *RetrieveProperties* operation, which will return an *ObjectContent* data object containing all of the information as defined by the *PropertyFilterSpec*.

- Additionally, you can get regular updates for any of those properties by invoking one of several operations. Those operations are *CreateFilter*, *CheckForUpdates*, and *WaitForUpdates*. These operations are similar in function to the *GetUpdates* operation in the VI SDK 1.x, but are more powerful. They require for input the *PropertyCollector* managed object reference, and return either a *PropertyFilter* managed object reference that you can work with later, or the updates you can work with directly in an *UpdateSet* data object.

During all of this, you may run into further complications as you deal with permissions in complex entities such as *Datacenter*, *ComputeResource*, or *ClusterComputeResource*. The complexity is usually related to the parent-child relationships they tend to form in the inventory tree and the corresponding ACLs of those child objects.

Developing Your Management Application

With all those formalities behind us, we're now ready to begin the coding process. The techniques and logic are similar to what you read in the section for VI SDK 1.x. However, with a new object model and some new features, the departure from the previous version is significant enough to spend some time reviewing code samples for some of the popular operations you may perform.

In this section, we will look at some unique tools VMware has provided to assist with SDK development, as well as more deeply explore the operations and processes you will incorporate into your management application.

Managed Object Browser and Other Tools

Before beginning, we should introduce you to an invaluable tool that VMware has included with every ESX host and VirtualCenter: the Managed Object Browser (MOB). We'll also look at a few useful tools in the Visual Studio IDE. The MOB, however, is a Web-based utility that is hosted on the VirtualCenter management server and host agents. To access the MOB, browse to one of the following URLs:

- For VirtualCenter: https://<*your_server*>:8443/mob
- For Host Agents: https://<*your_server*>/mob

> **NOTE**
>
> The TCP port references in the URL (8443 for VirtualCenter and the standard 443 for the host agent) assume that the default ports are being used. If you have changed the ports, please account for this in the URL.

Once you successfully authenticate to the MOB, you will be presented with a page similar to that shown in Figure 3.16. This page represents the instantiation of the *ServiceInstance* object, the main gateway to the exposed managed and data objects. For each object that you view through the MOB, you will see a list of the properties and methods associated with that object.

Figure 3.16 The *ServiceInstance* Object Displayed in the Managed Object Browser

Home		
Managed Object Type: ManagedObjectReference:ServiceInstance		
Managed Object ID: **ServiceInstance**		

Properties

NAME	TYPE	VALUE
capability	Capability	capability
content	ServiceContent	content
serverClock	DateTime	"2006-08-20T04:26:27.400819Z"

Methods

RETURN TYPE	NAME
DateTime	CurrentTime
HostVMotionCompatibility[]	QueryVMotionCompatibility
ServiceContent	RetrieveServiceContent
Event[]	ValidateMigration

In some cases, as defined in the data model for that particular datatype or managed entity, properties are references to another object, usually a data object. The value of such properties is the name of the data object, which is displayed in the Value column as a hyperlink (such as *capability* and *content* in Figure 3.16). Similarly, you can invoke methods by clicking the corresponding sub-object in the Name column, also displayed as a hyperlink.

TIP

To work with the Managed Object Browser, you must have pop-ups disabled completely or at least for the URL of your MOB in your Web browser.

Let's explore the power of the MOB by reviewing a simple walk-through. We will gather information about our Web service host by performing the following steps:

1. Connect to the Managed Object Browser by browsing the appropriate URL and entering in valid credentials when prompted.

2. Click the **RetrieveServiceContent** hyperlink under Methods. A new window will open.

3. Click **Invoke Method**.

At this point, you will see the Method Invocation Result displaying various items in table form, as shown in Figure 3.17. The Name column represents the actual name of the managed or data object in the SDK. The Type column tells you more about that object and can help you map the object back to the appropriate data model for additional information. The Value column will either display the actual value or collection of values (for data objects) or a link to another data object or managed object. Remember that managed objects are never passed directly. Instead, a reference to that managed object is returned by operations. In this example, we see the value of the AboutInfo data object. This value is represented as a collection and gives you plenty of information about the Web service.

Figure 3.17 Method Invocation Result from Invoking the *RetrieveServiceContent* Operation

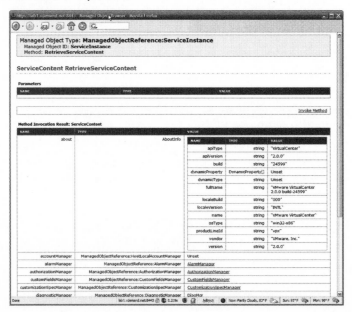

Although not much has been documented about the MOB, it will still serve as a great test or troubleshooting tool. If you need more information

about the value you must pass, such as a reference to managed objects that are required as input to an operation call, capture some samples of the returned managed object references to ensure that your input data is compliant with the WSDL schema for all complex types.

Microsoft has also provided some useful tools and functionality in the Visual Studio IDE that you will find handy. As we discussed earlier in the chapter, the Object Browser, as shown in Figure 3.18, can prove to be useful as a quick reference to the various properties, methods, and datatypes of VimService2005. The following figure shows the *VimApi* namespace and associated classes. Highlighting any class will reveal the properties and methods defined by that class, as well as their input and return values.

Figure 3.18 Visual Studio 2005 Object Browser Showing the *VimAPI* Namespace

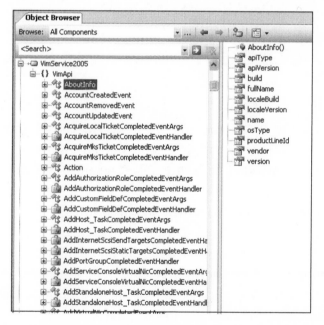

Another great feature about developing in Visual Studio is Intellisense, as shown in Figure 3.19. The IDE is ever mindful about objects that get instantiated, and as you code with those objects, the IDE will present you with the valid methods and properties related to your location of the object-oriented hierarchy, as well as hints on the syntax and datatypes expected. In the following figure, the IDE is aware of that *_service* as an instance of the *VimService* object and is helping to identify valid properties, methods, and events based on what has been typed so far, "_service.QueryVM".

Figure 3.19 Visual Studio 2005's Intellisense Feature Enumerating Properties and Methods of *VimService*

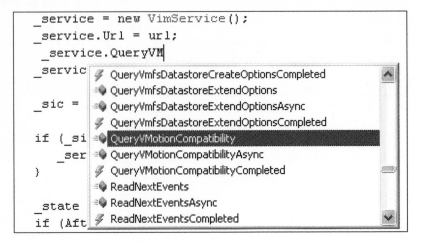

The Connection Process

Now you are ready to start some simple coding exercises. Although we step through some code snippets in this section, you can find complete applications in the samples included with the SDK. Our purpose here is to break down a lot of that complicated code to explore the various operations you may perform in your own management applications.

As the first step, you will need to connect the client to the Web service either using the stub you created or using the one that came with the SDK package. Assuming you have already created a new project, you will want to make a reference to the VimService2005.dll in your project. This will present the *VimApi* namespace for us to use in our code.

To log on to the Web service, perform the following steps:

1. Create a new managed object reference.

2. Create a reference to the Web service URL. Optionally, you can define how to handle cookies as part of the HTTP-based SOAP interaction.

3. Retrieve the ServiceContent data object from the service instance.

4. Obtain the session manager reference to be used when invoking the login operation

5. Call the *Login* operation, passing the referenced session manager, username, and password.

Code Listings 3.19 and 3.20 demonstrate a simple logon process and assume you have captured the values of *url*, *username*, and *password* as input or arguments to work with. Remember that the URL to the Web service is https:// <your_server>/sdk.

Code Listing 3.19 C# Script for Logging on to the Web Service

```
using System;
using VimApi;


protected VimService _service;
protected ServiceContent _sic;
protected ManagedObjectReference _svcRef;


public void Connect(string url, string username, string password) {
    _service = new VimService();
    _service.Url = url;
    _service.CookieContainer = new System.Net.CookieContainer();

    _svcRef = new ManagedObjectReference();
    _svcRef.type = "ServiceInstance";
    _svcRef.Value = "ServiceInstance";

    _sic = _service.RetrieveServiceContent(_svcRef);

    if (_sic.sessionManager != null) {
        _service.Login(_sic.sessionManager, username, password, null);
    }
}
```

Code Listing 3.20 VB.NET Script for Logging on to the Web Service

```
Imports System

Imports VimApi


protected _service As VimService

protected _sic As ServiceContent

protected _svcRef as ManagedObjectReference


Public Function connect(url As string, username as String, password As _

  String)

    _service = New VimService

    _service.Url = url

    _service.CookieContainer = New System.Net.CookieContainer


    _svcRef = New ManagedObjectReference

    _svcRef.type = "ServiceInstance"

    _svcRef.Value = "ServiceInstance"


    _sic = _service.RetrieveServiceContent(_svcRef)


    if (_sic.sessionManager != null)

        _service.Login(_sic.sessionManager, username, password, null)

    End if

End Function
```

In this example, we reference the *VimAPI* namespace that will facilitate access to the various objects needed in our management application. We declare and instantiate three variables. *_service* serves as a primary object of type *VimService*. *_sic* serves as our *ServiceContent* managed object. *_svcRef* represents an instance of the *ManagedObjectReference* object type. Upon instantiation, we set the appropriate values for the URL and cookie container for the client and invoke the Login operation. You will notice that we must pass the reference to the *sessionManager* managed object as one of the input parameters of the login operation.

Handling SSL Certificates

With VI SDK 2.0, we are faced with the same potential problems surrounding PKI management and certificate issues for your management application that we experienced with earlier SDKs. In most cases, you will connect to the Web service through the HTTPS listener instead of HTTP. The default certificate used by the VI Web service is not a valid one for production use since it was not issued by a trusted root certificate authority (CA). You can choose to handle this condition one of two ways. First, you can replace the certificate with a valid one from a trusted CA and update the vpx configuration as reviewed earlier in this chapter. Another option would be to handle the "bad" certificate programmatically in your application. Although the certificate cannot be trusted, it can still be used to encrypt the HTTP data payload transmitted between the management client and the Web service.

The latter option is the most common and still provides adequate security for situations where the Web service is only accessible on your internal network. The examples found in the SDK package all include a sample workaround which we will discuss briefly. The key component is the CertPolicy.cs file, which can be copied from any sample and added to your project. Using the *System.Security.Cryptography.X509Certificates* namespace and hashtables, the *CheckValidationResult* function is passed the certificate and assesses its validity. If the function detects any issues with the certificate, it will then display a message box stating any problems that were found, presenting the management client user the option to continue regardless.

To take advantage of this certificate validation functionality, you can implement *ICertificatePolicy*. Then you must pass *ICertificatePolicy* to *ServicePointManager.CertificatePolicy* before any Web service method calls are made. Include the following code in the client code. Before you make the Web Service method call from the client code, the following statement must be executed:

```
System.Net.ServicePointManager.CertificatePolicy = new CertPolicy();
```

In addition to using the *CertPolicy* distributed in the SDK package, you can create you own *CertPolicy* that will validate, for example, all certificates. The following sample code implements *ICertificatePolicy* and then accepts every request under SSL:

```
using System.Net;
using System.Security.Cryptography.X509Certificates;

public class CertPolicy : ICertificatePolicy {
    public bool CheckValidationResult(
          ServicePoint svcPnt
        , X509Certificate cert
        , WebRequest req
        , int certProblem) {
        return true;
    } // end CheckValidationResult
} // class CertPolicy
```

Retrieving Property Information

Collecting information from any managed objects requires that you create a *PropertyFilterSpec* data object. This object contains two properties: *propSet*, a set of *PropertySpec* data objects, and *objectSet*, a set of *ObjectSpec* data objects (see Table 3.17).

Table 3.17 Details Concerning the Definition of These Properties as Required for the *PropertyFilterSpec*

Item	Object	Comprised Object Properties
propSet	PropertySpec	**type** Value that represents the type of managed object being collected.
		all Boolean value that tells the *PropertySpec* to retrieve all available properties of the managed object (is set to TRUE).

Continued

Table 3.17 continued Details Concerning the Definition of These Properties as Required for the *PropertyFilterSpec*

Item	Object	Comprised Object Properties
		pathSet Comma-separated list of property names identifying the properties whose values should be retrieved for the managed object. This implies that the "all" property was set to FALSE or omitted.
objectSet	ObjectSpec	**obj** Defines the managed object reference where the collection begins.
		skip Boolean value that tells the *ObjectSpec* whether the object defined in "obj" is part of the selection for property retrieval.
		selectSet (Optional) Is made up of one or more *SelectionSpec* data objects, which in turn contain *TraversalSpec* data objects. Each managed object is a property of the original managed object defined in "obj", and can be traversed or have its properties retrieved as well.
selectSet	SelectionSpec TraverseSpec	**type** Value that represents the type of managed object for the *TraversalSpec*.
		path The property name that contains the managed object reference as a value. This reference is where the traversal will go next.
		skip Boolean value that tells the *SelectionSpec* or *TraversalSpec* whether the referenced object is part of the selection for property retrieval.
		selectSet An array of *SelectSpec* objects defining the next step of the traversal. The *SelectionSpec* can be a *TraversalSpec* if further traversing is necessary.

Mastering the *PropertyCollector*, filters, and inventory traversal will be key to developing efficient and powerful management applications. With this latest release, the frontier is still fairly unexplored, but in time you will develop a strategy that works best for you in your development efforts.

Since property management is such an important area in the new SDK, we will review two examples in C# that should help demonstrate the basic techniques. The first example demonstrates a simple *PropertyFilterSpec* with no traversal. In this example, we will monitor a task by retrieving specific information about it.

We start by declaring *pSpec* as a new instance of *PropertySpec*. Setting the type to "Task", we can focus on managed objects of the desired type. We also set the *all* property to FALSE because we only want to retrieve specific information, "info.state", as defined in the array *pathSet*.

```
PropertySpec pSpec = new PropertySpec();

pSpec.Type = "Task";

pSpec.all = false; pSpec.allSpecified = true;

pSpec.pathSet = new String[] { "info.state" };
```

Next, we declare *oSpec* as a new instance of *ObjectSpec*. By setting the property *obj* to the managed object reference of the specific task that we are focusing on, we define it as the starting point. Since the skip property is not set to TRUE and *selectSet* is not defined, the managed object referenced in *obj* will be checked to see if it matches *pSpec.Type*, or "type", and there will be no traversal to other managed objects. Consequently, this will be the only object that is checked.

```
ObjectSpec oSpec = new ObjectSpec();

oSpec.Obj = taskMgdObjRef;
```

With *pSpec* and *oSpec* defined, we can now construct the *PropertyFilterSpec*. We do so by declaring *_pfsec* as a new instance of *PropertyFilterSpec*, setting its *ObjectSpec* property to *oSpec* and its *PropertySpec* to *pSpec*.

```
PropertyFilterSpec _pfSpec = new PropertyFilterSpec();

_pfSpec.ObjectSet = new ObjectSpec[] { oSpec };

_pfSpec.PropSet = new PropertySpec[] { pSpec };
```

We have everything we need to retrieve the results of the collection. First, we need to declare a *PropertyCollector* managed object reference from the *ServiceContent* data object.

```
ManagedObjectReference _svcRef = new ManagedObjectReference();

_svcRef.type = "ServiceInstance";

_svcRef.Value = "ServiceInstance";


ServiceContent _sic = VimService.RetrieveServiceContent(_svcRef);


ManagedObjectReference pCollector = _sic.PropertyCollector();
```

Next, we invoke the *retrieveProperties* operation, passing it the *PropertyCollector* managed object reference and the *PropertyFilterSpec* that we constructed. The resulting *ObjectContent* is then used alongside a *DynamicProperty* array to store the values retrieved, which we then write to the console. Note that the variable *_service* was declared and defined upon establishing a connection with the Web service.

```
ObjectContent[] ocary = vimService.retrieveProperties(pCollector,
  new PropertyFilterSpec[] { pfSpec });


if (ocary != null) {
  ObjectContent oc = null;
  ManagedObjectReference mor = null;
  DynamicProperty[] pcary = null;
  DynamicProperty pc = null;
  oc = ocary[0];
  mor = oc.obj;
  pcary = oc.propSet;

  Console.WriteLine("Object Type : " + mor.type);
  Console.WriteLine("Reference Value : " + mor.Value);

  if (pcary != null) {
```

```
    pc = pcary[0];

    Console.WriteLine("   Property Name : " + pc.name);

    Console.WriteLine("   Property Value : " + pc.val);

  }

}
```

When simple property retrieval isn't wanted or it doesn't fit the situation, you must incorporate object traversal through the entity inventory to collect the information you need. This is particularly true when you do not know where the object you desire to manage is located and you need to traverse the inventory recursively. The following example reviews the steps you will need in order to enumerate all of the virtual machines in the inventory regardless of where they are located. Our objective is to collect the properties *guest.hostName* and *guest.guestFullName*.

We begin by creating a new *PropertySpec* instance, followed by a single *ObjectSpec* property:

```
PropertySpec pSpec = new PropertySpec();

pSpec.Type = "VirtualMachine";

pSpec.all = false; pSpec.allSpecified = true;

pSpec.pathSet = new String[] { "guest.hostName", "guest.guestFullName" };


ObjectSpec oSpec = new ObjectSpec();

oSpec.Obj = refDataCenter;

oSpec.Skip = FALSE;
```

We supposed that the variable *refDataCenter* was declared and defined earlier as a managed object reference to a datacenter managed object. We now define the traversal path. The *TraversalSpec* objects will use the *Datacenter* managed object as a starting point and will cover the six possible paths through the hierarchy, as shown in the following list:

- Folder to childEntity (*folderTSpec*)
- Datacenter to hostFolder (*dc2HostTSpec*)
- Datacenter to vmFolder (*dc2VmTSpec*)

- ComputeResource to resourcePool (*cr2RpTSpec*)

- ComputeResource to host (*cr2HostTSpec*)

- resourcePool to resourcePool (*rp2RpTSpec*)

Code Listing 3.21 demonstrates how the TraversalSpec objects are defined.

Code Listing 3.21 Defining TraversalSpec Objects

```
TraversalSpec dc2HostTSpec = new TraversalSpec();

dc2HostTSpec.Type = "Datacenter";

dc2HostTSpec.Path = "hostFolder";

dc2HostTSpec.SelectSet = new SelectionSpec[]{recursiveSpec};


TraversalSpec dc2VmTSpec = new TraversalSpec();

dc2VmTSpec.Type = "Datacenter";

dc2VmTSpec.Path = "vmFolder";

dc2VmTSpec.SelectSet = new SelectionSpec[]{recursiveSpec};


TraversalSpec cr2RpTSpec = new TraversalSpec();

cr2RpTSpec.Type = "ComputeResource";

cr2RpTSpec.Path = "resourcePool";


TraversalSpec cr2HostTSpec = new TraversalSpec();

cr2HostTSpec.Type = "ComputeResource";

cr2HostTSpec.Path = "host";


TraversalSpec rp2rpTSpec = new TraversalSpec();

rp2rpTSpec.Type = "ResourcePool";

rp2rpTSpec.Path = "resourcePool";


TraversalSpec folderTSpec = new TraversalSpec();

folderTSpec.Type = "Folder";

folderTSpec.Path = "childEntity";
```

```
folderTSpec.SelectSet = new SelectionSpec[]{recursiveSpec,
                                            dc2VmTSpec,
                                            dc2HostTSpec,
                                            cr2RpTSpec,
                                            cr2HostTSpec,
                                            rp2rpTSpec};
```

In order to finalize the declaration of the *PropertyFilterSpec*, we must next define the *ObjectSpec* and referencing *folderTSpec* as the *SelectSet* property. This will be the starting point of the traversal at every possible path, collecting data along the way. At that point, we can construct the *PropertyFilterSpec*, as shown Code Listing 3.22.

Code Listing 3.22 *PropertyFilterSpec*

```
oSpec.SelectSet = new SelectionSpec[]{folderTSpec};

PropertyFilterSpec pfSpec = new PropertyFilterSpec();
pfSpec.PropSet = new PropertySpec[] {pSpec};
pfSpec.ObjectSet = new ObjectSpec[] {ospec};
```

Other Retrieval Mechanisms

In addition to these techniques, you can also retrieve information through several other mechanisms. You can search for managed object by *SearchIndex* API rather than the *PropertyCollector*. There are some inherent differences between the two, as shown in the following list:

- *SearchAPI* returns the first managed entity match, while *PropertyCollector* returns as many items as matched within the scope of its search.

- *SearchAPI* only works with a small group of managed entities, while *PropertyCollector* works with all managed objects.

- SearchAPI is much easier to work with.

The SearchAPI allows a client to query the entity inventory for a specific management object using a variety of search attributes. The common managed objects types retrieved using this mechanism are *VirtualMachine* and *HostSystem*. One thing to keep in mind, though, is that a user cannot find a managed object that it does not have access, so ensuring the proper setting for the ACLs of the objects in question is important. The SearchAPI has the following six operations associated with it:

- FindByDatastorePath
- FindByDnsName
- FindByInventoryPath
- FindByIp
- FindByUuid
- FindChild

You can also retrieve updates for previously collected properties. This is done using one of three operations, as shown in Table 3.18. Each operation has its pros and cons, however, so you must match these characteristics against the goal of your code and the functional and efficiency requirements you may have.

Table 3.18 Three Operations to Get Updates on Properties

Operation	Pros	Cons
RetrieveProperties	Same process as retrieving the original values for the targeted properties.	Retrieves all of the properties as defined in the *PropertyFilterSpec*, whether they have changed or not; least efficient use of network bandwidth.
CheckForUpdates	Efficient use of network bandwidth; only returns properties that have changed.	Runs synchronously, so it returns immediately, whether there were any changes or not.

Continued

Table 3.18 continued Three Operations to Get Updates on Properties

Operation	Pros	Cons
WaitForUpdates	Efficient use of network bandwidth; only returns properties that have changed.	Runs asynchronously, so it does not return until a change has occurred; will wait or listen indefinitely if change is not detected or *CancelWaitForUpdates* is called.

Performing Advanced Operations

Now that you know how to retrieve information about managed objects and obtain the value of data objects found within your inventory, you are ready to tackle performing management operations against those managed entities. This is where the power of any SDK comes in, as you can build powerful applications that analyze properties of the managed objects and, in turn, invoke the appropriate set of operations as a response.

In this section, we will discuss a few of the common operations that can be accomplished programmatically with the SDK. Reviewing each of the operations in this chapter would be lengthy and is beyond the scope of this book. However, both the *Virtual Infrastructure SDK Programming Guide* and the *Virtual Infrastructure SDK Reference Guide* will help tremendously and serve as a great look-up guide when needed.

Power Operations

To control the power state of a particular virtual machine, you can call any of the following operations: *PowerOnVM_Task*, *PowerOffVM_Task* (for "hard" shutdowns), or *ShutdownGuest* (for "cold" shutdowns), *SuspendVM_Task*, and *ResetVM_Task*. Code Listing 3.23 demonstrates the PowerOffVM_Task operation.

Code Listing 3.23 *PowerOffVM_Task*

```
ManagedObjectReference MgdObjRef_VM =

    _service.findByInventoryPath(_sic.SearchIndex(), pathVM);

ManagedObjectReference MgdObjRef_Host =

    _service.findByInventoryPath(_sic.SearchIndex(), pathHost);

ManagedObjectReference MgdObjRef_Task =

    _service.PowerOffVM(MgdObjRef_VM, MgdObjRef_Host);
```

Virtual Machine Migration

The *MigrateVM_Task* operation is used to migrate an existing virtual machine, regardless of power state. Migrating a virtual machine from one host to another is different than moving a virtual machine because the disk files themselves are not migrated, just the ownership of the virtual machine. The operation has the following required and options parameters that are passed when being invoked:

- **VirtualMachine managed object reference** The reference to the VirtualMachine managed object.

- **Pool** A reference to a ResourcePool managed object.

- **Host** A reference to a HostSystem managed object.

- **Priority** The priority level that you want to set for the migration task.

- **State** If specified, the migration will only proceed if the power state of the virtual machine matches this parameter.

Code Listing 3.24 demonstrates the MigrateVM_Task operation.

Code Listing 3.24 *MigrateVM_Task*

```
ManagedObjectReference MgdObjRef_VM =

    _service.findByInventoryPath(_sic.SearchIndex(), pathVM);

ManagedObjectReference MgdObjRef_Host =

    _service.findByInventoryPath(_sic.SearchIndex(), pathHost);

ManagedObjectReference MgdObjRef_RPool =
```

```
    _service.findByInventoryPath(_sic.SearchIndex(), pathResourcePool);
ManagedObjectReference MgdObjRef_Task =
    _service.MigrateVM(MgdObjRef_VM, MgdObjRef_RPool, MgdObjRef_Host
    VirtualMachineMovePriority.highPriority,
    VirtualMachinePowerState.poweredOn);
```

Working with Snapshots

New to Virtual Infrastructure 3 is the ability to create multiple points-in-time snapshots and to revert back to other snapshots—a functionality similar to that available in the VMware Workstation product. The operations *CreateSnapshot_Task*, *RevertToSnapshot_Task*, and *RemoveSnaphost_Task* can be used to manage your snapshot processes programmatically. Each operation has its own set of parameters that are passed upon invocation. For example, the *CreateSnapshot_Task* has the following for parameters:

- **Name** A friendly string value to name the snapshot.

- **Description** A user-defined string value that describes the snapshot, such as "Pre-SP1 Snapshot #3 Created on 2006/08/20".

- **Memory** A Boolean value that tells the operation whether a memory dump should be included with the snapshot

- **Quiesce** A Boolean value that tells the virtual machine, via VMware Tools, to quiesce the file system prior to taking the snapshot. If set to TRUE, the snapshot will be power-down consistent, rather than crash-consistent, as with previous versions of the ESX Server product.

Refer to the Virtual Infrastructure SDK Programming Guide for more information about each of these operations. Code Listing 3.25 demonstrates the *CreateSnapshot_Task* operation.

Code Listing 3.25 *CreateSnapshot_Task*

```
ManagedObjectReference MgdObjRef_VM =
    _service.findByInventoryPath(_sic.SearchIndex(), pathVM);
boolean memoryDump = false;
```

```
boolean quiesceFileSys = true;

string snapName = "Pre-SP1 Snapshot #3";

string snapDescription = "Pre-SP1 Snapshot #3 Created on 2006/08/20";

ManagedObjectReference MgdObjRef_Task =

    _service.CreateSnapshot_Task(MgdObjRef_VM, snapName, snapDescription,

    memoryDump, quiesceFileSys);
```

Working with Scheduled Tasks

You can programmatically create scheduled tasks. To do this, you invoke the
CreateScheduledTask operation and configure the task with the
ScheduledTaskSpec data objects. This operation has the following parameters:

- **ScheduledTaskManager managed object reference** This reference
  is derived from the *scheduledTaskManager* property of the
  ServiceContent data object.

- **ManagedEntity managed object reference** The target entity for
  the action in the task.

- **Spec** The *ScheduledTaskSpec* object.

The *ScheduledTaskSpec* also has various parameters that are defined as
properties of the data object. Those properties are

- **Action** Defines the action performed against the targeted managed
  entity.

- **Scheduler** A *TaskScheduler* data object that is used to define when
  the action takes place.

- **Enabled** A Boolean property for whether the task is enabled or disabled.

- **Name** A user-friendly name for the task.

- **Description** A user-defined description of the task.

- **Notification** A string value for the e-mail notification associated
  with the task.

Code Listing 3.26 demonstrates the *CreateScheduledTask* operation.

Code Listing 3.26 *CreateScheduledTask*

```
ManagedObjectReference MgdObjRef_VM =

    _service.FindByInventoryPath(_sic.SearchIndex(), pathVM);


MethodActionArgument[] mActArgumnt = new MethodActionArgument();

MethodAction mAction = new MethodAction();

mActArgumnt.Value = MgdObjRef_VM;

ma.Argument = mActArgumnt;

ma.Name = "MigrateVM";


DailyTaskScheduler dtScheduler = new DailyTaskScheduler();

dtScheduler.Hour = 12;

dtScheduler.Minute = 0;


ScheduledTaskSpec tSpec = new ScheduledTaskSpec();

tSpec.Action = mAction;

tSpec.Scheduler = dtScheduler;

tSpec.Enabled = true;

tSpec.Name = "Migrate virtual machine";

tSpec.Description = "Migrate virtual machine at noon");

tSpec.Notification = "VMAdmin@syngress.com";


_service.createScheduledTask(_sic.ScheduledTaskManager,MgdObjRef_VM,tSpec);
```

For more information, download and review the *VMware Virtual Infrastructure SDK Programming Guide* and the HTML–based *VMware Virtual Infrastructure SDK Reference Guide*.

Other VMware SDKs

In an effort to give developers and administrators even more control over their Virtual Infrastructure, VMware has provided additional SDKs designed to meet specific management needs. In addition to the VMware Scripting

APIs and the Virtual Infrastructure SDK, VMware also offers the VMware Guest SDK and the CIM SDK. We will review each of these SDKs briefly.

VMware Guest SDK

Newly introduced with Virtual Infrastructure 3 is the VMware Guest SDK or Guest API. This interface provides access to certain data for the guest operating system running inside a virtual machine. The SDK is facilitated by the VMware Tools, implying that the tools must be installed in order for your management application to be able to hook into the API. In addition, the Guest SDK is a read–only API, intended only to provision a mechanism for data collection.

Using the VMware Guest SDK, you can monitor and collect data for the statistics (shown in Table 3.19) about the virtual machine environment.

Table 3.19 Statistics Available Through the Guest SDK

Item	Statistic
Memory	The total amount of memory allocated to the guest OS. The amount of memory in use at the time of data collection. The upper limit of memory available to the guest OS, if not equal to the total amount of memory allocated. The number of shares allocated for memory resources.
CPU	The amount of CPU resources guaranteed. Minimum reserved rate that the virtual machine is allowed to run, even when idle. The number of shares allocated for CPU resources. CPU time scheduled on the hosting ESX Server for the virtual machine's CPU resources.
Miscellaneous	The runtime since the last power-on event or reset of the virtual machine. The ability of the API to provide accurate data.

The Guest API run-time component exists as a library that is installed with VMware Tools version 3.0 and higher. For Windows guest operating systems, the library file is *vmGuestLib.dll*; for Linux, the library is *libvmGuestLib.so*.

TIP

By default, the run-time component of the Guest API is enabled. Even at idle, this causes the virtual machine to consume CPU cycles, although the amount may be negligible. You may want to consider disabling this component to avoid utilizing unnecessary resources.

To disable the run-time component, edit the config file by either adding the following line or, if it already exists, changing the value as shown in the following:

```
isolation.tools.guestlibGetInfo.disable = "TRUE"
```

The run-time component exposes several data types, functions, and a library of Error Messages that you can use to troubleshoot the environment. As a read-only set of API calls, it does not support any operations to perform actions within the virtual machine, such as reconfiguration, power operations, or interaction with other members of the virtual infrastructure. If you need to perform operations, you should utilize the Virtual Infrastructure SDK (preferred) or Scripting APIs.

For more information, please consult the *VMware Guest SDK Programming Guide*.

VMware CIM SDK

Available as 1.0 or 2.0 releases for ESX 2.x or ESX 3, respectively, the VMware CIM SDK is the final offering to developers and administrators for managing components of the virtual infrastructure. This SDK is compliant with Common Information Model (CIM) standards and supports the Storage Management Initiative Specification (SMI-S) schema for storage management. Since the focus of the SDK is on storage, it allows developers and administrators to:

- View and identify logical storage resources using a CIM-compliant application, whether it be "home-grown" or a commercially available tool.

- View allocation of storage resources to virtual machines.

- View the physical layer of the storage presented to the hosts associated with the managed virtual machines.

- Monitor the components responsible for facilitating access to storage, including, but not limited to, host bus adapters, CIM/SMS-S–compliant connectivity devices, and compliant storage servers/arrays themselves.

The CIM SDK is based on standards defined by the DMTF and WBEM bodies, even though it is targeted to storage management and not the overall management of the ESX hosts. The SDK is provisioned by two components as listed next and as illustrated in Figure 3.20:

- **Pegasus CIMOM** A popular open-source CIMOM application that is installed with, and runs inside, the Service Console of ESX hosts.

- **Set of Managed Object Format (MOF) files** MOF files that can be compiled and used on management clients to interact with the CIMOM process on the server.

Figure 3.20 The CIM SDK Process for Communication

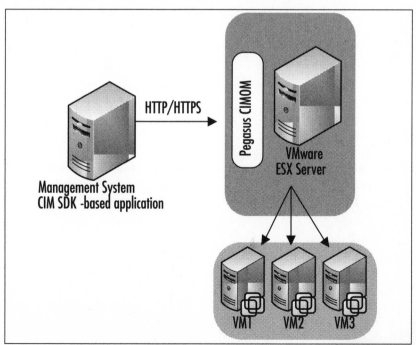

Covering the CIM SDK in detail is beyond the scope of this chapter. If you are interested in developing management applications that take advantage of the SDK for storage management purposes, you will want to make sure you are familiar with CIM concepts and principles as well as the SMI-S schema profile. For more information about the VMware CIM SDK, please see the *VMware CIM SDK Programming Guide*. If you are looking for additional information regarding CIM and SMI-S, visit the following sites:

- **Distributed Management Task Force (DMTF)** www.dmtf.org
- **Common Information Model (CIM)** www.dmtf.org/standards/cim/
- **OpenPegasus** www.openpegasus.org
- **Storage Networks Industry Association (SNIA)** www.snia.org/home
- **Storage Management Initiative Specification (SMI-S)** www.snia.org/smi/tech_activities/smi_spec_pr/spec/

Summary

Beginning with the release of ESX Server 2.x and evolving into the Virtual Infrastructure 3 product line, VMware has uniquely positioned their virtualization technology in such a way that clearly distinguishes them from their competition. Combined with the inherit flexibility and performance that ESX Server and VirtualCenter provide at a functional level, the ability to develop custom management client applications to help administer, manage, and monitor your virtual infrastructure makes their technology the choice for many operations. Even with a limited background in scripting or programming, you can develop programs that will help automate and ease your administration through the VMware Scripting APIs, Virtual Infrastructure SDK, Guest SDK, and CIM SDK.

## Chapter 4

Building a VM

Topics in this chapter:

- Creation of Virtual Machines Utilizing Command-Line Tools
- Scripting Creation of Virtual Machines in ESX Shell
- Scripting Creation of Virtual Machines in Perl Scripts
- Cloning Virtual Machines Utilizing ESX Shell Scripts
- Cloning Virtual Machines Utilizing VmPerl Scripts

Introduction

VMware provides many useful command-line tools for the creation and cloning of virtual machines. In this chapter, you will gain a working understanding of these tools and how to leverage them to automate virtual machine creation. At the end of this chapter, you will be able to script the creation and cloning of virtual machines to automate your virtual machine setup.

Creation of Virtual Machines Utilizing Command-Line Tools

VMware ESX Server has tools available for command-line creation and cloning of virtual machines. These tools are available via the service console and require that you access the service console with root-level privileges.

TIP

Remote access to ESX Server by default is disabled for the root account. Create an additional account on your ESX server. Log in with this new account and use the **su – root** command. This command will allow you to assume root level privileges.

Three main steps are involved to create a virtual machine utilizing the command-line tools.

- Creation of a virtual machine configuration file
- Creation of a virtual machine disk file
- Registering the virtual machine with ESX Server

We accomplish the preceding tasks by utilizing the following tools:

- text editor such as VI
- *vmkfstools*
- *vmware-cmd*

Creation of a Virtual Machine Configuration File

Virtual machine configurations are stored as files with a .vmx extension. The VMX file is just a text file with specific fields that define the virtual machine's configuration. A very short vmx file only needs 14 lines to support a virtual machine that encompasses one CPU, one hard drive, and one network adapter. You could create a VMX file with just three lines but it would be of minimal value. Code Listings 4.1 and 4.2 show sample VMX configurations.

Code Listing 4.1 ESX 2.x VMX Code

```
guestOS = "winnetenterprise"
config.version = "6"
virtualHW.version = "3"
scsi0.present = "true"
scsi0.sharedBus = "none"
scsi0.virtualDev = "lsilogic"
memsize = "512"
scsi0:0.present = "true"
scsi0:0.fileName = "ESX Created VM.vmdk"
scsi0:0.deviceType = "scsi-hardDisk"
ethernet0.present = "true"
ethernet0.allowGuestConnectionControl = "false"
ethernet0.networkName = "VM Network"
ethernet0.addressType = "vpx"
```

Code Listing 4.2 ESX 3.x VMX Code

```
guestOS = "winnetenterprise"
config.version = "8"
virtualHW.version = "4"
scsi0.present = "true"
scsi0.sharedBus = "none"
scsi0.virtualDev = "lsilogic"
memsize = "512"
```

```
scsi0:0.present = "true"
scsi0:0.fileName = "ESX Created VM.vmdk"
scsi0:0.deviceType = "scsi-hardDisk"
ethernet0.present = "true"
ethernet0.allowGuestConnectionControl = "false"
ethernet0.networkName = "VM Network"
ethernet0.addressType = "vpx"
```

As you can tell from Code Listings 4.1 and 4.2, the only difference is in the values of the config.version and virtualHW.version entries. These values relate to the version of ESX Server you are running. To check the values for these fields, open up an existing virtual machine's configuration file in a text editor.

NOTE

It doesn't matter whether you use upper- or lowercase, but always make sure to use " " for the values in an (VMX) file.

Once you start a VM using a VMX configuration file like the ones shown in Code Listings 4.1 and 4.2, VMware will generate additional entries in the VMX. These entries identify the virtual machine and set default values for the virtual machine. Examples of these types of entries are shown in Code Listing 4.3

Code Listing 4.3 VMware Autogenerated VMX Entry Examples

```
uuid.bios = "56 4d ee 3c 52 06 a3 de-be 4a 73 9c cc 79 25 2b "
ethernet0.generatedAddress = "00:50:56:a7:42:e2"
powerType.powerOff = "default"
powerType.powerOn = "default"
powerType.suspend = "default"
powerType.reset = "default"
```

NOTE

Configuration files for virtual machines created with VMware ESX Server 2.0 and later use the .vmx extension. Earlier versions of ESX Server used the .cfg extension.

Creating Your Virtual Machine Configuration File

You now have a basic understanding of how a virtual machine configuration file is constructed and are ready to build your own. The steps that follow detail how to create a new virtual machine configuration file.

- Log in locally or connect to your ESX server remotely.

- Log in with an ID that has root privileges (see the Tip in the previous section), as shown in Figure 4.1.

Figure 4.1 Gaining Root Level Access on ESX Server

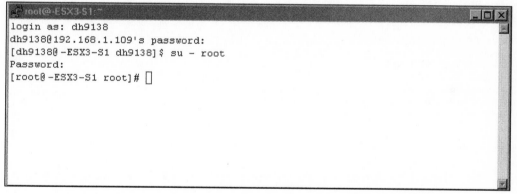

```
login as: dh9138
dh9138@192.168.1.109's password:
[dh9138@-ESX3-S1 dh9138]$ su - root
Password:
[root@-ESX3-S1 root]# []
```

- Change to the location of where you want to put your new virtual machine. Virtual machine configuration files (VMX) have to be stored in the same location as the other virtual machine files (VSWP, VMDK, and so on). See Figure 4.2.

Figure 4.2 Virtual Machine Storage Location

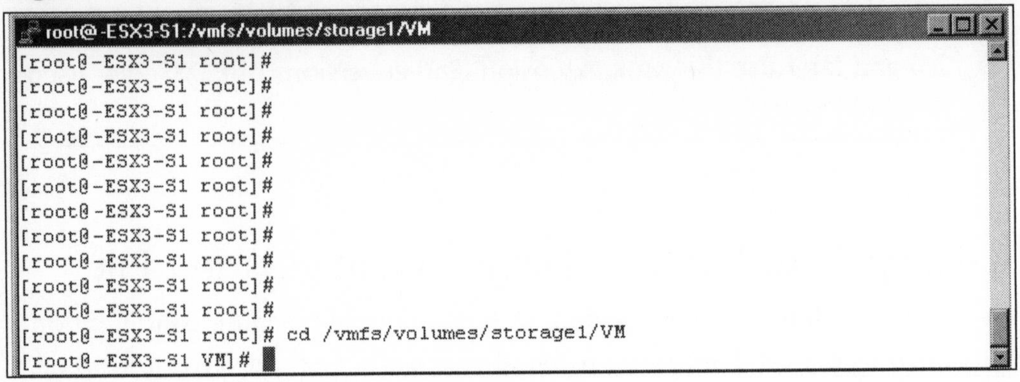

```
root@-ESX3-S1:/vmfs/volumes/storage1/VM                        _ □ X
[root@-ESX3-S1 root]#
[root@-ESX3-S1 root]#
[root@-ESX3-S1 root]#
[root@-ESX3-S1 root]#
[root@-ESX3-S1 root]#
[root@-ESX3-S1 root]#
[root@-ESX3-S1 root]#
[root@-ESX3-S1 root]#
[root@-ESX3-S1 root]#
[root@-ESX3-S1 root]#
[root@-ESX3-S1 root]# cd /vmfs/volumes/storage1/VM
[root@-ESX3-S1 VM]#
```

- Create a new directory to store your new virtual machine in newvm and change to that directory (see Figure 4.3).

Figure 4.3 Virtual Machine Working Directory

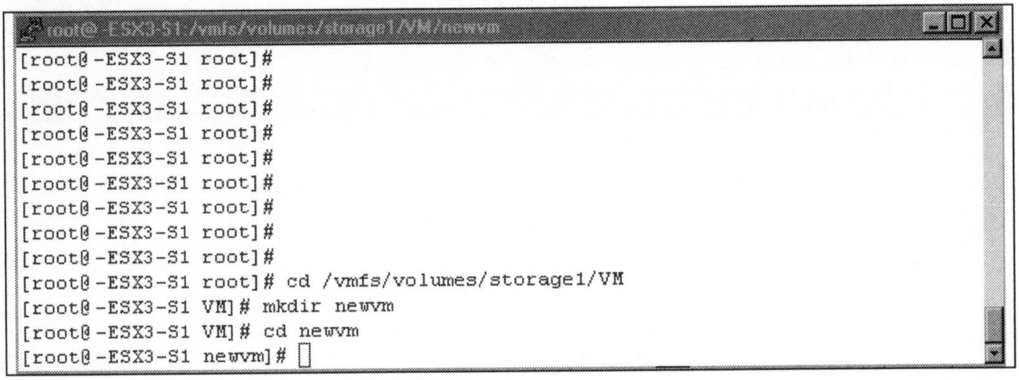

```
root@-ESX3-S1:/vmfs/volumes/storage1/VM/newvm                  _ □ X
[root@-ESX3-S1 root]#
[root@-ESX3-S1 root]#
[root@-ESX3-S1 root]#
[root@-ESX3-S1 root]#
[root@-ESX3-S1 root]#
[root@-ESX3-S1 root]#
[root@-ESX3-S1 root]#
[root@-ESX3-S1 root]#
[root@-ESX3-S1 root]#
[root@-ESX3-S1 root]# cd /vmfs/volumes/storage1/VM
[root@-ESX3-S1 VM]# mkdir newvm
[root@-ESX3-S1 VM]# cd newvm
[root@-ESX3-S1 newvm]# []
```

- You are now ready to create your new virtual machine configuration file. We are going to use the built-in text editor VI to create our configuration file. Type **vi newvm.vmx** and press **Enter** (see Figure 4.4).

Figure 4.4 Creating a New Virtual Machine Configuration File in VI

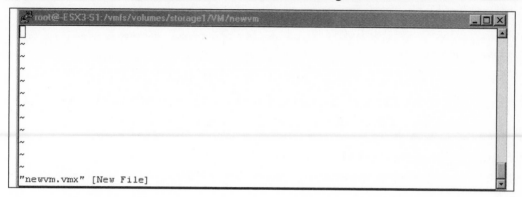

- Press **I** to turn on inserting (you will see the word insert at the bottom of the screen).

- Type in the following example virtual machine configuration file (see Code Listing 4.4).

Code Listing 4.4 Example Virtual Machine Configuration File

```
config.version = "6"

virtualHW.version = "3"

memsize = "256"

floppy0.present = "false"

displayName = "newVM"

guestOS = "winNetStandard"

ide0:0.present = "TRUE"

ide0:0.deviceType = "cdrom-raw"

ide:0.startConnected = "false"

floppy0.startConnected = "FALSE"

floppy0.fileName = "/dev/fd0"

Ethernet0.present = "TRUE"

Ethernet0.connectionType = "monitor_dev"

Ethernet0.networkName = "VM Network"

Ethernet0.addressType = "vpx"

scsi0.present = "true"

scsi0.sharedBus = "none"
```

```
scsi0.virtualDev = "lsilogic"

scsi0:0.present = "true"

scsi0:0.fileName = "newvm.vmdk"

scsi0:0.deviceType = "scsi-hardDisk"
```

- Press the **Esc** key to exit the insert mode, then press and hold **Shift** and press **ZZ** to save and exit (see Figure 4.5).

Figure 4.5 Saving the VMX File in VI

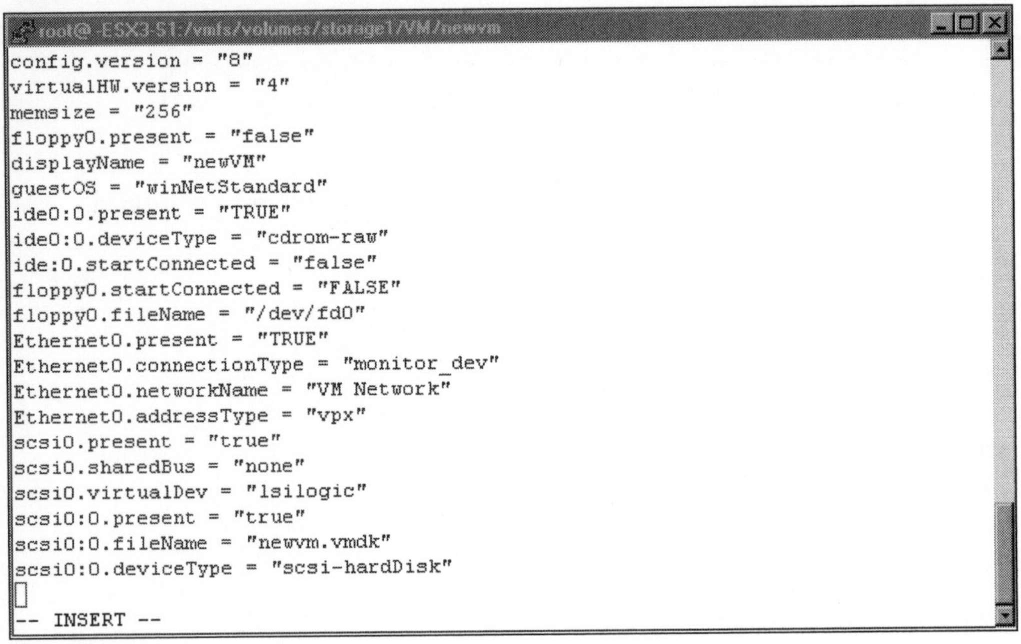

```
root@-ESX3-S1:/vmfs/volumes/storage1/VM/newvm                    _□X
config.version = "8"
virtualHW.version = "4"
memsize = "256"
floppy0.present = "false"
displayName = "newVM"
guestOS = "winNetStandard"
ide0:0.present = "TRUE"
ide0:0.deviceType = "cdrom-raw"
ide:0.startConnected = "false"
floppy0.startConnected = "FALSE"
floppy0.fileName = "/dev/fd0"
Ethernet0.present = "TRUE"
Ethernet0.connectionType = "monitor_dev"
Ethernet0.networkName = "VM Network"
Ethernet0.addressType = "vpx"
scsi0.present = "true"
scsi0.sharedBus = "none"
scsi0.virtualDev = "lsilogic"
scsi0:0.present = "true"
scsi0:0.fileName = "newvm.vmdk"
scsi0:0.deviceType = "scsi-hardDisk"

-- INSERT --
```

- Type **ls –l** to get a directory listing. You should now see your new virtual machine configuration file (see Figure 4.6).

Figure 4.6 Completed Creation of VMX File

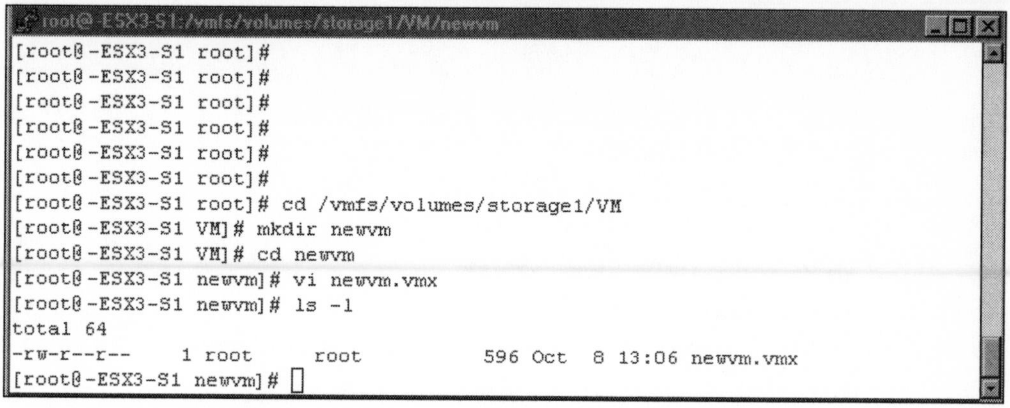

```
root@-ESX3-S1:/vmfs/volumes/storage1/VM/newvm                    _ □ ×
[root@-ESX3-S1 root]#
[root@-ESX3-S1 root]#
[root@-ESX3-S1 root]#
[root@-ESX3-S1 root]#
[root@-ESX3-S1 root]#
[root@-ESX3-S1 root]#
[root@-ESX3-S1 root]# cd /vmfs/volumes/storage1/VM
[root@-ESX3-S1 VM]# mkdir newvm
[root@-ESX3-S1 VM]# cd newvm
[root@-ESX3-S1 newvm]# vi newvm.vmx
[root@-ESX3-S1 newvm]# ls -l
total 64
-rw-r--r--    1 root      root          596 Oct  8 13:06 newvm.vmx
[root@-ESX3-S1 newvm]# []
```

You are now ready to go on to the next section to create the virtual disk newvm.vmdk that you will be referencing in your configuration file.

NOTE

Do not log out or close your ESX session just yet. You will continue from this point in the next section.

Creation of a Virtual Machine Disk File

VMware has a command-line utility, called *vmkfstools*, which can be used for the creation of VMFS file systems and virtual machine disk files. In this chapter, we will only focus on the options that pertain to virtual disks. For a full listing of command options, type **vmkfstools** in a console session or **man vmkfstools**. Code Listing 4.5 lists the *vmkfstools* options that pertain to virtual disks.

Code Listing 4.5 *vmkfstools* Command Options for Virtual Disks

```
vmkfstools

OPTIONS FOR VIRTUAL DISKS:

vmkfstools -c --createvirtualdisk #[gGmMkK]

              -d --diskformat [zeroedthick|
```

```
                              eagerzeroedthick|

                              thick|

                              thin]

                -a --adapterType [buslogic|lsilogic]

          -w --writezeros

          -j --inflatedisk

          -U --deletevirtualdisk

          -E --renamevirtualdisk srcDisk

          -i --clonevirtualdisk srcDisk

                -d --diskformat [rdm:<device>|rdmp:<device>|

                                 raw:<device>|thin|2gbsparse]

          -X --extendvirtualdisk #[gGmMkK]

          -M --migratevirtualdisk

          -r --createrdm /vmfs/devices/disks/...

          -q --queryrdm

          -z --createrdmpassthru /vmfs/devices/disks/...

          -Q --createrawdevice /vmfs/devices/generic/...

          -v --verbose #

          -g --geometry

    vmfsPath
```

In our example, we will create a 4GB virtual disk called newvm.vmdk and assign it a SCSI LSI Logic adapter. In the console, type the following: **vmkfs-tools –c 4g newvm.vmdk –a lsilogic**. Then, press **Enter** (see Figure 4.7).

Figure 4.7 Creating the Virtual Disk

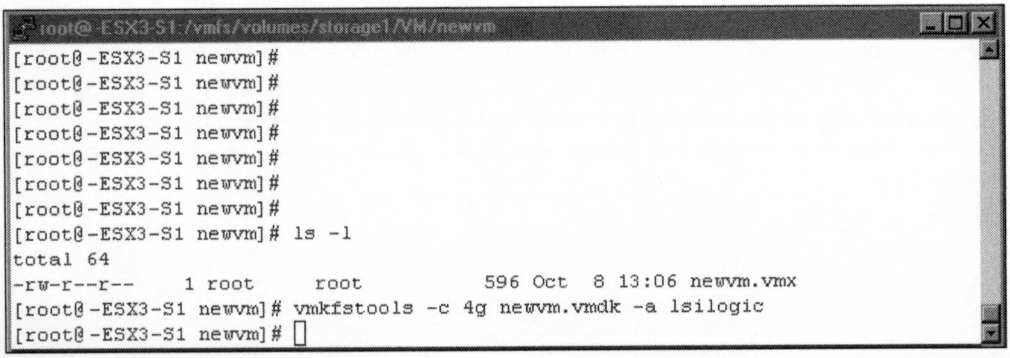

```
root@-ESX3-S1:/vmfs/volumes/storage1/VM/newvm                              _ □ X
[root@-ESX3-S1 newvm]#
[root@-ESX3-S1 newvm]#
[root@-ESX3-S1 newvm]#
[root@-ESX3-S1 newvm]#
[root@-ESX3-S1 newvm]#
[root@-ESX3-S1 newvm]#
[root@-ESX3-S1 newvm]#
[root@-ESX3-S1 newvm]# ls -l
total 64
-rw-r--r--    1 root      root          596 Oct  8 13:06 newvm.vmx
[root@-ESX3-S1 newvm]# vmkfstools -c 4g newvm.vmdk -a lsilogic
[root@-ESX3-S1 newvm]# ▯
```

We have now created a virtual disk file newvm.vmdk in the same location as our virtual machine configuration file. The last step is to register this new virtual machine with ESX Server.

Registering Virtual Machines with ESX Server

VMware includes the *vmware-cmd* command tool for performing various operations on virtual machines and the server. In this chapter, we will focus on the virtual machine registration option of this tool *-s register*. For more information on all available tool options, type **vmware-cmd** at the console command prompt.

Type the following all on one line in the console window to register the new virtual machine with the ESX server:

```
vmware-cmd -s register "Your Path"/newvm/newvm.vmx
```

"Your Path" should be in a similar format to */vmfs/volumes/storage1/* (see Figure 4.8).

Figure 4.8 Registering a Virtual Machine with ESX

```
root@-ESX3-S1:/vmfs/volumes/storage1/VM/newvm                      _ □ ×
[root@-ESX3-S1 newvm]#
[root@-ESX3-S1 newvm]#
[root@-ESX3-S1 newvm]#
[root@-ESX3-S1 newvm]#
[root@-ESX3-S1 newvm]#
[root@-ESX3-S1 newvm]#
[root@-ESX3-S1 newvm]#
[root@-ESX3-S1 newvm]#
[root@-ESX3-S1 newvm]#
[root@-ESX3-S1 newvm]#
[root@-ESX3-S1 newvm]#
[root@-ESX3-S1 newvm]# vmware-cmd -s register /vmfs/volumes/storage1/VM/newvm
/newvm.vmx
register(/vmfs/volumes/storage1/VM/newvm/newvm.vmx) = 1
[root@-ESX3-S1 newvm]# []
```

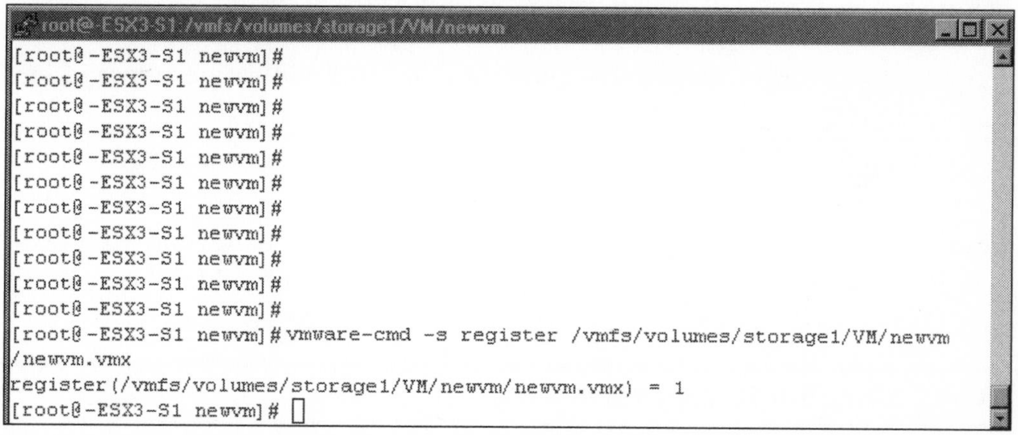

A returned value of "1" after running this command indicates a successful registration of the virtual machine. Open up the GUI of your ESX server to verify that the new VM is listed. At this point, you are ready to power on the virtual machine and install your operating system. You have successfully created a new virtual machine utilizing the VMware command-line tools.

WARNING

If when turning on the virtual machine for the first time you receive the error message "Cannot open disk <diskname.vmdk>:The system cannot find the file specified. Bad value for scsi0:0.virtualDev," this means your virtual machine configuration file has the wrong values for config.version and virtualHW.version. Update the values for these two fields with the appropriate ones for your version of ESX.

Scripting Creation of Virtual Machines in ESX Shell

Scripting the creation of virtual machines is simpler than one might think. We will leverage you new gained experience from previous sections on utilizing the VMware tools to automate the VM creation process. In the previous section, you manually created a virtual machine configuration file and virtual disk. You then registered the virtual machine with ESX Server. We're going to now essentially take all those commands and steps and automate them in a script that you can run repeatedly and customize to build various types of virtual machines.

The VMware ESX shell is simply the service console operating system. This operating system is a custom version of Linux that VMware created. In Linux, you can create a simple text file to automate commands and then execute it. If you are familiar with DOS batch files, then this will be easy for you. Code Listing 4.6 shows an example of scripted VM creation.

Code Listing 4.6 Scripted VM Creation

```
##### VM Creation Script ###################################
#Script Version 1.1
#Author David E. Hart
#Date 10-05-06
#
#--------+
# Purpose|
```

```
#--------+----------------------------------------------------
# This script will create a VM with the following attributes;
# Virtual Machine Name = ScriptedVM
# Location of Virtual Machine = /VMFS/volumes/storage1/ScriptedVM
# Virtual Machine Type = "Microsoft Windows 2003 Standard"
# Virtual Machine Memory Allocation = 256 meg
#
#----------------------------------------+
#Custom Variable Section for Modification|
#----------------------------------------+--------------------
#NVM is name of virtual machine(NVM). No Spaces allowed in name
#NVMDIR is the directory which holds all the VM files
#NVMOS specifies VM Operating System
#NVMSIZE is the size of the virtual disk to be created
#-------------------------------------------------------------
###############################################################

### Default Variable settings - change this to your preferences
NVM="ScriptedVM"        # Name of Virtual Machine
NVMDIR="ScriptedVM"     # Specify only the folder name to be created; NOT the
complete path
NVMOS="winnetstandard"  # Type of OS for Virtual Machine
NVMSIZE="4g"            # Size of Virtual Machine Disk
VMMEMSIZE="256"         # Default Memory Size

### End Variable Declaration

mkdir /vmfs/volumes/storage1/$NVMDIR # Creates directory
exec 6>&1                            # Sets up write to file
exec 1>/vmfs/volumes/storage1/$NVMDIR/$NVM.vmx # Open file
# write the configuration
echo config.version = '"'6'"'      # For ESX 3.x the value is 8
echo virtualHW.version = '"'3'"'   # For ESX 3.x the value is 4
echo memsize = '"'$VMMEMSIZE'"'
```

```
echo floppy0.present = '"'TRUE'"' # setup VM with floppy
echo displayName = '"'$NVM'"'       # name of virtual machine
echo guestOS = '"'$NVMOS'"'
echo
echo ide0:0.present = '"'TRUE'"'
echo ide0:0.deviceType = '"'cdrom-raw'"'
echo ide:0.startConnected = '"'false'"'   # CDROM enabled
echo floppy0.startConnected = '"'FALSE'"'
echo floppy0.fileName = '"'/dev/fd0'"'
echo Ethernet0.present = '"'TRUE'"'
echo Ethernet0.networkName = '"'VM Network'"' # Default network
echo Ethernet0.addressType = '"'vpx'"'
echo
echo scsi0.present = '"'true'"'
echo scsi0.sharedBus = '"'none'"'
echo scsi0.virtualDev = '"'lsilogic'"'
echo scsi0:0.present = '"'true'"'    # Virtual Disk Settings
echo scsi0:0.fileName = '"'$NVM.vmdk'"'
echo scsi0:0.deviceType = '"'scsi-hardDisk'"'


echo
# close file
exec 1>&-


# make stdout a copy of FD 6 (reset stdout), and close FD6
exec 1>&6
exec 6>&-


# Change permissions on the file so it can be executed by anyone
chmod 755 /vmfs/volumes/storage1/$NVMDIR/$NVM.vmx


#Creates 4gb Virtual disk
cd /vmfs/volumes/storage1/$NVMDIR   #change to the VM dir
```

```
vmkfstools -c $NVMSIZE $NVM.vmdk -a lsilogic
```

```
#Register VM
```

```
vmware-cmd -s register /vmfs/volumes/storage1/$NVMDIR/$NVM.vmx
```

NOTE

The standard format for values for the VMX file are to encase them in double quotes, such as memsize = "256". When scripting the creation of the VMX, you need to use single quote, double quote, single quote. So the previous example would be memsize = '"256"'. You must do this for VMX values.

The script in Code Listing 4.6 will create a virtual machine that has the following characteristics:

- A VM called ScriptedVM in a directory named ScriptedVM on storage1

- A VM that will be assigned 256MB of memory

- A VM that will have a 4GB SCSI hard drive (lsilogic controller)

- A VM configured for a Windows 2003 standard operating system

- A floppy drive assigned, not connected at startup

- A CD-ROM attached to the ESX server's CD-ROM drive, not connected at startup

- An Ethernet adapter connected to the VM Network, enabled at startup

The *exec* commands in the script are system-level commands in Linux to set up the writing to, and saving of, the script file. It redirects the console screen's output to the script file. The use of the *echo* commands in the script sends the commands to the screen which are redirected to the file for writing. The file is then closed and the virtual configuration file, VMX, is saved. The permissions are changed on the configuration file so any user on ESX can access the virtual machine. Then the script creates the virtual disk and registers the VM with the ESX server.

Use the following process to set up your script on the ESX server:

- Log in locally or connect to your ESX server remotely.

- Log in with an ID that has root privileges (see Figure 4.9).

Figure 4.9 Gaining Root Level Access on ESX Server

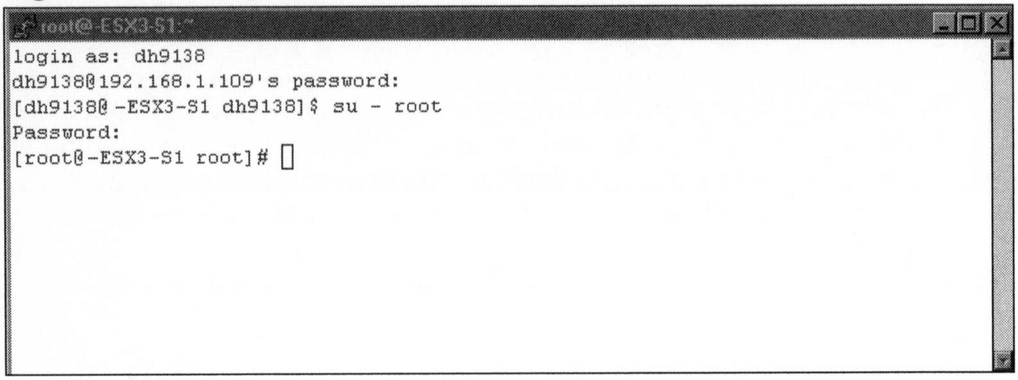

```
root@-ESX3-S1:~                                              _ □ X
login as: dh9138
dh9138@192.168.1.109's password:
[dh9138@-ESX3-S1 dh9138]$ su - root
Password:
[root@-ESX3-S1 root]# []
```

- Change to the location or create a location of where you would like to store your scripts (see Figure 4.10).

Figure 4.10 Script Storage Location

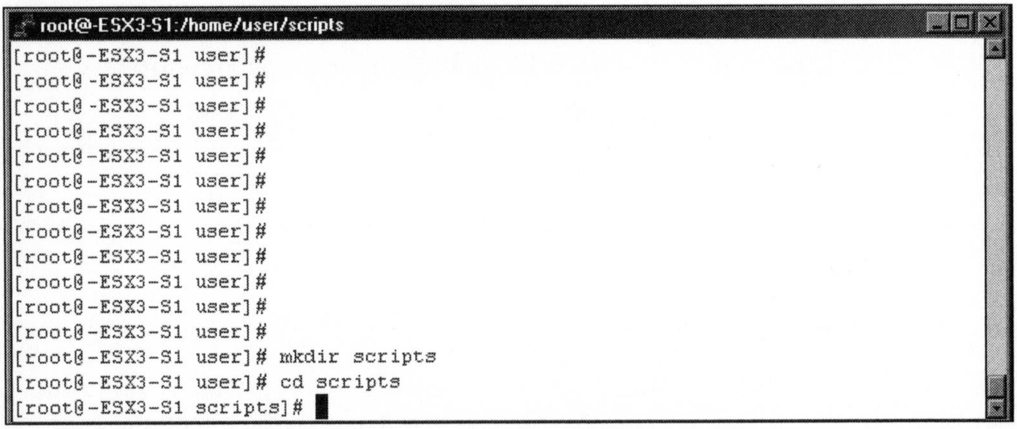

```
root@-ESX3-S1:/home/user/scripts                             _ □ X
[root@-ESX3-S1 user]#
[root@-ESX3-S1 user]#
[root@-ESX3-S1 user]#
[root@-ESX3-S1 user]#
[root@-ESX3-S1 user]#
[root@-ESX3-S1 user]#
[root@-ESX3-S1 user]#
[root@-ESX3-S1 user]#
[root@-ESX3-S1 user]#
[root@-ESX3-S1 user]#
[root@-ESX3-S1 user]#
[root@-ESX3-S1 user]#
[root@-ESX3-S1 user]# mkdir scripts
[root@-ESX3-S1 user]# cd scripts
[root@-ESX3-S1 scripts]# █
```

- Type **VI newvm.script** and press **Enter**.

- Press **I** for insert and type in the script as shown in Code Listing 4.6 (see Figure 4.11).

Figure 4.11 Using VI to Create Shell Script

```
root@ESX3-S1:/home/user/scripts                                    _ □ ×
# make stdout a copy of FD 6 (reset stdout), and close FD6
exec 1>&6
exec 6>&-

# Change permissions on the file so it can be executed by anyone
chmod 755 /vmfs/volumes/storage1/$NVMDIR/$NVM.vmx

#Creates 4gb Virtual disk
cd /vmfs/volumes/storage1/$NVMDIR    #change to the VM dir
vmkfstools -c $NVMSIZE $NVM.vmdk -a lsilogic

#Register VM
vmware-cmd -s register /vmfs/volumes/storage1/$NVMDIR/$NVM.vmx

-- INSERT --
```

- Press **Esc** and then press and hold **Shift** while pressing **ZZ** to exit and save.

- You should now have a file called newvm.script listed. Before you run the script, you must set permissions on it. To do this, type **chmod 755 newvm.script** (see Figure 4.12).

Figure 4.12 Setting Permissions on Script File

```
root@ESX3-S1:/home/user/scripts                                    _ □ ×
[root@-ESX3-S1 scripts]#
[root@-ESX3-S1 scripts]#
[root@-ESX3-S1 scripts]#
[root@-ESX3-S1 scripts]#
[root@-ESX3-S1 scripts]#
[root@-ESX3-S1 scripts]#
[root@-ESX3-S1 scripts]#
[root@-ESX3-S1 scripts]#
[root@-ESX3-S1 scripts]#
[root@-ESX3-S1 scripts]#
[root@-ESX3-S1 scripts]#
[root@-ESX3-S1 scripts]# ./newvm.script
-bash: ./newvm.script: Permission denied
[root@-ESX3-S1 scripts]# chmod 755 newvm.script
[root@-ESX3-S1 scripts]# █
```

- Run the script by typing **./newvm.script** (see Figure 4.13).

Figure 4.13 The Execution of Shell Script

```
root@-ESX3-S1:/home/user/scripts                              _ □ X
[root@-ESX3-S1 storage1]#
[root@-ESX3-S1 storage1]#
[root@-ESX3-S1 storage1]# cd /
[root@-ESX3-S1 /]# cd home
[root@-ESX3-S1 home]# ls
dh9138   lost+found   user
[root@-ESX3-S1 home]# cd user
[root@-ESX3-S1 user]# ls
scripts
[root@-ESX3-S1 user]# cd scripts
[root@-ESX3-S1 scripts]# ls
newvm.script
[root@-ESX3-S1 scripts]# ./newvm.script
register (/vmfs/volumes/storage1/ScriptedVM/ScriptedVM.vmx) = 1
[root@-ESX3-S1 scripts]# []
```

The virtual machine has now been created and registered with ESX. The next steps are for you to power it on and install the guest operating system. Creating scripts in ESX shell will save you time and effort in creating new virtual machines in your environment.

TIP

VMware ESX shell is just a customized version of Linux. For more information on scripting in shell, reference Linux shell information and examples.

Swiss Army Knife…

Creating Templates with the Scripted VM Creation Script

You can create multiple copies of the Scripted VM Creation script all with unique configurations. Save each of these customized scripts with a descriptive name such as **2003std512m4g.script** or **2003ent1g4g.script**. You could use the ESX shell command **cp Source.script Target.script** to copy the first script and then use **VI** to customize the second one. Change

Continued

each script to store its VMs in a staging area and each VM with a unique name. Now when you need to build those types of VMs you have template scripts to do it with. You could even chain together running of these scripts so you can create complete virtual system setups.

If you are not comfortable with utilizing VI as a text editor, you could also use a text editor such as Notepad on your PC to create your script. Once you have completed your script, highlight the whole script and select **copy**. Connect to your ESX server with a tool like **Putty** and run the **VI** command. Select I for input, and then paste in your script. All the script examples in this book were created on ESX Server using that method. Alternatively, you could also create the script file locally and then use a tool like WinSCP to copy the file to your ESX server.

Scripting Creation of Virtual Machines in Perl Scripts

VMware ESX Server supports additional scripting languages such as VmPerl. VmPerl is VMware's version of the Perl programming language. VMware has designed VmPerl to provide task automation and simple, single-purpose user interfaces. VmPerl's main purpose is to interact with the virtual machines on ESX Server. You can query status, start and stop virtual machines, as well as manage snapshots. With some creative scripting we can have VmPerl create our virtual machines for us as well. Scripting in VmPerl is not for beginners. If you've never scripted in Perl before then review the sample VmPerl Script and note the code comments in the script. VmPerl is a customized version of Perl, so research the Perl language in general for more information on how to program in Perl. The example script in Code Listing 4.7 was written so it could be easily modified to suit your particular needs. It is a basic VmPerl script with a menu-driven interface. Leveraging the knowledge you've gained in the previous sections will help you understand the script interactions. Novices in scripting should find the next script example very easy to understand and follow. Experienced scripters may find the script rudimentary and know of alternate ways to accomplish similar tasks. Whatever your scripting experience, I hope you find the example scripts in this chapter thought provoking and insightful.

> **NOTE**
>
> VMware in its latest release of ESX Server 3.0 is moving toward more mainstream scripting languages. Scripting APIs such as VmCom and VmPerl are being deprecated. What this means is that VMware prefers that you use a new set of APIs for programming languages such as Java, Visual .NET, and so on. ESX 3.0 will continue to support VmPerl and ESX shell scripting, and all the sample scripts in the chapter have been tested on ESX 3.0.

VmPerl allows for flexibility on how you go about creating your virtual machines. In our example script (see Code Listing 4.7), I used VmPerl's user input and file manipulation commands to accomplish the three primary tasks when creating virtual machines.

- Creating the virtual machine configuration file (VMX)

- Creating the virtual machine disk file (VMDK)

- Registering the virtual machine with ESX Server

> **NOTE**
>
> The script shown in Code Listing 4.7 is meant to be used for educational purposes. Further development in the area of "error checking" and "handling" should be done prior to utilizing it in a production environment. It is meant only to show what can be done with VmPerl.

Code Listing 4.7 Scripted VM Creation with Perl

```perl
#!/usr/bin/perl -w


use VMware::VmPerl;

use VMware::VmPerl::Server;

use VMware::VmPerl::ConnectParams;

#use strict;
```

```
##### VM Menu Driven Creation Script ############
#Script Version 1.8
#Author David E. Hart
#Date 10-05-06
#
#----------+
#Purpose   |
#-----------
# This script presents a menu for automatically building
# virtual machine config files (VMX) and Dis files (VMDK)
# This script demonstrates how to automate the setup
# of virtual environments
#--------------------------+
#Custom Variables Section  |
#--------------------------+
#vmname = virtual machine name, will be used for disk as well
#vmmem = amount of memory assigned to VM
#vmos = OS that VM is configured for
#vmdisk = size of VM disk
##################################################


main:     # main menu


system("clear");
print "                     MAIN MENU \n";
print "------------------ Virtual Machine Creation --------- \n";
print "\n";
print "\n";
print "\n";
print "               1) Create a Custom VM \n";
print "\n";
print "               2) Create VM's from Defined Templates \n";
print "\n";
```

```perl
print "                     3) View ESX's registered VM's \n";
print "\n";
print "                     4) Exit \n";
print "\n";
print "        Your Selection - ";
$menuopt = <>; chomp $menuopt;      # Get user selection
if ($menuopt == 1) {    # Get input for custom VM
         system("clear");
         print "What do you want to name your VM? ";
         $vmname = <>; chomp $vmname;    # use chomp to remove carriage return
         print "How much memory do you want to assign? ";
         $vmmem = <>;chomp $vmmem;
         print "Do you want to run Windows 2003STD as the OS? (y/n) ";
         $vmos = <>;chomp $vmos;
         if ($vmos eq "y") {
             $vmos = "winNetStandard";
             }            # Only 2 options for this example
         else {
             print "Do you want to run Windows 2003Ent as the OS? (y/n) ";
             $vmos2 = <>;chomp $vmos2;
             if ($vmos2 eq "y") {
                 $vmos = "winnetenterprise";
              }
             }
         print "What size hard disk do you want to set up (gb)? ";
         $vmdisk = <>;chomp $vmdisk;
         print "\n";
         $x = writevmx();    # Subrouting for creating VMX file
         if ($x == 1) {
             print "VMX File written successfully \n";
              }
         $w = setper();      # Subroutine to set permissions so anyone can
use VM
         if ($w == 1) {
```

```
          print "Permissions set successfully \n";
             }
      $y = createdisk();  # subrouting to create VMDK disk file
      if ($y == 1) {
          print "Virtual disk created successfully \n";
             }
      $z = registervm();  # subroutine to register VM with ESX
      if ($z == 1) {
          print "VM registered successfully \n";
             }
      print "Press the ENTER key to continue ...";
      $pause = <STDIN>;
      goto main


          }
if ($menuopt == 2) {   # option to displays the templates
menu1:
      system("clear");
      print "                Defined Templates \n";
      print "                ---------------- \n";
      print "\n";
      print "\n";
      print "         1) Windows 2003std VM with 256m, 4gb drive \n";
      print "\n";
      print "         2) Windows 2003ent VM with 1gig, 8gb drive \n";
      print "\n";
      print "\n";
      print "\n";
      print "\n";
      print "   Your Selection - ";
      $menu1opt = <>; chomp $menu1opt;
      if ($menu1opt == 1) {
          $vmname = "2003std25m4gb";
          $vmmem = "256";  # change and add on similar sections
```

```
$vmdisk = "4";    # to create templates for your environment
$vmos = "winnetstandard";
$x = writevmx();
   if ($x == 1) {
   print "VMX File written successfully \na";
   }
$w = setper();
   if ($w == 1) {
   print "Permisions set successfully \na";
   }
$y = createdisk();        # Call subroutines to create VMs
   if ($y == 1) {
   print "Virtual disk created successfully \na";
   }
$z = registervm();
   if ($z == 1) {
   print "VM registered successfully \na";
   }
 print "Press the ENTER key to continue ...";
 $pause = <STDIN>;
 goto main
 }
if ($menu1opt == 2) {
 $vmname = "2003Ent1gb8gb";
 $vmmem = "1024";
 $vmdisk = "8";
 $vmos = "winnetenterprise";
 $x = writevmx();
    if ($x == 1) {
    print "VMX file written successfully \na";
    }
 $w = setper();
    if ($w == 1) {
    print "Permissions set successfully \na";
```

```
            }
        $y = createdisk();
          if ($y == 1) {
          print "Virtual disk created successfully \na";
          }
        $z = registervm();
          if ($z == 1) {
          print "VM registered successfully \na";
          }
        print "Press the ENTER key to continue ...";
        $pause = <STDIN>;
        goto main
          }
      else {
          goto menu1;
      }


        }
if ($menuopt == 3) {    # Use a function of VmPerl to display registered VMs
      system("clear");
      my ($server_name, $user, $passwd) = @ARGV;  # Assume running in ESX
server
      my $port = 902;                             # with appropriate
rights

VMware::VmPerl::ConnectParams::new($server_name,$port,$user,$passwd);
      VMware::VmPerl::ConnectParams::new(undef,$port,$user,$passwd);
      my $connect_params = VMware::VmPerl::ConnectParams::new();



      # Establish a persistent connection with server
      my $server = VMware::VmPerl::Server::new();
      if (!$server->connect($connect_params)) {
          my ($error_number, $error_string) = $server->get_last_error();
```

```perl
            die "Could not connect to server: Error $error_number:
$error_string\n";
        }

        print "\nThe following virtual machines are registered:\n";

        # Obtain a list containing every config file path registered with the
server.
        my @list = $server->registered_vm_names();
        if (!defined($list[0])) {
            my ($error_number, $error_string) = $server->get_last_error();
            die "Could not get list of VMs from server: Error $error_number:
".

            "$error_string\n";
        }

        print "$_\n" foreach (@list);

        # Destroys the server object, thus disconnecting from the server.
        undef $server;
        print "Press the ENTER key to continue ...";
        $pause = <STDIN>;
        goto main

}
if ($menuopt == 4) {
    goto end1
    }


sub writevmx {        # Subroutine to Create VM's VMX config file


#        $file = '/vmfs/volumes/storage1/perlvm/perlvm.vmx';              #
Name the file
        $file = "/vmfs/volumes/storage1/perlvm/" . $vmname . ".vmx";
        open(INFO, ">$file");    # Open for output
```

```perl
        print INFO 'config.version = "6" ' . "\n";

        print INFO 'virtualHW.version = "3" ' . "\n";

        print INFO 'memsize = "' . $vmmem . '" ' . "\n";

        print INFO 'floppy0.present = "TRUE" ' . "\n";

        print INFO 'displayName = "' . $vmname . '" ' . "\n";

        print INFO 'guestOS = "' . $vmos . '" ' . "\n";

        print INFO 'ide0:0.present = "TRUE" ' . "\n";

        print INFO 'ide0:0.deviceType = "cdrom-raw" ' . "\n";

        print INFO 'ide:0.startConnected = "false" ' . "\n";

        print INFO 'floppy0.startConnected = "FALSE" ' . "\n";

        print INFO 'floppy0.fileName = "/dev/fd0" ' . "\n";

        print INFO 'Ethernet0.present = "TRUE" ' . "\n";

        print INFO 'Ethernet0.connectionType = "monitor_dev" ' . "\n";

        print INFO 'Ethernet0.networkName = "VM Network" ' . "\n";

        print INFO 'Ethernet0.addressType = "vpx" ' . "\n";

        print INFO 'scsi0.present = "true" ' . "\n";

        print INFO 'scsi0.sharedBus = "none" ' . "\n";

        print INFO 'scsi0.virtualDev = "lsilogic" ' . "\n";

        print INFO 'scsi0:0.present = "true" ' . "\n";

        print INFO 'scsi0:0.fileName = "' . $vmname . '.vmdk" ' . "\n";

        print INFO 'scsi0:0.deviceType = "scsi-hardDisk" ' . "\n";


        close(INFO);                    # Close the file
}


sub createdisk {    # Subroutine to create virtual disk
        $cr = "vmkfstools -c " . $vmdisk . "g " . "
/vmfs/volumes/storage1/perlvm/". $vmname . ".vmdk -a lsilogic";
        system("$cr");
    };



sub registervm {    # Subroutine to register VM with ESX Server
```

```
        $rg = "vmware-cmd -s register /vmfs/volumes/storage1/perlvm/" .
$vmname . ".vmx";

        system("$rg");

    }


sub setper{         # Subroutine to set permission on VMX file

        $pm = "chmod 755 /vmfs/volumes/storage1/perlvm/" . $vmname .
".vmx";

        system("$pm");

    }


end1:
```

Modifying Scripted VM Creation with Perl

The script shown in Code Listing 4.7, and later in Code Listing 4.11, provides static mapping for VM creation. This is sufficient for an example, but
not very practical for real-world scenarios. We will modify the script to support end-user input of VM destination pathing. We will accomplish this by
adding a new variable *$vmpath* to our script and adding the appropriate fol-
lowing sections.

- Add new variable *vmpath* to scripts variable notes section

```
#-------------------------+
#Custom Variables Section   |
#-------------------------+
#vmname = virtual machine name, used for disk as well
#vmmem = amount of memory assigned to VM
#vmos = OS that VM is configured for
#vmdisk = size of VM disk
#vmpath = path to VM directory, (must already exist)
####################################################
```

- Add new prompt in Custom VM Creation section, "option 1."

```
print "What size hard disk do you want to set up (gb)? ";
```

```
$vmdisk = <>;chomp $vmdisk;

print "\n";

print "Path to Save VM (ie. /vmfs/volumes/storage1/vm/";

$vmpath = <>;chomp $vmpath;

print "\n";
```

- Add new prompt in Defined Templates section, "option 2."

```
$vmos = "winnetstandard";

print "Path to Save VM (ie. /vmfs/volumes/storage1/vm/";

$vmpath = <>;chomp $vmpath;

print "\n";
```

- Update subroutine "writevmx".

```
$file = $vmpath . $vmname . ".vmx";
```

- Update subroutine "createdisk".

```
$cr = "vmkfstools -c " . $vmdisk . "g " . $vmpath . $vmname . ".vmdk
-a lsilogic";
            system("$cr");
```

- Update subroutine "registerVM".

```
$rg = "vmware-cmd -s register " .$vmpath  . $vmname . ".vmx";
 system("$rg");
```

- Update subroutine "setper".

```
$pm = "chmod 755 " . $vmpath . $vmname . ".vmx";
system("$pm");
```

The script will now prompt you for VM destination when creating new VMs. Please note that when entering the destination file path, you should include the leading and trailing "/".

When the script in Code Listing 4.7 is executed on the ESX server, a menu will be displayed (see Figure 4.14).

Figure 4.14 The Perl Script VM Creation Menu

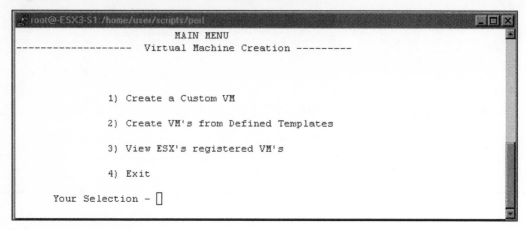

```
root@-ESX3-S1:/home/user/scripts/perl                              _ □ ×
                            MAIN MENU
------------------- Virtual Machine Creation ---------

           1) Create a Custom VM

           2) Create VM's from Defined Templates

           3) View ESX's registered VM's

           4) Exit

     Your Selection - []
```

Perl Script Components

Utilizing the script in Code Listing 4.7, you can do the following tasks:

- Create a custom VM with parameters that you supply.
- Create VMs from predefined templates.
- View listing of VMs currently registered on the ESX server.
- Exit the script.

This script was written to be easily customized by you, the reader. Variables have been set up for key VM-related options enabling simple modifications. Let's dissect this script to get a better understanding of VmPerl. Code Listing 4.8 shows the key variables.

Code Listing 4.8 Scripted Creation of VM with Perl Key Variables

```
$vmname = virtual machine name, will be used for disk as well
$vmmem = amount of memory assigned to VM
$vmos = OS that VM is configured for
$vmdisk = size of VM disk
```

These variables in the program are either dynamic or static depending upon which option in the script you choose. The first option presented on the menu shown in Figure 4.14 is Create A Custom VM. This option will prompt you for the variables listed in Code Listing 4.8, as shown in Figure 4.15.

Figure 4.15 Perl Script Custom Creation of VM

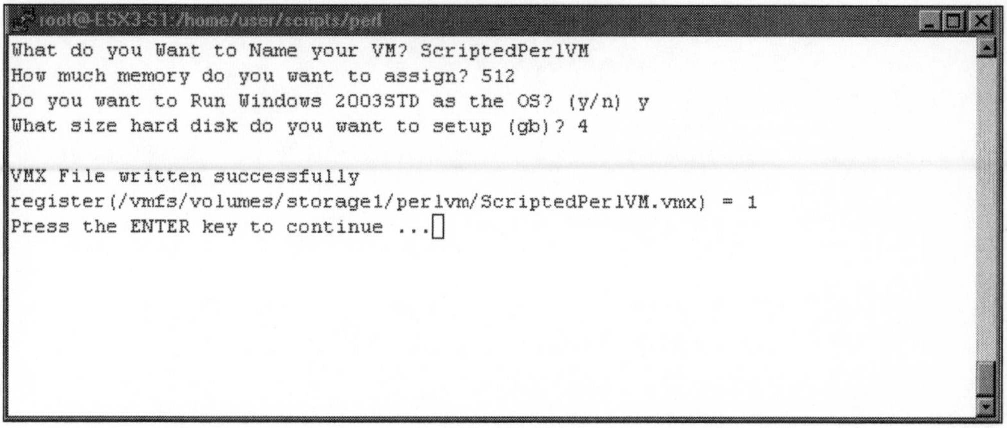

```
root@-ESX3-S1:/home/user/scripts/perl                          _ □ ×
What do you Want to Name your VM? ScriptedPerlVM
How much memory do you want to assign? 512
Do you want to Run Windows 2003STD as the OS? (y/n) y
What size hard disk do you want to setup (gb)? 4

VMX File written successfully
register(/vmfs/volumes/storage1/perlvm/ScriptedPerlVM.vmx) = 1
Press the ENTER key to continue ...□
```

If you select the second option, **Create VM's from Defined Templates**, the values are set statically in that section. Code Listing 4.9 shows an example where these values are set in the code.

Code Listing 4.9 Perl Script Static Variables for Template VM Creation

```
if ($menu1opt == 1) {
        $vmname = "2003std25m4gb";

        $vmmem = "256";

        $vmdisk = "4";

        $vmos = "winnetstandard";
```

It's a simple task to add additional menu options for more templates. Adding sections like those in Code Listing 4.9 will enable to you to define a bigger selection of templates for your environment.

Master Craftsman...

VM Procurement Automation

The example script provides basic VM procurement with two templates and a custom VM creation option. Typical production environments have a multitude of system types and requirements. You can modify the script to meet your needs and provide for procurement of VMs for varying situations such as:

- Procurement of new virtual machines for customers
- Procurement of groups of servers
- Automated environment setups (lab testing, and so on)

Because the script is written in VmPerl, which is just a VMware-customized version of Perl, you can leverage Perl's additional features and characteristics. Perl code can be executed from within a Web browser enabling you to create a VM procurement Web site. You could host this new Web site on the ESX server itself, and create a "Self-Service" procurement architecture. These are just some suggestions and ideas to get you thinking about the possibilities that VmPerl provides.

The third menu choice option in the script is View ESX's Registered VM's. This section utilizes the VmPerl API to access the ESX server. For more information on the VmPerl API, download the ESX server SDK. This section of the code connects to the local ESX server with your current userid and password on port 902. It then queries ESX Server for a listing of registered VMs. Figure 4.16 shows the output generated by this option.

Figure 4.16 Perl Script Query of ESX Server for Registered VMs

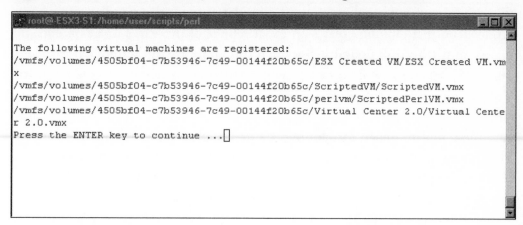

```
root@-ESX3-S1:/home/user/scripts/perl                              _□×
The following virtual machines are registered:
/vmfs/volumes/4505bf04-c7b53946-7c49-00144f20b65c/ESX Created VM/ESX Created VM.vm
x
/vmfs/volumes/4505bf04-c7b53946-7c49-00144f20b65c/ScriptedVM/ScriptedVM.vmx
/vmfs/volumes/4505bf04-c7b53946-7c49-00144f20b65c/perlvm/ScriptedPerlVM.vmx
/vmfs/volumes/4505bf04-c7b53946-7c49-00144f20b65c/Virtual Center 2.0/Virtual Cente
r 2.0.vmx
Press the ENTER key to continue ...
```

VmPerl Commands

VmPerl by itself cannot create virtual machine files or register virtual machines. To accomplish these tasks, we must use the tools available. The sample VmPerl script utilizes the command "system" to access the following VMware tools:

- *vmkfstools*
- *vmware-cmd*

Do those tools sound familiar? By now you've become quite adept at utilizing these tools for the creation of virtual machines. The latter sections of the code contain the subroutines that handle the virtual machine disk creation *createdisk*, and VM registration *registervm*. It is in these subroutines that we use the tools listed earlier.

Utilizing the example script, and with your working knowledge of the VMware tools from previous sections, you should have a competent understanding of how to create virtual machines from a VmPerl script.

Cloning Virtual Machines Utilizing ESX Shell Scripts

As we've seen in previous sections, VMware provides you with built-in tools to accomplish most virtualization tasks. Cloning is the process of copying an existing virtual machine's virtual disk to a new file for a new virtual machine to use. The source virtual machine is considered to be the template VM. Understand that cloning creates an exact replica of the VM's disk contents. It is very similar to disk imaging. So when this clone is configured and turned on in ESX Server it will come up with all the same attributes as the template VM. To address this, the template VM should be prepared in advanced for cloning. For Microsoft Windows–based servers, you would use *Sysprep* to prepare the template image for cloning. Using template images saves an enormous amount of time when procuring servers for all types of situations. Because the template VM has the operating system preinstalled and configured, setup time for new systems is drastically reduced.

To clone an existing template virtual machine, we will use the VMware utility *vmkfstools*. We will use the *-i* option which instructs *vmkfstools* to import an existing template VM's disk file (VMDK) and copy it. The command syntax is as follows:

```
Vmkfstools -I /pathtoTemplateVM/template.vmdk
/pathtoDestinationVM/newvm.vmdk
```

The cloning process does not create a virtual machine configuration file or register the new virtual machine with ESX Server. We will leverage what you've learned in the previous sections to modify the ESX shell script from Code Listing 4.6.

We need to modify the part of the script that calls *vmkfstools* to create the 4GB virtual disk. We are instead going to use the *-i* command and clone an existing virtual disk. If you've been implementing the scripts in the previous sections, then you will have an example virtual machine disk that we can use for this section. If not, create a quick empty VM via any of the ESX GUI methods: Virtual Client, Virtual Infrastructure Client (ESX 3.0), Web, and so on.

Once you have your source template virtual disk ready, go ahead and edit the code to support cloning (see Code Listing 4.10).

Code Listing 4.10 ESX Shell Script VM Creation Utilizing Cloning

```
##### VM Creation Script Utilizing Cloning ###################
#Script Version 1.2
#Author David E. Hart
#Date 10-05-06
#
#--------+
# Purpose|
#--------+----------------------------------------------------
# This script will create a VM utilizing the cloning option of # the
vmkfstools command tool;
# The New Virtual Machine Configuration will be set as follows
# Virtual Machine Name = ScriptedCloneVM
# Location of Virtual Machine = /VMFS/volumes/storage1/ScriptedVM
# Virtual Machine Type = "Microsoft Windows 2003 Standard"
# Virtual Machine Memory Allocation = 256 meg
#
#---------------------------------------+
#Custom Variable Section for Modification|
#---------------------------------------+--------------------
#NVM is name of virtual machine(NVM). No Spaces allowed in name
#NVMDIR is the directory which holds all the VM files
#NVMOS specifies VM Operating System
#-------------------------------------------------------------
###############################################################


### Default Variable settings - change this to your preferences
NVM="ScriptedCloneVM"        # Name of Virtual Machine
NVMDIR="ScriptedCloneVM"     # Specify only the folder name to be created;
NOT the complete path
NVMOS="winnetstandard" # Type of OS for Virtual Machine
VMMEMSIZE="256"          # Default Memory Size


### End Variable Declaration
```

```
mkdir /vmfs/volumes/storage1/$NVMDIR # Creates directory
exec 6>&1                            # Sets up write to file
exec 1>/vmfs/volumes/storage1/$NVMDIR/$NVM.vmx # Open file
# write the configuration
echo config.version = '"'6'"'        # For ESX 3.x the value is 8
echo virtualHW.version = '"'3'"'   # For ESX 3.x the value is 4
echo memsize = '"'$VMMEMSIZE'"'
echo floppy0.present = '"'TRUE'"' # setup VM with floppy
echo displayName = '"'$NVM'"'        # name of virtual machine
echo guestOS = '"'$NVMOS'"'
echo
echo ide0:0.present = '"'TRUE'"'
echo ide0:0.deviceType = '"'cdrom-raw'"'
echo ide:0.startConnected = '"'false'"'   # CDROM enabled
echo floppy0.startConnected = '"'FALSE'"'
echo floppy0.fileName = '"'/dev/fd0'"'
echo Ethernet0.present = '"'TRUE'"'
echo Ethernet0.networkName = '"'VM Network'"' # Default network
echo Ethernet0.addressType = '"'vpx'"'
echo
echo scsi0.present = '"'true'"'
echo scsi0.sharedBus = '"'none'"'
echo scsi0.virtualDev = '"'lsilogic'"'
echo scsi0:0.present = '"'true'"'    # Virtual Disk Settings
echo scsi0:0.fileName = '"'$NVM.vmdk'"'
echo scsi0:0.deviceType = '"'scsi-hardDisk'"'


echo
# close file
exec 1>&-


# make stdout a copy of FD 6 (reset stdout), and close FD6
```

```
exec 1>&6
exec 6>&-

# Change permissions on the file so it can be executed by anyone
chmod 755 /vmfs/volumes/storage1/$NVMDIR/$NVM.vmx

#Clone existing Template VM's VMDK into current directory
cd /vmfs/volumes/storage1/$NVMDIR   #change to the VM dir
vmkfstools -i /vmfs/volumes/storage1/ScriptedVM/ScriptedVM.vmdk $NVM.vmdk

#Register VM
vmware-cmd -s register /vmfs/volumes/storage1/$NVMDIR/$NVM.vmx
```

When you execute the script, the status of the cloning process will be displayed (see Figure 4.17).

Figure 4.17 Cloning Process

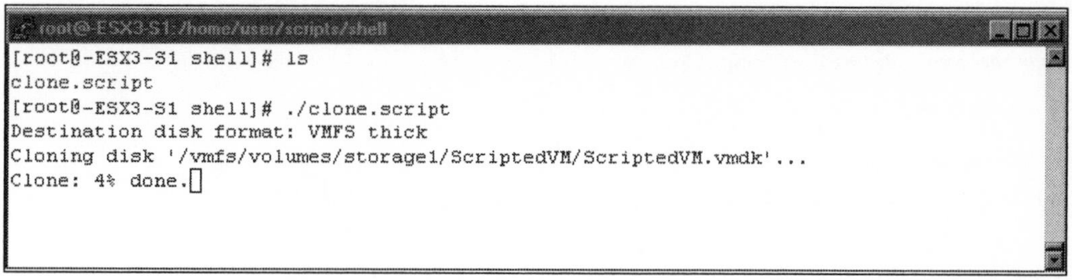
root@-ESX3-S1:/home/user/scripts/shell
[root@-ESX3-S1 shell]# ls
clone.script
[root@-ESX3-S1 shell]# ./clone.script
Destination disk format: VMFS thick
Cloning disk '/vmfs/volumes/storage1/ScriptedVM/ScriptedVM.vmdk'...
Clone: 4% done.

When the script finishes, you will have a new cloned copy of the template VM ready for use. Log on to the ESX GUI and validate that the new VM is registered and available.

The ability to script the cloning of existing template VMs allows you to pre-stage your virtual environments for your particular needs. For instance, you could have a Windows Lab of four servers pre-staged. Just run the WindowsLab script and all four VMs are created and ready to go. In the next chapter, you will learn how to perform operations on VMs such as starting and stopping VMs via scripting.

Cloning Virtual Machines Utilizing VmPerl Scripts

You already know the benefits of cloning, but by utilizing the VmPerl scripting language you can build scripted procurement systems. VmPerl provides you more flexibility and more functionality than shell scripting. This allows you to be more creative in your approach to VM creation. We will add the cloning functionality to the example script in Code Listing 4.7. We will also add a new menu option for cloning and a new subroutine. In addition, we will use the VMware command tool *vmkfstools* with the *-i* option for cloning as we did in the previous chapter. Code Listing 4.11 shows the new Perl script with cloning.

Code Listing 4.11 Scripted VM Creation with Perl Utilizing Cloning

```
#!/usr/bin/perl -w

use VMware::VmPerl;
use VMware::VmPerl::Server;
use VMware::VmPerl::ConnectParams;
#use strict;


##### VM Menu Driven Creation Script with Cloning ###########
#Script Version 1.3
#Author David E. Hart
#Date 10-05-06
#
#----------+
#Purpose   |
#----------
# This script presents a menu for automatically building
# virtual machine config files (VMX) and disk files (VMDK)
# This script demonstrates how to automate the setup
# of virtual environments and includes cloning of VMs
#--------------------------+
```

```
#Custom Variables Section   |
#--------------------------+
#vmname = virtual machine name, will be used for disk as well
#vmmem = amount of memory assigned to VM
#vmos = OS that VM is configured for
#vmdisk = size of VM disk
#################################################


main:     # main menu


system("clear");
print "                         MAIN MENU \n";
print "------------------- Virtual Machine Creation --------- \n";
print "\n";
print "\n";
print "\n";
print "              1) Create a Custom VM \n";
print "\n";
print "              2) Create VM's from Defined Templates \n";
print "\n";
print "              3) View ESX's registered VM's \n";
print "\n";
print "              4) Clone an Existing VM \n";
print "\n";
print "              5) Exit \n";
print "\n";
print "     Your Selection - ";
$menuopt = <>; chomp $menuopt;      # Get user selection
if ($menuopt == 1) {   # Get input for custom VM
        system("clear");
        print "What do you Want to Name your VM? ";
        $vmname = <>; chomp $vmname;   # use chomp to remove carriage return
        print "How much memory do you want to assign? ";
        $vmmem = <>;chomp $vmmem;
```

```
        print "Do you want to run Windows 2003STD as the OS? (y/n) ";
        $vmos = <>;chomp $vmos;
        if ($vmos eq "y") {
            $vmos = "winNetStandard";
            }           # Only 2 options for this example
        else {
            print "Do you want to run Windows 2003Ent as the OS? (y/n) ";
            $vmos2 = <>;chomp $vmos2;
            if ($vmos2 eq "y") {
                $vmos = "winnetenterprise";
              }
            }
        print "What size hard disk do you want to set up (gb)? ";
        $vmdisk = <>;chomp $vmdisk;
        print "\n";
        $x = writevmx();    # Subrouting for creating VMX file
        if ($x == 1) {
            print "VMX file written successfully \n";
              }
        $w = setper();      # Subroutine to set permissions so anyone can
use VM
        if ($w == 1) {
            print "Permissions set successfully \n";
              }
        $y = createdisk();  # subrouting to create VMDK disk file
        if ($y == 1) {
            print "Virtual disk created successfully \n";
              }
        $z = registervm();  # subroutine to register VM with ESX
        if ($z == 1) {
            print "VM registered successfully \n";
              }
        print "Press the ENTER key to continue ...";
        $pause = <STDIN>;
```

```
        goto main


            }
if ($menuopt == 2) {    # option to display the templates
menu1:
        system("clear");
        print "                    Defined Templates \n";
        print "                    ----------------- \n";
        print "\n";
        print "\n";
        print "        1) Windows 2003std VM with 256m, 4gb drive \n";
        print "\n";
        print "        2) Windows 2003ent VM with 1gig, 8gb drive \n";
        print "\n";
        print "\n";
        print "\n";
        print "\n";
        print "   Your Selection - ";
        $menu1opt = <>; chomp $menu1opt;
        if ($menu1opt == 1) {
            $vmname = "2003std25m4gb";
            $vmmem = "256";  # change and add on similar sections
            $vmdisk = "4";   # to create templates for your environment
            $vmos = "winnetstandard";
            $x = writevmx();
              if ($x == 1) {
              print "VMX file written successfully \na";
              }
          $w = setper();
              if ($w == 1) {
              print "Permissions set successfully \na";
              }
            $y = createdisk();        # Call subroutines to create VM's
              if ($y == 1) {
```

```
         print "Virtual disk created successfully \na";

         }

    $z = registervm();

      if ($z == 1) {

      print "VM registered successfully \na";

      }

     print "Press the ENTER key to continue ...";

     $pause = <STDIN>;

     goto main

     }

  if ($menu1opt == 2) {

     $vmname = "2003Ent1gb8gb";

     $vmmem = "1024";

     $vmdisk = "8";

     $vmos = "winnetenterprise";

     $x = writevmx();

       if ($x == 1) {

       print "VMX file written successfully \na";

       }

     $w = setper();

       if ($w == 1) {

       print "Permissions set successfully \na";

       }

     $y = createdisk();

       if ($y == 1) {

       print "Virtual disk created successfully \na";

       }

     $z = registervm();

       if ($z == 1) {

       print "VM registered successfully \na";

       }

     print "Press the ENTER key to continue ...";

     $pause = <STDIN>;

     goto main
```

```
            }
        else {
            goto menu1;
            }


          }
if ($menuopt == 3) {     # Use a function of VmPerl to display registered VMs
        system("clear");
        my ($server_name, $user, $passwd) = @ARGV;   # Assume running in ESX
server
        my $port = 902;                               # with appropriate
rights

VMware::VmPerl::ConnectParams::new($server_name,$port,$user,$passwd);
        VMware::VmPerl::ConnectParams::new(undef,$port,$user,$passwd);
        my $connect_params = VMware::VmPerl::ConnectParams::new();



        # Establish a persistent connection with server
        my $server = VMware::VmPerl::Server::new();
        if (!$server->connect($connect_params)) {
            my ($error_number, $error_string) = $server->get_last_error();
            die "Could not connect to server: Error $error_number:
$error_string\n";
        }


        print "\nThe following virtual machines are registered:\n";


        # Obtain a list containing every config file path registered with the
server.
        my @list = $server->registered_vm_names();
        if (!defined($list[0])) {
            my ($error_number, $error_string) = $server->get_last_error();
            die "Could not get list of VMs from server: Error $error_number:
".
```

```perl
                    "$error_string\n";
        }


        print "$_\n" foreach (@list);


        # Destroys the server object, thus disconnecting from the server.
        undef $server;
        print "Press the ENTER key to continue ...";
        $pause = <STDIN>;
        goto main


}
if ($menuopt == 4) {
        system("clear");
        print "                    Clone Existing VM.s \n";
        print "                    ------------------- \n";
        print "\n";
        print "\n";
        print "          1) Clone ScriptedVM \n";
        print "\n";
        print "          2) Clone ScriptedPerlVM \n";
        print "\n";
        print "\n";
        print "\n";
        print "\n";
        print "   Your Selection - ";
        $menu4opt = <>; chomp $menu4opt;
        if ($menu4opt == 1) {
            $vmname = "ScriptedPerlCloneVM";
            $vmmem = "256";   # change and add on similar sections
            $vmdisk = "4";    # to create templates for your environment
            $vmos = "winnetstandard";
            $vmpath ="/vmfs/volumes/storage1/ScriptedVM/ScriptedVM.vmdk";
            $x = writevmx();
```

```perl
       if ($x == 1) {

       print "VMX file written successfully \na";

       }

    $w = setper();

       if ($w == 1) {

       print "Permissions set successfully \na";

       }

    $y = clonedisk();           # Call subroutines to create VM's

       if ($y == 1) {

       print "Virtual disk cloned successfully \na";

       }

    $z = registervm();

       if ($z == 1) {

       print "VM registered successfully \na";

       }

     print "Press the ENTER key to continue ...";

     $pause = <STDIN>;

     goto main

    }

if ($menu4opt == 2) {

    $vmname = "ScriptedPerlVMClone";

    $vmmem = "1024";

    $vmdisk = "8";

    $vmos = "winnetenterprise";

    $vmpath ="/vmfs/volumes/storage1/perlvm/ScriptedPerlVM";


    $x = writevmx();

       if ($x == 1) {

       print "VMX file written successfully \na";

       }

    $w = setper();

       if ($w == 1) {

       print "Permifsions set successfully \na";

       }
```

```perl
         $y = clonedisk();
           if ($y == 1) {
           print "Virtual disk cloned successfully \na";
           }
         $z = registervm();
           if ($z == 1) {
           print "VM registered successfully \na";
           }
         print "Press the ENTER key to continue ...";
         $pause = <STDIN>;
         goto main
           }
       else {
           goto menu1;
         }


   }



if ($menuopt == 5) {
   goto end1
   }



sub writevmx {         # Subroutine to create VM's VMX config file


#         $file = '/vmfs/volumes/storage1/perlvm/perlvm.vmx';                    #
Name the file
         $file = "/vmfs/volumes/storage1/perlvm/" . $vmname . ".vmx";
         open(INFO, ">$file");    # Open for output
         print INFO 'config.version = "6" ' . "\n";
         print INFO 'virtualHW.version = "3" ' . "\n";
         print INFO 'memsize = "' . $vmmem . '" ' . "\n";
         print INFO 'floppy0.present = "TRUE" ' . "\n";
         print INFO 'displayName = "' . $vmname . '" ' . "\n";
```

```
        print INFO 'guestOS = "' . $vmos . '" ' . "\n";

        print INFO 'ide0:0.present = "TRUE" ' . "\n";

        print INFO 'ide0:0.deviceType = "cdrom-raw" ' . "\n";

        print INFO 'ide:0.startConnected = "false" ' . "\n";

        print INFO 'floppy0.startConnected = "FALSE" ' . "\n";

        print INFO 'floppy0.fileName = "/dev/fd0" ' . "\n";

        print INFO 'Ethernet0.present = "TRUE" ' . "\n";

        print INFO 'Ethernet0.connectionType = "monitor_dev" ' . "\n";

        print INFO 'Ethernet0.networkName = "VM Network" ' . "\n";

        print INFO 'Ethernet0.addressType = "vpx" ' . "\n";

        print INFO 'scsi0.present = "true" ' . "\n";

        print INFO 'scsi0.sharedBus = "none" ' . "\n";

        print INFO 'scsi0.virtualDev = "lsilogic" ' . "\n";

        print INFO 'scsi0:0.present = "true" ' . "\n";

        print INFO 'scsi0:0.fileName = "' . $vmname . '.vmdk" ' . "\n";

        print INFO 'scsi0:0.deviceType = "scsi-hardDisk" ' . "\n";


        close(INFO);                    # Close the file
}


sub createdisk {    # Subroutine to create virtual disk
        $cr = "vmkfstools -c " . $vmdisk . "g " . "
/vmfs/volumes/storage1/perlvm/". $vmname . ".vmdk -a lsilogic";
        system("$cr");
    };


sub clonedisk {     # Subroutine to create virtual disk
        $cr = "vmkfstools -i " . $vmpath . " " . "
/vmfs/volumes/storage1/perlvm/" . $vmname . "vmdk";
        system("$cr");
    };


sub registervm {    # Subroutine to register VM with ESX server
        $rg = "vmware-cmd -s register /vmfs/volumes/storage1/perlvm/" .
$vmname . ".vmx";
```

```
        system("$rg");

    }


sub setper{          # Subroutine to set permission on VMX file

        $pm = "chmod 755 /vmfs/volumes/storage1/perlvm/" . $vmname .
".vmx";

        system("$pm");

    }


end1:
```

The preceding code is highlighted with the changes necessary to support cloning. When the code is executed, you now have a new menu option #4, for cloning of virtual machines. The code currently clones ScriptedVM.vmdk and ScriptedPerlVM.vmdk, created from previous sections. You can easily modify the code to request the name of the VMs to clone. You could even have the code generate a list of VMs registered with the ESX server and then you would select from this list. The script is provided as an example of how you would go about setting up your own VMs to use as templates and how to automate creating clones of these. Go ahead and expand the sample script to include other options such as "lab setup" where the option clones a series of virtual templates to set up a virtual test environment.

Master Craftsman...

Using Clones to Set Up Virtual Environments

The example script provides basic VM procurement via custom entry, templates, and cloning. Custom VM entry and templates provide you new VMs ready for the installation of an operating system, while cloning provides you with a prebuilt virtual machine ready for use. Create clone templates of your most common server types in your environment for fast deployment in your virtual infrastructure. You can, in essence, set up virtual labs in a matter of minutes versus hours.

Summary

In this chapter, you learned how to use the built-in command-line tools from VMware—namely, *vmkfstools* and *vmware-cmd*—to build and clone virtual machines. You also learned how to use ESX shell scripting to incorporate these tools and automate the VM and cloning process. We showed you how to employ VmPerl for advanced scripting of VM creation and cloning. We then showed you how to use the code examples to build a rough VM creation and cloning architecture for you to expand on. You should now have a good understanding of what you can script on the ESX server as it relates to virtual machine creation.

## Chapter 5

Modifying VMs

Topics in this chapter:

- **The Virtual Machine VMDK File**
- **The Virtual Machine Configuration vmx File**
- **Converting IDE Drives to SCSI Drives**
- **Dynamic Creation of Virtual Machines**

Introduction

This chapter expands on the virtual machine's creation that was introduced in Chapter 4. To begin, we will discuss the two main components of a virtual machine, the .vmx and the .vmdk files. Then we will look at the hardware and version level of these files, as well as how we can change the files to be able to migrate a virtual machine's disk file from one VMware platform to another.

Virtual machines are made up of two files. The vmx file is the virtual machine's configuration file, while the virtual machine disk format (VMDK) file is the virtual machine's disk file or hard drive. We will examine these files and the different settings that can be used. Afterward, as an example, we will change a virtual machine's IDE disk to a SCSI disk.

To conclude, we will dynamically create a virtual machine using a script, as well as modify the script to build the virtual machine in a few different ways.

TIP

As a best practice, *always* make a backup of the files you are going to edit *before* you edit.

The Virtual Machine VMDK File

When working with virtual machines, there are two main components or files that need to be understood. The first is the VMDK file. But what exactly *is* the VMDK file? A virtual machine disk (VMDK) file is an encapsulation of an entire server or desktop environment in a single file. In a way, it can be seen as the hard drive for a virtual machine.

The VMDK file can have four different forms. Type 0 (monolithic sparse disk), Type 1 (growable; split into 2GB files), Type 2 (single pre-allocated; monolithic sparse disk), and Type 3 (pre-allocated; split into 2GB files). Types 1, 2, and 3 use a disk descriptor file, while type 0 does not. To make changes to the VMDK file, you need to be able to open and view the disk descriptor;

otherwise, with the type 0 single disk, you would need to edit a very large binary file with a hex editor—an unwise choice. A better option, if you have the VMDK file on a VMFS file system, is to use vmkfstools to easily export the file in a Type 3 format.

For example:

```
Vmkfstools -e /mnt/bigspace/toputfile/thedisk.vmdk
vmhba0:0:0:1:thedisk.dsk
```

If you mount a file share to ESX and use the VMware File Manager to copy the VMDK file to this share, ESX uses the preceding command automatically when making the copy.

TIP

VMware does not support the use of VMDK files moved from a VMFS volume to a non-VMFS file system using SCP or FTP without first employing the vmkfstools export command or the file manager in the VMware Management Interface.

We should now have the VMDK file in a Type 1 growable split or a Type 3 preallocated split. You should now see a 1KB VMDK file. This is your disk descriptor file (see Figure 5.1).

Figure 5.1 The Disk Descriptor File

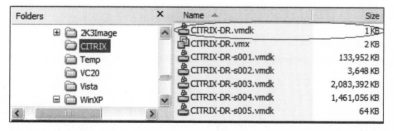

Using a text editor, we can open the disk descriptor file and view its contents. Code Listing 5.1 is one example of a disk descriptor file.

Code Listing 5.1 A Disk Descriptor File

```
# Disk DescriptorFile

version=1

CID=2af6d34d

parentCID=ffffffff

createType="twoGbMaxExtentSparse"


# Extent description

RW 4192256 SPARSE "Windows-s001.vmdk"

RW 4192256 SPARSE "Windows-s002.vmdk"

RW 4096 SPARSE "Windows-s003.vmdk"


# The Disk Data Base
#DDB


ddb.adapterType = "ide"

ddb.geometry.sectors = "63"

ddb.geometry.heads = "16"

ddb.geometry.cylinders = "8322"

ddb.virtualHWVersion = "4"

ddb.toolsVersion =
```

VMDK Components

In the following subsections, we'll discuss the various parameters, settings, and commands related to VMDKs.

Version=1

The version parameter is the version of the disk descriptor file and not the VMDK file. Currently, in all VMware products, the disk descriptor version is 1.

```
# Disk DescriptorFile
version=1
```

CID=2af6d34d

Every time a VMware product opens up the vmx file, it creates a random 32-bit value and uses that value for the content identification or CID value.

parentCID=ffffffff

This parameter is the parent content identification which is used to specify whether the disk descriptor file is part of a snapshot file. If no snapshot file is being used, the value of this parameter is ffffffff.

file.createType="twoGbMaxExtentSparse"

The createType describes which type of file this is. There are currently 11 different values for this depending on the format of the data. Many values that exist in some products do not exist in others. The three values you see most often, especially with VMware's ESX server, are **"twoGbMaxExtentSparse"**, **"monolithicSparse"**, and **"monolithicFlat"**. Performing a manual change would make the disk unusable and has caused my VMware workstation host to crash. If you need to change the type of file, use the tool vmware-vdiskmanager to change the type.

```
# Extent description
RW 4192256 SPARSE "Windows-s001.vmdk"
RW 4192256 SPARSE "Windows-s002.vmdk"
RW 4096 SPARSE "Windows-s003.vmdk"
```

The preceding list shows files (typically VMDKs) that are used to store data blocks for the guest operating system.

The values in those lines reveal the access mode of the VMDK, the size in sectors of the VMDK, the type of the extent, and the location of the VMDK data file.

The Size in Sectors Value

The Size in Sectors value is required for a VMware Server to properly initialize the VMDK file. This value must be calculated based on the total byte size of the VMDK file and the number of bytes per sector. The Bytes per

Sector is a static value of 512. The equation to calculate this value, as shown next, is quite simple.

Size in Sectors = (VMDK Byte Size – 512) / Bytes per Sector

The Disk Data Base Command

The Disk Data Base command will tell the virtual machine's hardware everything it needs to know to access the VMDK files. This is the actual disk geometry that the VMDK represents as a disk to the virtual machine. In Code Listing 5.2, this disk descriptor represents an IDE virtual disk with 63 sectors on 16 heads with 8,322 cylinders. It is important that the proper disk geometry be chosen to prevent "geometry mismatch" errors on the restored virtual machine (see Table 5.1).

Code Listing 5.2 A Disk Descriptor for an IDE Virtual Disk

```
# The Disk Data Base
#DDB

ddb.adapterType = "ide"
ddb.geometry.sectors = "63"
ddb.geometry.heads = "16"
ddb.geometry.cylinders = "8322"
ddb.virtualHWVersion = "4"
ddb.toolsVersion = "6404"
```

Table 5.1 Disk Geometry

Disk Size	Heads	Sectors
<=1GB	64	32
>1GB and <=2GB	128	32
>2GB	255	63

Cylinders = (VMDK ByteSize – 512) / (Heads * Sectors * Bytes per Sector)

Three different adapter types can currently be used with virtual machines.

- **ide** For an IDE drive
- **buslogic** For a buslogic SCSI controller driver
- **lsilogic** For a lsilogic SCSI controller driver

One particular thing to notice in this section is the ddb.virtualHWVersion. This version number is the VMware platform the virtual machine is running on.

Swiss Army Knife…

Scripting the Backup of Virtual Machine's Configuration Files

In the next section, we will dig into the vmx configuration file for the virtual machines. Before that, however, let's put together a script to take care of one of the most important things we can do with these files: backing them up. This script is what I am using in my VMware ESX servers. They will back up all the configuration files for all the virtual machines, compress them into a tar file along with the vm-list file, and put them on a share on the network. The vm-list file is the list of registered virtual machines on an ESX server. This script runs daily and if I were to lose one of the ESX hosts, I could grab the backup file, register the virtual machines, and I am all set.

```
#!/bin/sh
# Virtual Machine VMX Backup
# Stephen Beaver
DOW=`date +%a` # Day of the week e.g. Mon
mount -t smbfs //server/share /mnt/smb -o
username=username/domain,password=password
SRC_DIR=/home/vmware/ #Directory will all vm configuration files
DST_DIR=/mnt/smb #Destination path which in this case is the mount
point
BASE_DIR=/home #Base directory to put the vmlist file
HOST="ESX-Server Name"
```

Continued

```
echo "src dir ="$SRC_DIR

echo "dst dir ="$DST_DIR

cp -f /etc/vmware/vm-list /home/vmware/vm-list

tar -czvf "$DST_DIR/vm_backup_$HOST-$DOW.tar.gz" "$SRC_DIR"

umount /mnt/smb

exit
```

The Virtual Machine Configuration vmx File

The vmx file is the configuration file that stores all the virtual machine's specific settings in one nice neat place. Code Listing 5.3 is an example of a vmx file.

Code Listing 5.3 A vmx File

```
#!/usr/bin/vmware

config.version = "6"

scsi0:0.present = "TRUE"

scsi0:0.name = "ESX_SAN4:2K900.vmdk"

scsi0:0.mode = "persistent"

scsi0.present = "true"

scsi0.virtualDev = "vmxbuslogic"

memSize = "512"

displayName = "2K900"

guestOS = "win2000Serv"

ethernet0.present = "true"

ethernet0.connectionType = "monitor_dev"

ethernet0.devName = "bond0"

ethernet0.networkName = "FH_Network"

Ethernet0.addressType = "vpx"

Ethernet0.generatedAddress = "00:50:56:9d:4d:10"

Ethernet0.virtualDev = "vmxnet"

floppy0.present = "true"

floppy0.startConnected = "false"

ide1:0.present = "true"

ide1:0.fileName = "/dev/cdrom"
```

```
ide1:0.deviceType = "atapi-cdrom"
ide1:0.startConnected = "FALSE"


draw = "gdi"
uuid.bios = "50 1d 07 5c a9 f3 2b dd-8b 3e 83 10 b2 ea 89 0b"
uuid.location = "56 4d b5 45 28 5a b0 20-29 52 da f8 22 74 60 1d"
uuid.action = "keep"
priority.grabbed = "normal"
priority.ungrabbed = "normal"


isolation.tools.dnd.disable = "TRUE"


suspend.Directory = "/vmfs/vmhba1:0:83:1"


autostart = "true"
autostop = "softpoweroff"


tools.syncTime = "FALSE"
```

This vmx file came from one of my virtual machines on a VMware ESX server. Let's take a look at the different settings in the file. As a rule, virtual machines will only read the full vmx file when the virtual machine is powered on. Thus, you should edit the virtual machine's vmx file when the virtual machine is off only. I have come across this scenario while playing around in the lab. There, I had a virtual machine and made a manual change to the configuration file. ESX knew I made a change and so it paused the virtual machine to ask me a question: "The configuration file for this VM has changed. Do you wish to reload the configuration file?" If the virtual machine in my production environment had instead been paused, I would have had a few people to answer to.

```
config.version = "6"
scsi0:0.present = "TRUE"
scsi0:0.name = "ESX_SAN4:2K900.vmdk"
scsi0:0.mode = "persistent"
```

```
scsi0.present = "true"
scsi0.virtualDev = "vmxbuslogic"
```

vmx File Components

In this subsection, we'll discuss the various parameters, settings, and commands related to vmx files.

config.version = ""

This is the hardware version level. When we talked about downgrading the disk descriptor file, this is what we must change to control the hardware version so it will work in the different products. What we see next are the settings for the SCSI drive. Scsi0:0 is the virtual machine's boot drive.

Scsi0:0.present = ""

This lets the host know that the virtual machine has a SCSI drive present. This can have an entry of True or False.

Scsi0:0.name = ""

This is the name and path of the VMDK file that the virtual machine will use. In the earlier example, "ESX_SAN4:2K900.vmdk" points to a common name of a LUN on the SAN called ESX_SAN4, and the 2K900.vmdk is the disk file located on the LUN.

Scsi0:0.mode = ""

This setting is the mode of the disk file. The following four disk modes are available.

- **Persistent** Changes are immediately and permanently written to the virtual disk.

- **Nonpersistent** Changes are discarded when the virtual machine powers off.

- **Undoable** Changes are saved, discarded or appended at your discretion.

- **Append** Changes are appended to a redo log when the virtual machine powers off.

scsi0.present = ""

This setting lets the host know this virtual machine has a SCSI controller. The value can be True for present, and False for no SCSI.

scsi0.virtualDev = ""

This setting determines what SCSI drivers the controller is using. Two different values can be used here.

- **vmxbuslogic** When using the buslogic SCSI driver
- **vmxlsilogic** When using the lsilogic SCSI driver

These are also the settings we would change on the vmx file to switch from an IDE disk to a SCSI.

The next part of the configuration vmx file is the memory, name, and guestOS, all of which do not need much explanation:

- **memSize = "512"** How much memory the virtual machine is allocated
- **displayName = "2K900"** The display name of the virtual machine
- **guestOS = "win2000Serv"** Which operating system the VM is running

The next part concerns the Ethernet adapter and whether Virtual Center is used to monitor this virtual machine (see the following example).

```
ethernet0.present = "true"
ethernet0.connectionType = "monitor_dev"
ethernet0.devName = "bond0"
ethernet0.networkName = "FH_Network"
Ethernet0.addressType = "vpx"
Ethernet0.generatedAddress = "00:50:56:9d:4d:10"
Ethernet0.virtualDev = "vmxnet"
```

ethernet0.present = ""

This value defines whether the network settings are read and processed. This value can be "true" or "false." If the value is "true," then all other parameters are then processed. If the value is "false," then all other network parameters for that device are ignored.

TIP

ethernet0.startConnected = "true"

**Ethernet0.present = "true" also sets startConnected to "TRUE",
though this may not appear in the vmx (another silent default).
So if you want the device to be present—but not at boot-time—you
must use
ethernet0.startConnected = "FALSE".**

---

ethernet0.connectionType = ""

This parameter concerns virtual networks. Your choices for this value are "bridged", "hostonly", "nat", "monitor_dev", and "custom". The custom settings are an expert way to use a combination of "connectionType" and "vne.t". A good example of this would be the following:

```
ethernet0.connectionType = "CUSTOM"
```

And the exact number of the VNET you want might look like:

```
ethernet0.vnet = "VMNET0"
```

ethernet0.devName = ""

This parameter is the actual name of the device being used. This could be one of the virtual ethernet cards like vmnic0, or in this case a bond of two ethernet cards together called "bond0".

ethernet0.networkName = ""

This is the name of the virtual switch that the virtual machine will be using for networking. In this example, the virtual switch's name is FH_Network.

Ethernet0.addressType = "vpx"

This parameter is only present when the virtual machine is on an ESX server that is controlled by Virtual Center.

Ethernet0.generatedAddress = ""

This parameter is the MAC address of the virtual machine. In this case, the MAC address is generated by the host application.

VMware has a special range of MAC addresses that are allocated for the virtual machines. The following lists the different ranges of addresses.

- **00:05:69:00:00:00** Automatically assigned by MUI when building a VM without VirtualCenter (ESX <2.0)

- **00:0c:29:00:00:00** Automatically assigned by MUI when building a VM without VirtualCenter as well as the other VMware products (ESX 2.0 +, all VMware)

- **00:50:56:00:00:00 – 00:50:56:3f:ff:ff** Manually configured MACs

- **00:50:56:80:00:00 – 00:50:56:bf:ff:ff** VirtualCenter-generated MACs

Ethernet0.virtualDev = "vlance" or "vmxnet" or "e1000"

This parameter is to define the virtual adapter itself. The choices available are

- **vlance** This is based on the AMD PCNet 32 and has the most backward compatibility. Take note that if you use vlance with your virtual machine, the VM will only show what it is connected at 10mb. This is presented for backward compatibility only and does not represent the actual speed with which the VM is communicating. The VM will use all the bandwidth given to it.

- **vmxnet** This is a VMware custom high-performance vmxnet virtual network adapter which allows for faster networking performance.

This is the adapter you should use whenever possible, given it offers better performance than the vlance driver and less overhead.

- **e1000** This is the Intel pro 1000 adapter, which is the default virtual NIC when choosing a 64-bit guest. It can be manually edited in the config file.

Floppy Drives and CD-ROMs for Virtual Machines

The following parameter is the configuration of the floppy and CD-ROM for the virtual machine. Notice that I have startConnected set to "false" for these devices. As a rule of thumb, I recommend leaving these disconnected until you need them.

```
floppy0.present = "true"
floppy0.startConnected = "false"
ide1:0.present = "true"
ide1:0.fileName = "/dev/cdrom"
ide1:0.deviceType = "atapi-cdrom"
ide1:0.startConnected = "false"
```

Notice that the parameter ide1:0.fileName is currently set to "dev/cdrom." This is the emulation of the CD-ROM device that shows up as a VMware CD-ROM and not the actual physical host CD-ROM device. By changing the fileName and deviceType values, you can also mount ISO images to the virtual machine.

```
ide1:0.fileName = "/iso/nameof.iso
ide1:0.deviceType = "cdrom-image"
```

Graphics Emulation, Unique Identifiers

VMware products offer two modes for host emulation of the graphics inside the virtual machine: GDI (Graphics Device Interface; the classic Windows graphics mode) and DirectDraw (a mode designed for games and other applications that write directly to the hardware).

```
draw = "gdi"
```

In general, Windows guest operating systems (Windows 95, Windows 98, Windows NT, and Windows 2000) perform better in GDI mode than in DirectDraw mode, while Linux guest operating systems (or any guest operating systems that use an X server) run much better in DirectDraw mode.

WARNING

DirectDraw on Windows 2000 is fairly buggy, so the virtual machine displays a cautionary message if you try to enable it. In addition, some specific issues have been identified on both Windows NT and Windows 2000 hosts when the virtual machine is using DirectDraw mode.

Once you start a virtual machine, the VMware host will then generate another two lines to identify the virtual machine. Whenever you change the path to the vmx-file, either by renaming or moving to a different location, VMware wants to update these lines to reflect that change (see the following example).

```
uuid.location = "56 4d ee 3c 52 06 a3 de-be 4a 73 9c cc 99 15 1f"
uuid.bios = "56 4d ee 3c 52 06 a3 de-be 4a 73 9c cc 99 15 1f"
```

If you've ever moved a virtual machine from one host to another, then when you start the machine you've probably seen a message similar to this:

> The virtual machine's configuration file has changed its location since its last poweron. Do you want to create a new unique identifier (UUID) for the virtual machine or keep the old one?

Your choices are Keep, Create, Always Keep, and Always Create. If you choose **Always Keep** or **Always Create**, then the parameter uuid.action is added to the vmx file (see the following example).

```
uuid.action = "Keep" or "Create"
```

The values you can use here are Keep or Create for Always Keep and Always Create.

Priority, VMware Tools Settings, and Suspend

The "grabbed: HIGH - ungrabbed: NORMAL" setting is useful if you have many background processes or applications and you do not care if they run with fairly low relative priority while a virtual machine is in the foreground. In return, you get a very noticeable performance boost using a virtual machine while another virtual machine is running or while some other processor-intensive task (a compile, for example) is running in the background (see the following example).

```
priority.grabbed = "high" or "normal"
```

The reverse is true of the "grabbed: NORMAL - ungrabbed: LOW" setting. If your host machine feels too sluggish when a virtual machine is running in the background, you can direct the virtual machine to drop its priority when it does not have control of the mouse and keyboard. As with the high setting, this is a heavy-handed change of priority, so the virtual machine (and any background applications inside) runs much more slowly.

```
priority.ungrabbed = "normal" or "low"
```

isolation.tools.dnd.disable = "True" or "False"

This setting is to enable/disable Host/Guest drag and drop interface. The values you can use here are "True" and "False".

suspend.Directory = "/vmfs/vmhba1:0:83:1"

This parameter is the location the host should use to "suspend" a virtual machine. The following example was taken from an ESX server that is attached to a SAN. Notice that the path is made up of the true path vmhba1:0:83:1 and not the friendly name that I set for the LUN: /vmfs/ESX_SAN4/.

Autostart, Autostop, and Time Sync Options

In this section, we'll discuss autostart, autostop, and time sync options that you can be used for configuring a virtual machine. The following example shows autostart and autostop command scripts.

```
autostart = "true" or "false"
```

```
autostop = "softpoweroff" or "poweroff"
autostart.order = ""
autostop.order = ""
```

You can configure a virtual machine to automatically begin when the host starts up from a reboot and also to automatically power off or shut down the guest OS when the host is being shut down. When you utilize this option, the autostart and autostop options are added to the virtual machine's vmx file. You can also take this a step further and define the startup and shutdown order of the virtual machines using the autostop.order and autostart.order. By default, it would use order number x10. To give you an example, if you wanted VM1 to be the first virtual machine started and the last virtual machine to shutdown, you would set the configuration this way:

```
autostart.order = "10"
autostop.order = "10"
```

To change this to be the third virtual machine started, change the number from 10 to 30.

```
tools.syncTime = "FALSE" or "TRUE"
```

The tools.syncTime Option

The last option in my vmx file is the tools.syncTime. This option is used to determine if the virtual machine is going to update its time with the host time via the VMware tools or not.

Virtual Machine Conversion from IDE to SCSI

You may find the need to be able to move virtual machines around from one platform to another. For example, I encourage people to utilize VMware Workstation in order to work on a virtual machine while on the go. I have had several instances where a virtual machine was created on VMware Workstation, but unfortunately was not created in legacy mode or had an IDE drive. As a result, when attempting to migrate to ESX, it would fail until some changes were made.

Therefore, here we will examine changing an IDE drive to a SCSI drive. Before we change the settings, we need to get the SCSI drivers in the system first. The easiest way to do this is to add another hard disk to the virtual machine as a secondary drive. Configure this drive to be a SCSI drive. Start the virtual machine with the new drive attached and, the SCSI drivers are now in place, allowing us to continue and really edit the files. When we open the descriptor file for a virtual machine using an IDE drive, it looks like the sample in Code Listing 5.4.

Code Listing 5.4 Descriptor File for a Virtual Machine Using an IDE Drive

```
# Disk DescriptorFile
version=1
CID=2af6d34d
parentCID=ffffffff
createType="twoGbMaxExtentSparse"


# Extent description
RW 4192256 SPARSE "Windows-s001.vmdk"
RW 4192256 SPARSE "Windows-s002.vmdk"
RW 4096 SPARSE "Windows-s003.vmdk"


# The Disk Data Base
#DDB


ddb.adapterType = "ide"
ddb.geometry.sectors = "63"
ddb.geometry.heads = "16"
ddb.geometry.cylinders = "8322"
ddb.virtualHWVersion = "4"
ddb.toolsVersion = "6404"
```

Starting with the ddb.adapterType you can see that this was indeed an IDE drive. There are a total of three different options for this setting. We'll discuss each in this section.

ddb.adapterType = "buslogic"

This entry converts the disk into a SCSI-disk with a BusLogic Controller. This is the standard for Windows 2000 virtual machines.

ddb.adapterType = "lsilogic"

This entry converts the disk into a SCSI-disk with LSILogic Controller. This is the standard for Windows 2003 virtual machines.

```
ddb.adapterType = "ide"
```

This entry converts the disk into an IDE-disk with Intel-IDE Controller.

Next, let's open the SCSI disk that we used to get the drivers in the virtual machine and use it to give us the section, heads, and cylinder values we need.

```
ddb.adapterType = "buslogic"
ddb.geometry.cylinders = "522"
ddb.geometry.heads = "255"
ddb.geometry.sectors = "63"
```

Put this all together and we have a new SCSI disk for our virtual machine.

There is one change left to be done, however. We will need to change the ddb.virtualHWVersion. The ddb.virtualHWVersion is dependent upon which VMware platform you are using. You may need to change the version number to get the virtual machine to start in certain cases, namely moving a virtual machine in to ESX Server.

Change the ddb.virtualHWVersion = "4" and make it ddb.virtualHWVersion = "3". You now have a legacy virtual machine disk file you have converted from IDE to SCSI. You've also brought the virtual machine disk file down to legacy mode so that it can run on ESX.

```
# Disk DescriptorFile
version=1
CID=826d3b6e
parentCID=ffffffff
createType="twoGbMaxExtentSparse"
```

```
# Extent description
RW 4192256 SPARSE "Windows-s001.vmdk"
RW 4192256 SPARSE "Windows-s002.vmdk"
RW 4096 SPARSE "Windows-s003.vmdk"


# The Disk Data Base
#DDB


ddb.adapterType = "buslogic"
ddb.geometry.sectors = "63"
ddb.geometry.heads = "255"
ddb.geometry.cylinders = "522"
ddb.virtualHWVersion = "3"
ddb.toolsVersion = "6309"
```

To complete this process we need to make an adjustment in the vmx file in order to change the IDE values to SCSI. Code Listing 5.5 is an example of a disk file that's been configured to use an IDE.

Code Listing 5.5 Configuring a Disk to Use an IDE

```
config.version = "8"
virtualHW.version = "4"
scsi0.present = "TRUE"
memsize = "200"
ide0:0.present = "TRUE"
ide0:0.fileName = "Windows.vmdk"
ide1:0.present = "TRUE"
ide1:0.fileName = "auto detect"
ide1:0.deviceType = "cdrom-raw"
floppy0.fileName = "A:"
ethernet0.present = "TRUE"
usb.present = "TRUE"
sound.present = "TRUE"
sound.virtualDev = "es1371"
```

```
displayName = "Windows XP Professional 1"

guestOS = "winxppro"

nvram = "winxppro.nvram"


ide0:0.redo = ""

ethernet0.addressType = "generated"

uuid.location = "56 4d b7 df d7 1d 42 ca-3e 81 5d a3 5e 05 7a f7"

uuid.bios = "56 4d b7 df d7 1d 42 ca-3e 81 5d a3 5e 05 7a f7"

tools.remindInstall = "FALSE"

ethernet0.generatedAddress = "00:0c:29:05:7a:f7"

ethernet0.generatedAddressOffset = "0"


ide1:0.autodetect = "TRUE"


ide1:0.startConnected = "TRUE"

tools.syncTime = "FALSE"
```

To finish the change from IDE to SCSI we need to adjust these lines in the vmx file (see Table 5.2).

Table 5.2 VMX Old and New Settings

From the Old Settings	To the New Settings
config.version = "8"	config.version = "6"
virtualHW.version = "4"	virtualHW.version = "3"
ide0:0.present = "TRUE"	scsi0.present = "TRUE"
ide0:0.fileName = "Windows.vmdk"	scsi0:0.present = "TRUE"
	scsi0:0.fileName = "Windows.vmdk"

Now we have completed downgrading the virtual hardware and also changed a virtual machine from using an IDE drive to a SCSI drive. This virtual machine will now start and run in VMWare ESX server. By using the example of taking a virtual machine from VMware Workstation and getting it to run to VMware ESX Server, we have gone from one extreme of the VMware product line (workstation) to the other extreme (ESX Server).

Scripted Disconnect of IDE Devices

As a general rule, you should always have the CD-ROM and floppy drive disconnect so they don't take away resources from the service console. This is also true if you place a CD-ROM in the physical host's drive, because all the virtual machines will not start to autorun the CD-ROM. VMotion also won't work if either the CD-ROM or the floppy is connected. The script shown in Code Listing 5.6 will disconnect all these devices in virtual machines that are registered on ESX Server. This script was originally posted on the VMware community forum by Stuart Thompson (aka, Mr-T) and Matt Pound, and it includes a few additions by me.

Code Listing 5.6 Disconnecting Devices in Virtual Machines Registered on an ESX Server

```bash
#!/bin/bash
# IDE / Floppy Disconnect Script
# Script by: Stuart Thompson and Matt Pound
# Edit by: Steve Beaver (Added floppy drive)

vmwarelist=`vmware-cmd -l`
vmwarelist=`echo $vmwarelist | sed -e 's/ /*/g'`
vmwarelist=`echo $vmwarelist | sed -e 's/.vmx/.vmx /g'`
for vm in $vmwarelist
do
    vm=`echo $vm | sed -e 's/*/ /g'`
    vm=`echo $vm | sed -e 's/ \//*/g'`

    if [ `vmware-cmd "$vm" getstate | sed -e 's/getstate() = //'` = "on" ]
    then
    echo Looking @ $vm
    IDEBUS=`seq 0 1`
    for i in $IDEBUS;
    do
        echo BUS : $i
            IDEDEVICE=`seq 0 1`
```

```
for j in $IDEDEVICE;
do
        PRESENT=`vmware-cmd "$vm" getconfig ide$i:$j.present | cut -f3
        -d " "`
        if [ $PRESENT = "true" ]
        then
                TYPE=`vmware-cmd "$vm" getconfig ide$i:$j.deviceType |
                cut -f3 -d " "`
                if [[ $TYPE == "atapi-cdrom" || $TYPE == "cdrom-image"]]
                then
                    echo Found CDROM on IDE$i:$j
                    vmware-cmd "$vm" disconnectdevice ide$i:$j
                fi
        fi
    done
  done
 fi
done
```

Swiss Army Knife...

vmwarelist=`vmware-cmd -l`

You can change this value to point to a specific path of a virtual machine
and have these scripts set up to run on only one virtual machine instead
of all virtual machines.
      Vmwarelist='/home/vmware/vmserver/vmserver.vmx

Employing this script as a base, you can choose many options using the
vmware-cmd to make a change to all of your registered virtual machines.
Take a look at Code Listing 5.7, which shows how you can start all your registered machines.

Code Listing 5.7 Starting All Registered Virtual Machines

```bash
#!/bin/bash
vmwarelist=`vmware-cmd -l`
vmwarelist=`echo $vmwarelist | sed -e 's/ /*/g'`
vmwarelist=`echo $vmwarelist | sed -e 's/.vmx/.vmx /g'`
for vm in $vmwarelist
do
    vm=`echo $vm | sed -e 's/*/ /g'`
    vm=`echo $vm | sed -e 's/ \//*/g'`

    if [ `vmware-cmd "$vm" getstate | sed -e 's/getstate() = //'` = "off" ]
    then
        echo Found $vm that is off, Starting $vm
        vmware-cmd "$vm" start
    fi
done
```

Now, let's take a look at a script to stop those virtual machines that are running.

```bash
#!/bin/bash
vmwarelist=`vmware-cmd -l`
vmwarelist=`echo $vmwarelist | sed -e 's/ /*/g'`
vmwarelist=`echo $vmwarelist | sed -e 's/.vmx/.vmx /g'`
for vm in $vmwarelist
do
    vm=`echo $vm | sed -e 's/*/ /g'`
    vm=`echo $vm | sed -e 's/ \//*/g'`

    if [ `vmware-cmd "$vm" getstate | sed -e 's/getstate() = //'` = "on" ]
    then
        echo Found $vm that is on, Stopping $vm
        vmware-cmd "$vm" stop trysoft
    fi
done
```

Code Listing 5.8 is one more example of this script, which will reboot all of the running virtual machines. This is very handy if you have installed updates or anything else and want to delay the reboot till later.

Code Listing 5.8 Script for Rebooting All Running Virtual Machines

```bash
#!/bin/bash
vmwarelist=`vmware-cmd -l`
vmwarelist=`echo $vmwarelist | sed -e 's/ /*/g'`
vmwarelist=`echo $vmwarelist | sed -e 's/.vmx/.vmx /g'`
for vm in $vmwarelist
do
   vm=`echo $vm | sed -e 's/*/ /g'`
   vm=`echo $vm | sed -e 's/ \//*/g'`

   if [ `vmware-cmd "$vm" getstate | sed -e 's/getstate() = //'` = "on" ]
   then
       echo Found $vm that is on, Rebooting $vm
       vmware-cmd "$vm" reset trysoft
   fi
done
```

Dynamic Creation of Virtual Machines

Now that we have looked at what makes up the vmx file, let's generate some scripts to dynamically create virtual machines. First, we'll take a script and modify it so we can create a virtual machine that will use a golden image as its base. We'll then make a couple of changes so we can take advantage of Altiris in the VM creation. We will then modify the script so that a virtual machine will be created and then start the VM with the installation CD mounted to begin the installation.

Code Listing 5.9 shows script that uses a golden image disk file. A golden image disk file is a fully loaded and patched virtual machine vmx file that has had sysprep run on it so it can be cloned.

WARNING

Please make sure you look through these scripts and make any changes needed to match your environment. Pay attention to the vmhba path and double-check these values with the values in your own environment.

Code Listing 5.9 Using a Golden Image Disk File to Dynamically Create a Virtual Machine

```bash
#!/bin/bash
#Scripting VMware Power Tools: Automating Virtual Infrastructure
Administration
#Dynamic Creation of a new Virtual Machine using a Golden Image
#Stephen Beaver
#####USER MODIFICATION################
#VMNAME is the name of the new virtual machine
#VMOS specifies which Operating System the virtual machine will have
#GLDIMAGE is the path to the "Golden Image" VMDK file
#DESTVMFS is the path to VMFS partition that the VMDK file
####################################
VMOS="winNetStandard"
VMMEMSIZE="256"
GLDIMAGE="/vmfs/FHVMFS1/Windows_2003_Standard.vmdk"
DESTVMFS="vmhba0:0:0:10"
#####END MODIFICATION#####
LOG="/var/log/$1.log"
echo "Start of Logging" > $LOG
echo "Importing Golden Image Disk File VMDK" >> $LOG
vmkfstools -i $GLDIMAGE $DESTVMFS:$1.vmdk
echo "Creating VMX Configuration File" >> $LOG
mkdir /home/vmware/$1
exec 6>&1
exec 1>/home/vmware/$1/$1.vmx
# write the configuration file
```

```
echo #!/usr/bin/vmware
echo config.version = '"'6'"'
echo virtualHW.version = '"'3'"'
echo memsize = '"'$VMMEMSIZE'"'
echo floppy0.present = '"'TRUE'"'
echo usb.present = '"'FALSE'"'
echo displayName = '"'$1'"'
echo guestOS = '"'$VMOS'"'
echo suspend.Directory = '"'/vmfs/vmhba0:0:0:10/'"'
echo checkpoint.cptConfigName = '"'$1'"'
echo priority.grabbed = '"'normal'"'
echo priority.ungrabbed = '"'normal'"'
echo ide1:0.present = '"'TRUE'"'
echo ide1:0.fileName = '"'auto detect'"'
echo ide1:0.deviceType = '"'cdrom-raw'"'
echo ide1:0.startConnected = '"'FALSE'"'
echo floppy0.startConnected = '"'FALSE'"'
echo floppy0.fileName = '"'/dev/fd0'"'
echo Ethernet0.present = '"'TRUE'"'
echo Ethernet0.connectionType = '"'monitor_dev'"'
echo Ethernet0.networkName = '"'Network0'"'
echo draw = '"'gdi'"'
echo
echo scsi0.present = '"'TRUE'"'
echo scsi0:1.present = '"'TRUE'"'
echo scsi0:1.name = '"'$DESTVMFS:$1.vmdk'"'
echo scsi0:1.writeThrough = '"'TRUE'"'
echo scsi0.virtualDev = '"'vmxlsilogic'"'
echo
# close file
exec 1>&-
# make stdout a copy of FD 6 (reset stdout), and close FD6
exec 1>&6
exec 6>&-
```

```
echo "VMX Configuration File Created Successfully" >> $LOG
#Change the file permissions
chmod 755 /home/vmware/$1/$1.vmx
#Register the new VM
echo "Registering .vmx Configuration" >> $LOG
vmware-cmd -s register /home/vmware/$1/$1.vmx
echo "VMX Initialization Completed Successfully" >> $LOG
```

NOTE

Notice that the preceding script uses a golden image file that is local to that machine. If your golden image is located on a network share, you can easily mount that share and import the file from there. To mount a network share you can use the following command:
    mount -t smbfs //server/share /mnt/smb -o
username=username/domain,password=password

Next, we'll take the same script and make a few changes so it will work with an ESX Server managed with Altiris. At the end of this script, the virtual machine is started and should boot PXE, which Altiris can then take over and use to install the operating system (see Code Listing 5.10).

Code Listing 5.10 Creating a New Virtual Machine to Use with an ESX Server Managed by Altiris

```
#!/bin/bash
#Scripting VMware Power Tools: Automating Virtual Infrastructure
Administration
#Creates a new Virtual Machine for use with Altiris
#Stephen Beaver
#####USER MODIFICATION################
#VMNAME is the name of the new virtual machine
#VMOS specifies which Operating System the virtual machine will have
#DESTVMFS is the path to the VMFS partition of the VMDK file
```

```
#VMDSIZE is the size of the Virtual Disk File being created ex (500mb) or
(10g)
####################################
VMNAME="vm_name"
VMOS="winNetStandard"
VMMEMSIZE="256"
DESTVMFS="vmhba0:6:0:1 #Must use the vmhba path
VMDSIZE="10g"
#####END MODIFICATION#####
LOG="/opt/altiris/deployment/adlagent/bin/logevent"
$LOG -l:1 -ss:"Creating VMX Configuration File"
mkdir /home/vmware/$VMNAME
exec 6>&1
exec 1>/home/vmware/$VMNAME/$VMNAME.vmx
# write the configuration file
echo #!/usr/bin/vmware
echo config.version = '"'6'"'
echo virtualHW.version = '"'3'"'
echo memsize = '"'$VMMEMSIZE'"'
echo floppy0.present = '"'TRUE'"'
echo usb.present = '"'FALSE'"'
echo displayName = '"'$VMNAME'"'
echo guestOS = '"'$VMOS'"'
echo suspend.Directory = '"'/vmfs/vmhba0:0:0:5/'"'
echo checkpoint.cptConfigName = '"'$VMNAME'"'
echo priority.grabbed = '"'normal'"'
echo priority.ungrabbed = '"'normal'"'
echo ide1:0.present = '"'TRUE'"'
echo ide1:0.fileName = '"'auto detect'"'
echo ide1:0.deviceType = '"'cdrom-raw'"'
echo ide1:0.startConnected = '"'FALSE'"'
echo floppy0.startConnected = '"'FALSE'"'
echo floppy0.fileName = '"'/dev/fd0'"'
echo Ethernet0.present = '"'TRUE'"'
```

```
echo Ethernet0.connectionType = '"'monitor_dev'"'
echo Ethernet0.networkName = '"'Network0'"'
echo draw = '"'gdi'"'
echo
echo scsi0.present = '"'TRUE'"'
echo scsi0:1.present = '"'TRUE'"'
echo scsi0:1.name = '"'vmhba0:0:0:5:$VMNAME.vmdk'"'
echo scsi0:1.writeThrough = '"'TRUE'"'
echo scsi0.virtualDev = '"'vmxlsilogic'"'
echo
# close file
exec 1>&-
# make stdout a copy of FD 6 (reset stdout), and close FD6
exec 1>&6
exec 6>&-
$LOG -l:1 -ss:"VMX Configuration File Created Successfully"
#Change the file permissions
chmod 755 /home/vmware/$VMNAME/$VMNAME.vmx
#Create the Virtual Disk
$LOG -l:1 -ss:"Creating Virtual Disk"
vmkfstools -c $VMDSIZE vmhba0:0:0:5:$VMNAME.vmdk
$LOG -l:1 -ss:"Virtual Disk Created Successfully"
#Register the new VM
$LOG -l:1 -ss:"Registering VMX Configuration"
#Registering .vmx Configuration
vmware-cmd -s register /home/vmware/$VMNAME/$VMNAME.vmx
$LOG -l:1 -ss:"VMX Initialization Completed Successfully"
#Starting the Virtual Machine
$LOG -l:1 -ss:"Starting the Virtual Machine"
vmware-cmd /home/vmware/$VMNAME/$VMNAME.vmx start
$LOG -l:1 -ss:"Virtual Machine Started"
$LOG -l:1 -ss:"Passing control to Altiris for PXE boot and install of VM"
```

Let's make one more change to the script so that when the virtual machine first boots up with a brand-new disk, it will boot from the virtual CD-ROM that has an ISO file mounted to it (see Code Listing 5.11).

Code Listing 5.11 Creating a New Virtual Machine That Boots to an ISO

```bash
#!/bin/bash
#Scripting VMware Power Tools: Automating Virtual Infrastructure
Administration
#Creates a new Virtual Machine booting to an ISO
#Stephen Beaver
#####USER MODIFICATION#################
#VMNAME is the name of the new virtual machine
#VMOS specifies which Operating System the virtual machine will have
#GLDIMAGE is the path to the "Golden Image" VMDK file
#DESTVMFS is the path to the VMFS partition of the VMDK file
#VMDSIZE is the size of the Virtual Disk File being created ex (500mb) or
(10g)
#ISOIMAGE is the path and file name of the ISO file you are using
#####################################
VMOS="winNetStandard"
VMMEMSIZE="256"
GLDIMAGE="/vmfs/FHVMFS1/Windows_2003_Standard.vmdk"
DESTVMFS="vmhba0:0:0:10"
VMDSIZE="10g"
ISOIMAGE"/vmfs/ESX_SAN/Windows2000.iso"
#####END MODIFICATION#####
LOG="/var/log/$1.log"
echo "Start of Logging" > $LOG
echo "Importing Golden Image Disk File VMDK" >> $LOG
vmkfstools -i $GLDIMAGE $DESTVMFS:$1.vmdk
echo "Creating VMX Configuration File" >> $LOG
mkdir /home/vmware/$1
exec 6>&1
exec 1>/home/vmware/$1/$1.vmx
```

```
# write the configuration file
echo #!/usr/bin/vmware
echo config.version = '"'6'"'
echo virtualHW.version = '"'3'"'
echo memsize = '"'$VMMEMSIZE'"'
echo floppy0.present = '"'TRUE'"'
echo usb.present = '"'FALSE'"'
echo displayName = '"'$1'"'
echo guestOS = '"'$VMOS'"'
echo suspend.Directory = '"'/vmfs/vmhba0:0:0:10/'"'
echo checkpoint.cptConfigName = '"'$1'"'
echo priority.grabbed = '"'normal'"'
echo priority.ungrabbed = '"'normal'"'
echo ide1:0.present = '"'TRUE'"'
echo ide0:0.present = '"'TRUE'"'
echo ide0:0.fileName = '"'$ISOIMAGE'"'
echo ide0:0.deviceType = '"'cdrom-image'"'
echo floppy0.startConnected = '"'FALSE'"'
echo floppy0.fileName = '"'/dev/fd0'"'
echo Ethernet0.present = '"'TRUE'"'
echo Ethernet0.connectionType = '"'monitor_dev'"'
echo Ethernet0.networkName = '"'Network0'"'
echo draw = '"'gdi'"'
echo
echo scsi0.present = '"'TRUE'"'
echo scsi0:1.present = '"'TRUE'"'
echo scsi0:1.name = '"'$DESTVMFS:$1.vmdk'"'
echo scsi0:1.writeThrough = '"'TRUE'"'
echo scsi0.virtualDev = '"'vmxlsilogic'"'
echo
# close file
exec 1>&-
# make stdout a copy of FD 6 (reset stdout), and close FD6
exec 1>&6
```

```
exec 6>&-
#Create the Virtual Disk
echo "Creating Virtual Disk" >> $LOG
vmkfstools -c $VMDSIZE vmhba0:0:0:5:$VMNAME.vmdk
echo "Virtual Disk Created Successfully" >> $LOG
echo "VMX Configuration File Created Successfully" >> $LOG
#Change the file permissions
chmod 755 /home/vmware/$1/$1.vmx
#Register the new VM
echo "Registering .vmx Configuration" >> $LOG
vmware-cmd -s register /home/vmware/$1/$1.vmx
echo "VMX Initialization Completed Successfully" >> $LOG
#Starting the Virtual Machine
echo "Starting the Virtual Machine" >> $LOG
vmware-cmd /home/vmware/$VMNAME/$VMNAME.vmx start
echo "Virtual Machine Started" >> $LOG
```

Summary

Let's review what we've covered. First, we took a solid look at the virtual disk files (*.vmdk). We opened up the disk descriptor file, reviewed its contents, and converted an IDE virtual disk file to a SCSI virtual disk file. We then took an in-depth look at the settings inside the virtual machine configuration files (*.vmx) and finished the IDE-to-SCSI conversion.

I presented a few scripts that covered backing up the configuration files of the virtual machines, and how to build virtual machines. I also discussed a few options for making changes to all (or one) virtual machines at the same time. You can use bits and parts of these different scripts to open the door to various types of automation. Using the native "sed" program, for example, you have the ability to script the edits to any of the files you need. This gives you a wide range of options that can be scripted and automated. The vmware-cmd tool also opens a lot of doors thanks to the different choices available. Run vmware-cmd from the service console to view all the options and syntax.

## Chapter 6

Instant Disk: How to P2V for Free

Topics in this chapter:

Introduction

Your overall goal is to consolidate that server room full of hardware into a more easily managed and less expensive to operate and maintain integrated system. Some of your current mission-critical servers may be hosted on older hardware that can't be, or are difficult to be, replaced. Virtualization is the answer, but how do you achieve this goal?

What Is a P2V?

A key component when building a virtual infrastructure is establishing a physical to virtual (P2V) migration process. As a guideline, the "do no harm" mantra is a very important concept when performing P2V migrations. What this means is that your source physical server should not be damaged in any way during your P2V process. This permits a fail-back strategy if the P2V does not complete for whatever reason. Some commercial P2V methods add directories into the file system and entries into the Registry. These changes remain, especially if the P2V process does not complete or fails, and can render the source physical server inoperable. No tool you use should ever cause harm to the original server, but amazingly there are tools that do exactly that and yet are out there gaining market share today.

Whether your P2V is successful or not, your original physical server must remain intact with no harm done. Again, you may need to go back to the original server for more reasons than you thought.

For example, suppose the physical server you P2V is a critical production server and you are creating a new development machine from a copy of the real one? If the P2V was unsuccessful, you just need to bring up the original production server and be confident that your process has in no way added directories, Registry entries, or anything that will render the source production server unusable or uncertified.

Another key reason you do not want to "touch" the source server and inject any potentially dangerous changes is illustrated with the following example. Let's say your P2V of a production or dev server is successful but the application owner says that errors exist within the Event log. Having your source server operational, you can turn it back on and parse the logs yourself to see if the problem was preexisting. Since we do a block-by-block transfer in our line of work, it has been our experience that the problem was already there and we simply carried it over into the newly created virtual machine. We have seen this many, many times. Thus, it is a very good idea to go through the logs prior to a migration and note any errors so as to have them corrected prior to the migration.

P2V Techniques

Many different P2V techniques and methods exist, but most involve software that must be purchased. The following subsections provide a brief description of how some of these tools work. This is not meant as a how-to guide for each of these methods, but an explanation of the underlying technology of each P2V process.

VMware P2V Tool

VMware P2V Tool is an easy-to-use, enterprise-class, market-proven tool that can take an image of an existing physical system and create a VMware virtual machine. While this tool is both fast and reliable, its cost as well as the fact that it's restricted to virtualizing only Windows NT 4 to Windows Server 2003 systems does limit its use except in very large enterprises.

The basic process is simple, as shown in Figure 6.1.

Figure 6.1 The Basic Process When Using the VMware P2V Tool

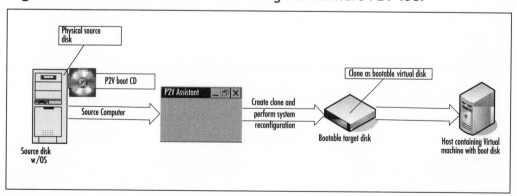

The VMware P2V Tool comes on a self-booting CD-ROM. The disk is placed in the target source computer's CD-ROM player and is run against the selected disk with its installed operating system. The P2V Assistant then creates the clone, performs the system reconfiguration, and now the clone is a bootable virtual disk being hosted on a system with new physical hardware.

Platespin PowerConvert

Currently in release 6.0, Platespin PowerConvert appears to be a much more sophisticated enterprise-class product than VMware's P2V tool. PowerConvert allows any kind of conversion and also supports Microsoft Virtual Server's format. As with VMware's offering, however, Platespin's product is also pricey. For that extra expense though, you get the following:

- The capability to drag and drop virtual machines from older VMware server technology into VMware Infrastructure 3.

- Limiting downtime for production servers running Windows 2000, Windows 2003, and Windows XP operating systems to only a brief (as little as one to five minutes) interruption by allowing the virtual machine to remain live as its OS, applications, and data are migrated to the new VMware Infrastructure 3 hosts.

- The capability to completely automate the Discover, Configure, and Convert functionality.

- The capability to reconfigure the CPU, the disk, and network and memory resources on the new target virtual machines.

- The capability to upgrade multiple virtual machines simultaneously onto new VMware Infrastructure 3 hosts.

In addition to the features previously mentioned, you can add hardware-independent images and Platespin becomes quite a power tool. How is it used? It's fully automated. Choose the source, the destination, and then start the process.

Barts/Ghost

A less-expensive enterprise-class alternative is the use of a boot CD-ROM such as Bart's Network Boot Disk (www.nu2.nu/bootdisk/network), which is free, and a cloning tool such as Symantec's Ghost, which is not. Adding another free tool, Ultimate-P2V (a plug-in for Bart) allows you to clone a physical machine to a virtual machine.

Several versions of tools are available that work in a similar fashion.

The "Big Secret" of P2V

Dozens of different ways exist to move data from a physical server to a virtual one and there are many different philosophies about how to reconfigure the hardware, but we've discovered that the easiest and most reliable method is to let Windows reconfigure itself. Sound too easy?

The Big Secret is that before we copy the source physical server, we install the VMware virtual SCSI driver. This applies to Windows 2000 and 2003. For Windows NT, we install the built-in NT BusLogic driver. But wait, doesn't this go against the "do no harm" mantra? Actually, no. Installing a built-in or supplied driver such as this is very minimal in its effect, but absolutely necessary in any P2V process since the operating system needs to have the SCSI driver in order to read the virtual disks. Initially, we weren't comfortable installing it either, but having installed it now literally thousands of times without any problems to speak of, we can say with confidence that the procedure is quite safe.

Once you install the virtual SCSI driver, you can copy the physical machine to your ESX host any way you like. This chapter explains the easiest way to do this without having to purchase any software. And the method described here is one of the safest and fastest.

After the new virtual machine boots, Windows will fix itself. Linux and Netware will need to be manually fixed. However, after the machine is up and running, you just need to clean up the drivers. By actually learning our methodology and understanding a little about the process, you should be able to achieve great success in your P2V migrations.

Instant Disk Overview

The next thing to do then is to examine the steps of the process. These steps are

1. Install the virtual VMware SCSI driver on the physical source machine.
2. Reboot the physical machine using a Linux boot disk, in rescue mode.
3. Cat (*cat* is like *type* in DOS) the hard drives (**/dev/sd[abcd]** or **/dev/hd**?) and FTP them directly to the /vmfs file system on your ESX host.
4. Reboot the virtual machine, and Windows will redetect the hardware.
5. Install the VMware tools.
6. Remove the old network and other hardware.
7. Optionally shrink or expand the virtual disk.
8. Test.

Once finished, you'll have an Instant Disk.

The Bad News

This Instant Disk method will not work on all machines, only on those physical servers that have modern RAID controllers. Original Compaq Smart Array 2 and Smart Array 3 controllers used special vendor-specific SCSI blocking, which is outside of the norm.

Prepping the ESX Host: Setting Up FTP on ESX Host

Before we start installing drivers and rebooting servers, let's start by making sure the ESX host is ready to be used. We use FTP to directly transfer the image of the hard drive from the physical source server that is being P2V'd onto the VMFS of the ESX host.

Why use FTP? Because FTP is the fastest way to move the raw data from the source server's hard drive. With FTP, we move data nearer to wire speed, or as fast as the physical source server can read it off its hard drives. Isn't secure FTP better? It may be secure, but it is not fast. Secure FTP goes through SSH, which greatly slows down the performance. We chose to use NCFTPPUT. Why, you might ask? We use NCFTPPUT because it will allow us to FTP a stream of data.

Let's start by making sure FTP is running on your ESX host server. If it isn't, you must turn it on. Either do it in the MUI or through the command line. If for security reasons you do not keep FTP running on your ESX Server, then you simply can turn it off.

Through the MUI you would go to the Options tab and then select Security settings. The best choice is to choose Custom. This way, you can turn on FTP without turning on Telnet or other services. Select the FTP check box and save your selection.

From the command line on your ESX host, type **ntsysv**.

Then go to the bottom (using the down arrow) and check the **wu-ftpd** box (see Figure 6.2).

Figure 6.2 Starting the FTP Daemon on the ESX Server

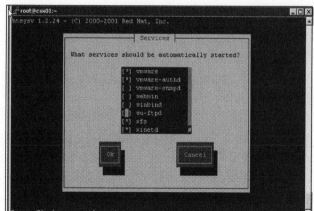

This is the FTP server service. Tab to **OK** and press **Enter** to save the changes.

From the command line, type **service xinetd restart**.

This command will tell the xinetd service to restart, which will then enable FTP.

> **NOTE**
>
> xinetd is the daemon used to manage the Internet daemon running on your ESX Server.

You need to create a user so you can FTP into the ESX host server. By default, ROOT cannot FTP in, and you do not want to change this. It's a good security practice to limit ROOT's access.

Since you need to check permissions and set up a user, it's easier to do all of this from the command line of your ESX host. For example, create a user named **PHD** from the command line, by typing **adduser phd**. Then type **passwd phd**.

You will be prompted to add the password for the user phd. You need to enter the password twice. If done correctly, the process should look something like the screenshot in Figure 6.3.

Figure 6.3 Creating User from the Command Line

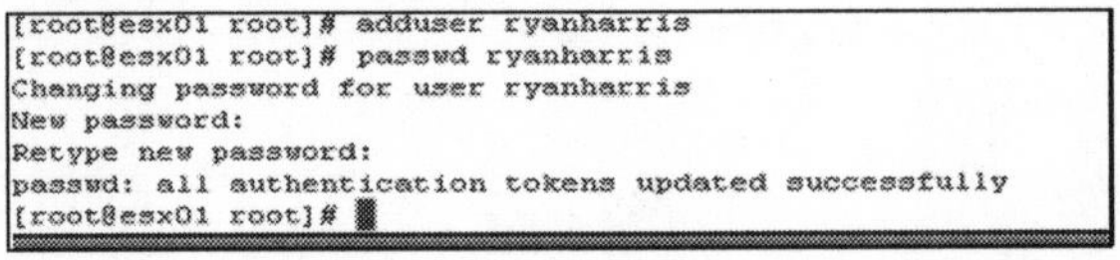

```
[root@esx01 root]# adduser ryanharris
[root@esx01 root]# passwd ryanharris
Changing password for user ryanharris
New password:
Retype new password:
passwd: all authentication tokens updated successfully
[root@esx01 root]# █
```

Now you need to test the FTP and make sure your user can log in successfully. From the command line of your ESX Server, type **ftp localhost**.

You should be prompted for the User and Password, use "phd" and the password you assigned to phd. Once you can successfully log in, change the directory to the /vmfs folder by typing **cd /vmfs/***your vmfs partition*. Ensure you can create new files on your VMFS of choice. For our example, we're going to use **/vmfs/LOCAL**.

You will probably need to change the permissions of the VMFS you want to use, which would be the vmhba$X$:X:X:X name.

To change the permissions on your VMFS partition, you should be at the ESX console, and then cd to your/vmfs folder.

From the command line, type **cd /vmfs**. Then type **ll** (same as ls –l).

Your vmhba folders should be shown, along with a nice name for each. For the VMFS you want to use, we'll change the permissions to 777, which will allow your phd user to write to them. Thus, type **chmod 1777 vmhba*X:X:X:X*** (use the correct name).

Now you need to test the FTP and make sure it works. Create a small test file, then FTP it to the /vmfs/LOCAL. Type the following:

cd /tmp

date > testfile

This is the *date* command and the greater than sign (>), then a new file name, such as testfile. Type **ll**.

You should see the newly created file, called **testfile**. If you were to cat this file, it should contain the current date string. Type **cat testfile**.

Now, from the /tmp folder, you're going to FTP into localhost and try to put this file on the /vmfs. Type **ftp localhost**.

You now want to log in as "phd" and put in the password, so type **cd /vmfs**. Then, type **dir**.

"dir" will give you a directory listing from the FTP command prompt. You should see your available vmfs file systems. You want to cd into the directory you are working with, so type **cd LOCAL** (use your name here; LOCAL is our example).

If this is successful and we do a *pwd* command, FTP will tell us our current folder. This should now be /vmfs/LOCAL. Type **pwd**.

You should get a response like 257 "/vmfs/LOCAL" is the current directory. Now you are going to "put" the testfile to the server. Type **put testfile** and press **Enter** and the local testfile will be transferred to the remote testfile. You'll then receive confirmation that this transfer has occurred and how long it took.

Now if you input a *dir* command again, you should see your testfile on your VMFS. Type **dir** and press **Enter**.

At this point, you have enabled FTP and verified that you can successfully put a file on your VMFS file system. You can delete the test file now. If you want to delete it from the FTP prompt. Type **del testfile**, or you can exit FTP and just delete the file /vmfs using the *rm* command. To exit FTP, type **bye**.

The last thing we want to do to make our work easier is to copy a few programs to our /home/phd folder. This is the home directory that was created when we added the user phd to the ESX host.

When doing our transfer of data form the source server, there are a few programs we need that are not included in a standard Linux rescue image. But all the programs we need already exist on the ESX host itself. Because we use the programs from the ESX host itself, we are limited to which versions of Linux rescue images we can use.

Let's create a p2v folder in our /home/phd folder to put copies of the programs we need to use. Type **mkdir /home/phd/p2v**. We also need to copy ncftpput and mii-tool to our /home/phd/p2v folder, so type **cp /usr/bin/ncftpput   /home/phd/p2v**. Then type **cp /sbin/mii-tool /home/phd/p2v**.

Other optional programs like **phdcat** should be copied to your /home/phd/p2v folder. At this point, the ESX host server should be ready for some P2V action.

Prepping the Source Machine: Install the SCSI Driver

Now you are ready to prep and get the physical source machine ready for Instant Disk P2V. You need the VMware SCSI driver, available from www.vmware.com/download/esx/ at the bottom of the page of SCSI Disk Drivers. VMware supplies this driver to be used in a virtual machine, but by installing in your physical first, it makes doing P2Vs very easy.

You need to load this driver onto your source server if you are using Windows 2000, Windows XP, or Windows 2003. You must do this for all machines, whether they are IDE and SCSI machines. The easiest thing to do is put the vmscsi.flp back onto a floppy or extract the contents and put them on a file share. If you copy this vmscsi.flp to your ESX host (or any Linux server), you can easily turn it back into a floppy. A FLP file is just a floppy ISO.

On the ESX host, you just cat the flp image to the floppy device. To do so, type **cat vmscsi.flp > /dev/fd0**. This will write the image in the flp file back to a floppy that you can use to install on the source servers. You can also turn the FLP file back into a real floppy using rawrite (Google it), an open-source utility that allows you to write raw floppy images to floppy drives in Windows.

Installing the SCSI Driver in Windows 2000/2003

When working with Windows 2000 or Windows 2003, you must install the vmscsi.sys driver using the specified method. On the source server, go to the Control Panel and select Add/Remove Hardware (see Figure 6.4).

Figure 6.4 Choose the Add/Remove Hardware Icon in the Control Panel

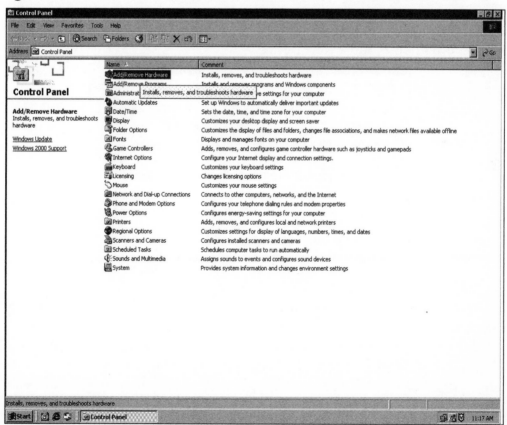

Next, choose **Add/Troubleshoot a Device** (see Figure 6.5).

Figure 6.5 Choose Add/Troubleshoot a Device

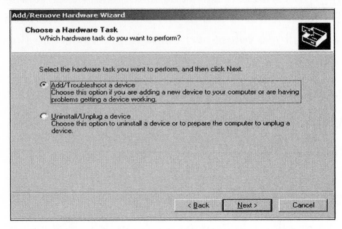

You then want to select **Add a New Device** (see Figure 6.6).

Figure 6.6 Choose Add a New Device

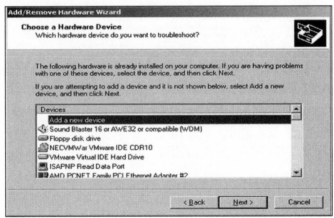

You do not want Windows to search for the new device, so select **No** (see Figure 6.7).

You are presented with a list of different types of hardware to install. You want to select **SCSI and RAID Controllers** (see Figure 6.8).

Figure 6.7 Choose the No Option to Select the Device from a Hardware List

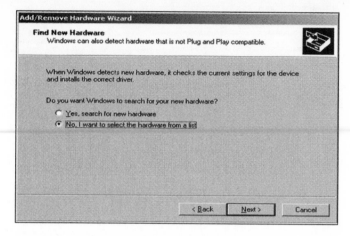

Figure 6.8 Choose the SCSI and RAID Controllers Option

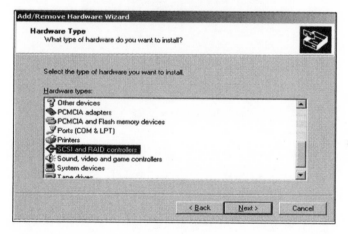

After clicking **Next**, you're shown a list of known SCSI drivers. Here you want to click **Have Disk** (see Figure 6.9).

After clicking **Have Disk**, you are asked for the location of the driver you want to install (see Figure 6.10). If you're using the vmscsi.sys driver on a floppy, you just need to insert the floppy and press **Enter**. Or you can browse to a network share and install the vmscsi.sys driver from there.

Figure 6.9 Choose the Have Disk Option

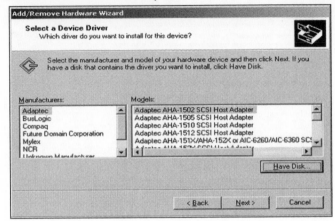

Figure 6.10 Enter or Browse to the Location of the Driver and Click OK

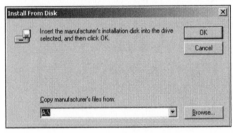

When you browse to the correct path, you are shown the vmscsi.inf file. Select this file and click **Open** (see Figure 6.11).

Figure 6.11 Select the File and Click the Open Button

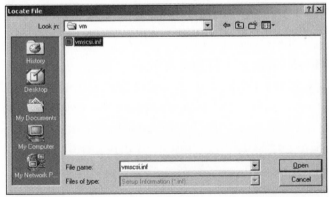

Then you are back to the Install from Disk prompt. Click **OK** (see Figure 6.12).

Figure 6.12 The Install from Disk Prompt

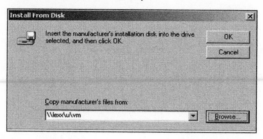

After clicking **OK**, you're asked if you want to install the VMware SCSI Controller. Select it and click **Next** (see Figure 6.13).

Figure 6.13 Click Next to Continue the Installation

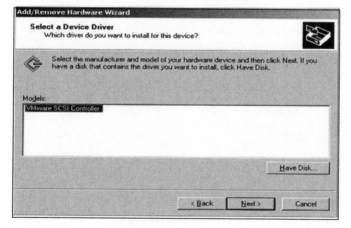

You then are asked to confirm that you want to install the VMware SCSI Controller. Click **Next** (see Figure 6.14).

Figure 6.14 Confirm the Installation

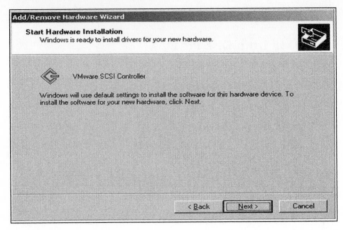

Windows might complain about it not being signed with a digital signature. Click **Yes** to continue (see Figure 6.15).

Figure 6.15 If Windows Complains, Click Yes to Continue the Installation

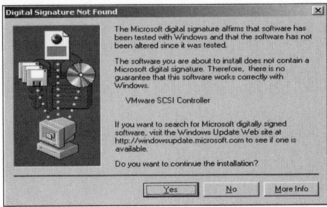

You're now done installing the vmscsi.sys driver (see Figure 6.16).

Figure 6.16 The Device Driver Is Installed

Afterward, you'll be asked if you want to reboot the server. Say No at this time.

If you're not sure if the vmscsi.sys driver is installed, you can right-click **My Computer**, go to Computer Management, and then click Device Manager (see Figure 6.17). You should see the VMSCSI Controller driver as a nonworking device. This is normal since you're not running a virtual machine yet.

Figure 6.17 The VMSCSI Controller Driver Is Seen as a Nonworking Device

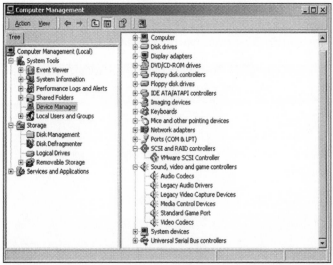

Installing the SCSI Driver in Windows NT

If you are doing a Windows NT P2V, then you need to use the built-in Buslogic SCSI driver from the Windows NT CD-ROM. You will probably need the Windows NT CD-ROM to do this.

Go to the Control Panel and select **SCSI Adapters** (see Figure 6.18).

Figure 6.18 Select SCSI Adapters

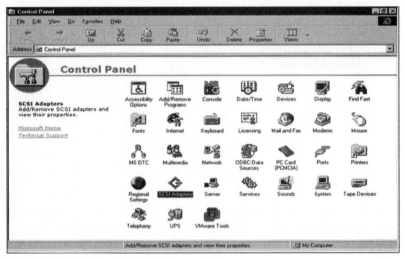

Add the new device. You want to select the **BusLogic MultiMaster PCI SCSI Host Adapters** (see Figure 6.19).

Figure 6.19 Choose the BusLogic MultiMaster PCI SCSI Host Adapters

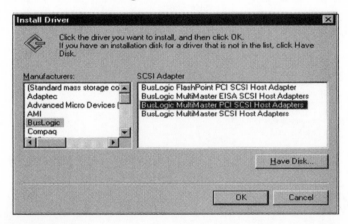

You have to add the ATAPI CD-ROM to the CD-ROM in the Control Panel, also. If you do not add the IDE CD-ROM driver now, and it is not installed, you will have difficulty installing the VMware Tools (see Figure 6.20).

Figure 6.20 Install the ATAPI CD-ROM

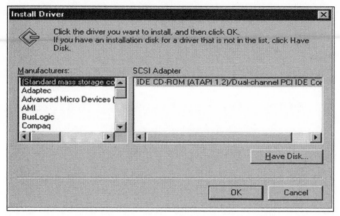

At this point the source server should be ready to go (see Figure 6.21). You may also have various other SCSI drivers installed. Leave these alone. Do not disable or remove any drivers at this time. Remember, cause no harm to your physical server.

Figure 6.21 The Two Adapters You Have Just Added Are Now Started

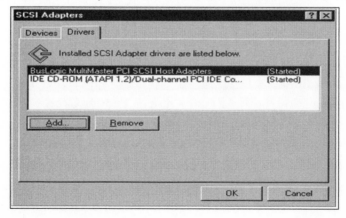

Once you have installed the BusLogic and the IDE CD-ROM drivers you will be asked to reboot. Do not reboot yet.

Continue Prepping the Source Machine: Validate

Once you have the correct SCSI driver installed in your physical machine, there are a few steps left to perform.

1. Run scandisk and make sure your drives have no problems. If you have scandisk errors, this can cause a problem in the new virtual machine.

2. Do not defrag at this time.

3. Note the existing network configuration.

4. Note the way the hard drives are lettered.

5. Note the drive letter of the CD-ROM drive.

Things to be concerned about:

If you are using Windows 2003 and employing the original build that came with your server, you might have to deal with Windows Licensing issues once you move it into a virtual machine. Be prepared with your License Key and the Microsoft Support phone number.

The Linux Rescue CD

Now that the source server has the VMware SCSI driver installed, we can reboot it using a Linux rescue cd and commence with the P2V.

Since we are working with ESX 2.x, we need to use a version of Linux boot CD with it that is binary-compatible. This is because we are going to use ncftpput from the ESX host. We've had good experience using the Fedora 3 Core rescue image or the Red Hat 9 disk 1. Fedora Core 4 is not binary-compatible with the ESX host, so you should download the Fedora Core 3 from http://download.fedora.redhat.com/pub/fedora/linux/core/3/. You can use disk 1 or the rescue image. Download this ISO and burn it to a CD using your favorite software. If you're going to do much older hardware, it's a good idea to burn the CD at a slow speed such as 4x. The Red Hat Linux 9 CD 1 can be downloaded from http://mirrors.kernel.org/redhat/redhat/linux/9/en/iso/i386/. Sometimes with really old hardware you need to use something older, like a Red Hat 7.2 CD.

Booting the Rescue CD

Put the Linux rescue CD into the CD-ROM drive and boot the physical source server from it. At the boot prompt, type **linux rescue** (see Figure 6.22). Unless you're using the FC3 rescue image, it will default to rescue mode.

Figure 6.22 To Enter the Rescue Mode, Press the Enter Key

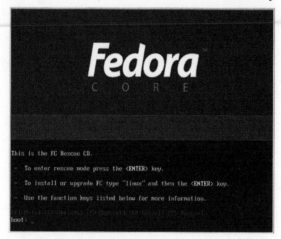

If you have screen issues, where the screen is unreadable after booting, you can try the no frame buffer option. To do so, type **linux rescue nofb**. The Linux kernel will start booting and will auto-detect the hardware.

The first question regards choosing your language. For our demonstration, we've chosen English (see Figure 6.23). At these Linux rescue prompts, you can click **OK** and continue by pressing the **F12** key.

Second question is choose the keyboard type, press **F12** to continue. Or choose your correct keyboard if it's different or nonstandard (see Figure 6.24).

Figure 6.23 Choose What Language You Will Use

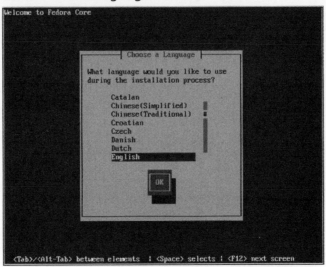

Figure 6.24 Choose Your Keyboard Type

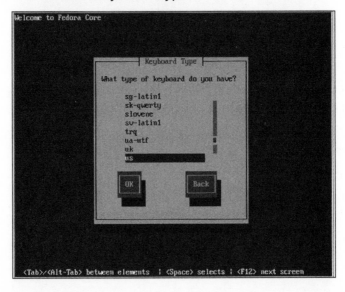

Third question is whether you want to start network services. You should choose **Yes** (see Figure 6.25), or just press **F12**.

Figure 6.25 Start Network Services

Set up and configure the first network card eth0. If you have DHCP enabled, choose it or enter the IP address. You should use the existing IP address of the physical server (see Figure 6.26).

Figure 6.26 Enable DHCP on the First Network Card eth0

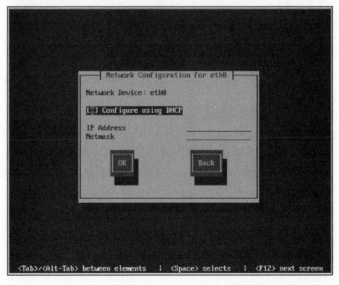

If you have more than one network card, it will ask you to configure them, too. If you do not use DHCP, you will also have to enter a default gateway and DNS servers. We usually just go by IP address. If our network doesn't seem to configure correctly, we'll take a look at it once rescue mode is booted.

Lastly, the rescue image will appear.

Choose **Skip**, which will give you a command-line prompt. Even if this is a Linux P2V, you should still choose **Skip** (see Figure 6.27).

Figure 6.27 Click the Skip Button to Get to the Command-Line Prompt

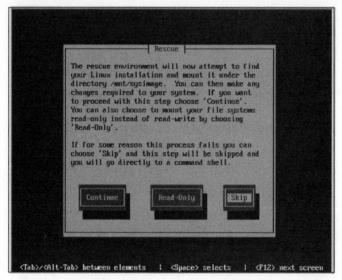

The other options will search for an existing Linux environment and try to mount it, as shown in Figure 6.28.

If you choose the Skip button, or if there are no Linux partitions to mount, you will be directed to a shell, as shown in Figure 6.29.

Figure 6.28 Other Options Will Try to Mount an Existing Linux Environment

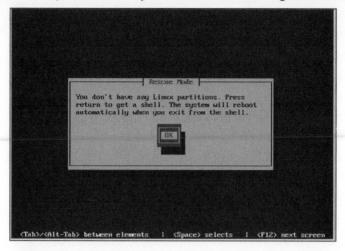

Figure 6.29 You're Now in the Shell

At the Command Prompt

Once you're at the command prompt, you want to make sure your networking is up and working. Try to ping your ESX host by name or IP address. If you did not enter a DNS server or used DHCP, then you will need to use the IP address instead.

If the network is not working, check the network configuration. Typing **ifconfig** will give you a list of your network adapters and their IP addresses. Sometimes with the rescue image it will default to using the highest numbered network adapter in your physical server, while you might be actually using the first one.

You can turn off a network card by typing **ifconfig eth0 down**.

This assumes we want to turn off eth0. If you want to rerun DHCP for an eth device, the command is **pump –i eth1**.

You can set the IP address manually by typing **ifconfig eth1** *xxx.xxx.xxx.xxx*. (For example: **ifconfig eth1 10.10.10.12**.)

This will default to a Class A address, but it should be okay. If your ESX host is not on the same segment as the source server, you will have to add a route to it. We're going to add the route for the ESX host directly, so type **route add <esx host IP> gw <default gateway IP>**. (For example: **route add 136.157.32.121 gw 10.10.10.1**.)

Try to ping your ESX host again. If you're able to ping it, we can move onto FTP. If you can't, then you're still having network problems. If you have more than one network adapter, try using the other one.

Remember, you can check the multiscreens and look for errors. By default, you're on screen 1, which is **Alt + F1**; screens **Alt + F3** and up show kernel output and possible error messages. Screen **Alt + F2** is another command line–like screen F1.

Next, you want to change directory to the /tmp folder (which is writable in the rescue image because it is a RAM drive) and download the contents of the p2v folder from the ESX host. To do so, type **cd /tmp**. Then type **ftp <ESX host IP>**.

You should be asked to log in to the FTP service. Log in as phd and make sure you can successfully connect. You should be in the phd home folder, which is /home/phd. By doing a **dir**, you should see the **p2v** folder. Change directory into the p2v folder by doing **cd p2v** and do a **dir** again. You should see the **ncftpput**, **mii-tool**, **phdcat**, and any other tools you put in this folder.

You'll want to get the contents of this folder. To get all programs, type **mget ***.

You will be prompted to confirm before each file. If you type **prompt** first, it will default to Yes for all files. For example, if you type:

prompt.
mget *.

FTP will transfer the files, placing them in the /tmp folder on your source machine. Remember, this is a RAM drive and does not touch the hard drives in the physical source server at all. *Do no harm!*

You need to make these programs you just downloaded executable by using the *chmod* command. You can *chmod* all the files in the /tmp folder because it's the easiest thing to do. So type **chmod 777 *.**

Now we can check the network connection and make sure we're running full duplex and that everything is the way it should be. By running **mii-tool**, you can check the speed and duplex of the network devices. If they are incorrect, you can change them by using mii-tool. To run mii-tool, you need to . / it. That again is dot slash and then the mii-tool. Or you could completely path the name /tmp/mii-tool. Type: **.**

/mii-tool.
or
./mii-tool –h

for the help and command options. The dot slash means to run the program from the current folder, which is /tmp. If our path was set up for /tmp, then this wouldn't be necessary. Once the network is all-good, we move onto the hard drives.

Finding the Hard Drives and Storage

Next, you need to find the hard drive devices, which are normally **/dev/sda** (/dev/sdb and so on). But some SCSI controllers do not use standard device names. This means most Compaq RAID cards and some other RAID cards such as Mylex are different from the norm. If you're going to P2V a SAN-attached drive, it should appear as a normal SCSI drive just like local attached storage.

By typing **fdisk −l**, you should get a list of all the known hard drive devices, which should look like the following example:

```
Disk /dev/sda: 41.9 GB, 41943040000 bytes
255 heads, 63 sectors/track, 5099 Cylinders
Units = cylinders of 16065 * 512 = 8225280 bytes

Device Boot    Start   End    Blocks       Id     System
/dev/sda1    *      1     5098    40949653+     7       HPFS/NTFS
```

If you have multiple hard drives, then they should all be listed. Compaq, HP, and other RAID controllers may not show when doing the **fdisk −l**. You will need to do the **fdisk −l** against the actual device name. For newer Compaq RAID controllers, try **fdisk −l /dev/ida/c0d0** (c = controller 0; d = drive 0); for older Compaqs, try **fdisk −l /dev/cciss/c0d0** (c = controller 0; d = drive 0).

For Mylex RAID cards, it would be **fdisk −l /dev/rd/c0d0** (c = controller 0; d = drive 0).

For Instant Disk, you are going to copy the whole hard drive, which means every sector, every byte, everything. Because Instant Disk copies the whole drive, the cylinders must be normal. If not, the partition boundaries will not line up and it won't work.

For the **/dev/sda** (or whatever drive), the cylinders must be **16065 * 512 = 8225280**. This is the same for IDE hard drives also since all IDEs should be this value. As mentioned previously, old Compaq computers using Smart Array 2/3s do not use standard cylinders. If your server has these values, then the Instant Disk methodology discussed in this chapter will not work for you. If your source server has dynamic disks or is using some form of software spanning or RAID, you can still use Instant Disk.

For example, your source server is an old NT server with three 4–gigabyte hard drives as a RAID 5. You just need to Instant Disk all the hard drives, and then add all three drives to the new virtual machine. It should work fine. Except that leaving it like this is not the best solution. However, once success-fully converted into a virtual machine, you can add another hard drive to it and use a Windows tool to copy the partition from the three-drive RAID 5 onto a normal basic single disk.

The greatest thing here is that you can P2V almost any server, then you can fix it, update it, and convert the hard drives. In fact, you can do anything you want to it.

Linux and Hardware

In Linux, hardware devices are accessed as if they were files. At least the ones we are going to deal with. Your first SCSI hard drive in Linux would be **/dev/sda**. The *a* means drive one, while *b*, as in /dev/sdb, would be drive 2, and so on. For IDE, it would be **/dev/hda** for your first drive.

By accessing this file, you access the hard drive at the hardware level, below the data and partitions. This allows you raw access to the drive. This is the fastest way to get data from the drive.

If you were to **cat /dev/sda**, you would get the raw dumping of that SCSI Hard drive. *Do not do this yet.*

The basic idea is that you **cat /dev/sda > newdisk.vmdk**, which means you are copying the raw hard drive (**/dev/sda**) and putting it into a file called **newdisk.vmdk**, except you're going to copy it across the network and write directly to the VMFS using FTP.

This newly created **newdisk.vmdk** is almost an ESX virtual disk file. The only difference between an ESX .vmdk (.dsk) file and a real hard drive image is a 512 record at the end of the file. This is how ESX knows the file is a virtual disk.

Virtual Disk Files on the VMFS

As mentioned before, there is little difference between a raw hard drive image and an ESX virtual disk file. (In Workstation and GSX, a pre-allocated virtual disk is the same as a raw hard drive, which is the same as an ESX virtual disk without the 512-byte record.)

Because of the format of an ESX virtual disk file, there is very little chance of corrupting a virtual disk (unlike Workstation or GSX) when using virtual cow disks or virtual hard drives split into pieces.

If you were to create a file on a VMFS file system and add the 512-byte record to the end it, it would be a valid ESX virtual disk file.

The following is a little exercise to show you how this works and how ESX manages the VMFS.

Create a small empty virtual disk file. You must path the complete file name. To do so, type **vmkfstools –c 1m /vmfs/LOCAL/test.vmdk**.

This will create an empty 1-megabyte virtual disk file named **test.vmdk**. Change directory to your VMFS file system and do an **ll** (ls –l). You should see the newly created virtual disk file. (For our example, this is **cd /vmfs/LOCAL**.) Then, type **ll**.

You should see output similar to that shown next:

```
-rw------    1    root   root   1049088      Jan 12 23:41 test.vmdk
```

The new virtual disk file you created has a size of 1,049,088 bytes. You created this file as 1 megabyte in size—that is, 1024 ? 1024 bytes = 1,048,576. If we add the 512 bytes—1,048,576 + 512 = 1,049,088—you get the same file size as the newly created file.

If you look at the last 2000 bytes of this file you will see a lot of NULLs and the VMware 512-byte record. Type **tail –c 2000 test.vmdk | cat –vet**.

The **cat –vet** will show us binary characters in a readable format. Notice all the ^@ (NULLS), and then some text that says "This is a VMware ESX server disk image." Those last 512 characters at the end are the VMware ESX 512-byte record. Not a lot of data in it.

Now if you were to echo some text on to the end of this file **test.vmdk**, ESX would know about it and re-add the 512-byte record to keep it as a valid virtual disk file. Once a file is a valid disk, ESX will try and keep it a valid disk. Let's do this. Type **echo THIS IS A TEST OF INSTANT DISK >> test.vmdk**.

The ">>," which is a greater than–greater than sign, means to append data onto the end of the file. Now, if you tail and cat the file again, you will see the original VMware record, followed by the message you echoed, followed again by a new VMware record at the end.

Before we start the FTP process, we need to create an empty virtual disk file in your VMFS that will be the virtual disk drive. By creating a valid disk file first, then FTPing on top of it, the file will remain a valid virtual disk. Because ESX does this for us, you can do an Instant Disk P2V almost anywhere without any special software.

Create a new virtual disk that will represent your physical source server. Our source drive is 40gig, so let's create an empty 40gig drive. You could create a 1M empty virtual drive, but creating it the same size as your physical source server is a good idea since you can make sure you have enough space to create it. Type **vmkfstools –c 40G /vmfs/LOCAL/newdisk.vmdk**.

Now that you created an empty virtual disk called **newdisk.vmdk**, you just have to make sure you use the same name when you FTP the source hard drive.

> **NOTE**
>
> If you copied your source hard drive to a local drive or USB drive instead, you can still use the tool from our Web site to convert the file into a valid virtual disk after you copy the file to the VMFS. Read about USB and other methods in the last few pages of this chapter.

Starting the FTP Process

Now we're going to FTP the raw hard drive into your VMFS on your ESX host and create an Instant Disk. If you have the phdcat program, use it instead of cat in the following command. It will give you the amount of data copied and the average speed. Without it, you get no feedback on the source server side.

Type:

cat /dev/sda | /tmp/ncftpput –u <username> -p <password> –c <remote esx host ip> <Full /vmfs
path and new file name>

For example:

cat /dev/sda | /tmp/ncftpput –u phdbot –p "p2v" –c 10.10.10.1 /vmfs/LOCAL/newdisk.vmdk.

With phdcat: **phdcat /dev/sda | /tmp/ncftpput –u phdbot –p
"p2v" –c 10.10.10.1
/vmfs/LOCAL/newdisk.vmdk**

If it is working, you won't see anything until it is done, but you can go check out your /vmfs/LOCAL on the ESX host and watch the newdisk.vmdk grow bigger.

If you are using phdcat, then you are getting a speed and total amount of data copied. You will see total megabytes copied and average megabytes per second. If you are on a 100MB network, the max wire speed will be 11MB a second. If you are on gigabit, you can see speeds much higher, getting 25MB to 35MB a second.

By pushing hard drive images to your ESX host, you can really test out your network performance. If you are getting 1MB/sec or less, then you are running at 10mb or running half duplex on 100mb. Or you're copying data from a really old server.

This speed is dependent on the physical source hard drive speed and your network speed. We say this is the fastest method for copying images because it reads the hard drive sequentially, block by block, as fast as it can go.

When using other P2V methods by other vendors to copy the data, they claim they are faster because they only copy the data and not the empty space. But this is not totally true. These other methods open the file system on the physical source server and proceed to copy all the files, one by one. For each and every file on your source server, the hard drive needs to seek and read each file. This can be incredibly slow when you have thousands of files.

If you are getting 10MB/sec (not bits), which means you are copying 10MB of real data each second, that is 30+ gigabytes an hour. You can run multiple Instant Disk conversions at the same time and you can really flex your network. But if you are going to do multiple conversions, only write to one VMFS file system at a time. If you have two conversions going to the same VMFS, it will be slower and it will fragment the virtual disk files on the VMFS as the new virtual VMDK files are being created.

After the FTP process is completed, you need to make a new virtual machine using the newly created virtual disk file as a preexisting disk.

Master Craftsman…

Instead of Using FTP

Besides using FTP to push the source hard drive image to the ESX host, you can copy the hard drives to another local drive or to a local USB drive.

Why would you do this? Suppose you have a remote location, you can have them attach an external USB drive and walk them through copying the hard drives to the USB drive. Then they mail you the USB drive, and you FTP the images to the ESX host server using Instant Disk.

If you're going to use a USB drive, then you have to use a Linux Rescue image that uses the 2.6 kernel, like the Fedora Core 4 rescue image. If not, by using regular USB, the speed is too slow, topping out at 1MB/sec if you're lucky. Using the FC4 rescue CD and a USB drive, you can achieve speeds like 25MB/sec.

You can literally go onsite with a laptop and an external USB drive and image lots of machines, and then come back to your data center and fire up some virtual machines.

Creating a New Virtual Machine and Pointing It to a New VMDK File

It's time now to create the new virtual machine. Here, too, there are a few items you need to make sure you have under control to insure a positive outcome.

Windows VMs

If you are creating a Windows 2003+ machine that normally uses the *lsibuslogic* SCSI driver, you must change it back to the *buslogic* in the configuration. You can always add it back later after the lsi fuson (lsibuslogic) driver has been loaded into the virtual server.

Remember to change the Network Adapter to the **vmxnet** instead of the *vlance* when you create the virtual machine (unless it is a NT4 virtual). Also, before you boot the virtual machine the first time, it's best to put the newly created virtual drive into UNDOABLE mode since it's quicker to commit all your changes than to re-FTP the physical hard drive again if something goes wrong.

When booting Windows 2003+, it may appear to hang for a while. This is normal for the first boot. If it really hangs, just power it off, and then back on.

NOTE

If you're using newer versions of Windows that require activation, they will need to be reactivated after you bring them up as a virtual machine. Be aware of your licensing and Microsoft product codes when starting.

After the virtual machine comes up, you should be able to log in and install VMware Tools. As a prerequisite, the admin password is needed.

After you log in, Windows will continue to redetect hardware and make changes. Keep hitting Yes or Continue. Afterwards, install VMware Tools and you can start some cleanup.

You usually do not have to remove the old devices except for the old network cards. It won't matter if you leave them in, but when you assign the same IP address to the new VMware NIC, it will warn you about it being the same as a disabled NIC. Plus, by leaving the old hardware drivers installed, you can always do a V2P (virtual to physical) conversion.

To remove unused hardware in Windows 2000, go to the Control Panel, select Add/Remove Hardware, choose Remove, then Show Hidden, and delete the old hardware.

In Windows 2003+, they changed it. However, even though it looks more detailed, it's actually quicker and easier. You'll need to open a **cmd** prompt.

Type **set devmgr_show_nonpresent_devices=1**. Then, type **devmgmt.msc**.

Now choose **Show Hidden** from the menu and you should see your hidden hardware. Delete what you want. Since you already installed VMware

Tools, you also will see a duplicate vmscsi.sys driver that's not being used. Delete it also.

Post-P2V

Finally, there are a few tasks you should deal with after completing the P2V process. While not a complete list, these tasks might include the following:

- Scandisk
- Defrag
- ZeroFill
- Install the VMware Tools
- Remove any legacy hardware drivers
- Disable legacy services
- NT hal.dll and kernels
- Enable automatic updates on NT
- Determine DSK per drive
- Move/resize any partitions needed
- Resize any drives/dsk

Summary

Hopefully, you are now on the way to virtualizing your server farm after completing this chapter. P2P is a vital and necessary component of your virtualization infrastructure.

## Chapter 7

Scripting Hot Backups and Recovery for Virtual Machines

Topics in this chapter:

- Anatomy of a VM Backup
- Existing VM Backup Tools
- VMX Backups
- Backup and Restore Methodology

Introduction

You probably picked up this book because you need to automate some functions in your virtual infrastructure. Scripting is all about automating our menial tasks. And no menial task begs for automation more than regular backups. Fortunately, VMware provides a rich platform for effective backup and restore solutions that can be controlled through scripts. In this chapter, we will exploit the functionality provided by VMware ESX Server to perform hot (that is, live, while VM is running) backups of our virtual machines. We'll show how to back up the data files and config files. In addition, we'll veer a bit out of the command line and into some consultative topics. We'll discuss the whys and hows of recovery planning for a virtual infrastructure. This will help you decide how you should implement a solution using the scripts and technologies presented in this chapter.

Anatomy of a VM Backup

Before getting into details, it is important to briefly discuss the fundamentals of a VM backup. The feature of virtualization that enables disaster recovery backup is encapsulation. In the VMware ESX world, this is the virtual hard disk, or VMDK. A VMDK file contains the entire contents of a hard disk, the partitions, boot sector, files, everything. A VMDK takes the thousands of files involved in a typical OS and bundles them all together in one VMDK file. We have the ability to create a copy of a VMDK and use this as a complete backup, then treat the backup as we would any file, choosing where to store the file and for how long.

For the purposes of this chapter, we will assume that a VMDK stored on a VMFS volume is a type 2 file, and an exported VMDK is type 1. They are the only file types supported by ESX 2.x. For review, a type 2 file is a preallocated virtual disk, and type 1 is a growable virtual disk split into 2GB files.

Because the data inside a live VMDK file may be constantly changing, simply making a copy of a VMDK file will result in corruption without some additional technology. Now it is not practical for most organizations to power off a virtual machine prior to backup. Instead a REDO log may be placed on the VMDK file prior to making a copy. The VMDK is placed in append mode, and all changes are written to an alternate file. The REDO log file has the extension .REDO.

Let's walk through a visual representation of the high-level backup process referencing native tools shipped with ESX to perform the operation. Figure 7.1 is a virtual machine in its simplest form. A VMX file references a single VMDK file on a VMFS volume.

Figure 7.1 Normal State, Persistent Disk

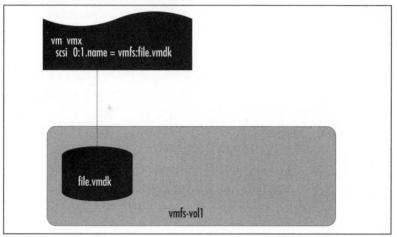

The first step of the process is to create a REDO log on the VMDK. The command *vmware-cmd* provides a quick and easy way to create a REDO log (see Figure 7.2):

```
vmware-cmd /home/vmware/vm/vm.vmx addredo scsi0:1
```

Figure 7.2 REDO Is Applied to the VMDK

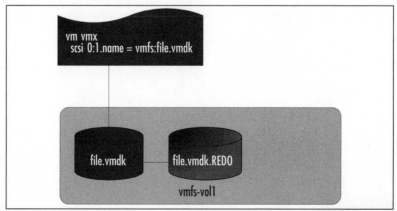

vmware-cmd is a command-line tool that ships with ESX and is for managing virtual machines. We are using one of many functions in this tool, addredo. The only argument to this function is the SCSI address of the VMDK in question. The command refers to the logical SCSI ID assigned to the disk file of the virtual machine, found in the VMX file. Don't confuse this SCSI ID with the physical SCSI ID of your hard disks or SAN LUNs. A number of ways exist to find the SCSI address, including Virtual Center, MUI, or the VMX. This command shows all SCSI lines in the VMX; only devices with the present flag set to TRUE are really there:

```
grep scsi /home/vmware/vm/vm.vmx
```

At this point, changes are being made to the REDO and the VMDK is static. You may now safely make a copy of this file. To keep things simple, we will export this VMDK to an ext3 filesystem (see Figure 7.3). Backup target options are discussed in more detail later in the chapter. The syntax of this command is a bit different than you might expect: vmkfstools −e <target> <source>. The result is a file on the ext3 /vmimages volume in a type 3 format.

```
vmkfstools -e /vmimages/file.vmdk /vmfs/vmfs-vol1/file.vmdk
```

Figure 7.3 VMDK Is Exported

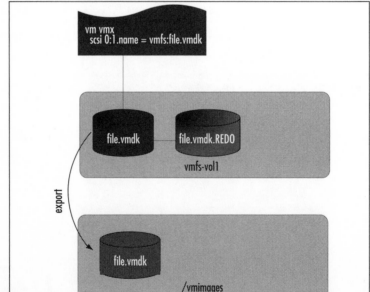

After the export is complete, your next step is to put things back into a normal operating state. This means applying all changes stored in the REDO file back to the VMDK file (see Figure 7.4). Again, *vmware-cmd* is the simplest tool to use.

```
vmware-cmd /home/vmware/vm/vm.vmx commit scsi0:1 0 1 1
```

Figure 7.4 REDO Is Committed

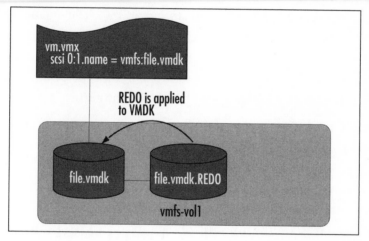

The syntax of this command is

```
vmware-cmd <cfg> commit <disk_device_name> <level> <freeze> <wait>
```

<level> only applies when you have more than one REDO. Actual usage of this option is covered in the "Layered REDO Logs" section of this chapter.

<freeze> is ignored and a freeze 0 is used unless <level> is 1.

<wait> 0 returns when commit begins; 1 returns after the commit is completed.

Limitations

It is important to discuss some of the limitations of this type of backup. The limitations include

- **Crash Consistent State** The most important thing to understand is that once a REDO log is placed on the disk file, the disk file is now in a crash consistent state. The guest operating system is not aware that this has happened. It is as reliable as pressing the power button on the machine, or crash consistent.

- **File-Level Recovery Challenges** Another limitation of this type of backup is the fact that doing a file-level restore can take a significant amount of time. The entire disk file must be restored and mounted somewhere before you can copy off the file in question. This is a function better left to an agent running inside the guest that is intended as a file-level recovery agent. File-level agents will also help with indexing, versioning and searching. If you must pursue a file-level restore without an agent, the VMware Diskmount utility is your friend. It will save you a significant amount of time mounting VMDK files and looking for the file in question.

- **Wall-Clock Time** We are talking about a significant amount of data here. Depending on the size of the environment, it may not be practical to copy entire VMDK files around on a regular basis. As your environment grows, you may be looking at a lack of wall clock time to accomplish your backups. Factors that will effect the time your backup takes are the amount of data inside a VMDK, the speed of the disk subsystem, available resources in the service console, and the type of transport used to move the backup data.

- **Performance Considerations** There are performance considerations when running with a REDO log. The REDO file grows 16MB at a time. Each file growth requires a SCSI reservation on the LUN. Also, the REDO log needs to be committed after you have a copy of the file. This will rewrite all changes back to the VMDK file. All of this activity requires CPU from the ESX service console and increases activity on the disk subsystem. Resources in the service console are generally limited to 1 CPU, < 1GB RAM, 1 NIC, and 1 SCSI/RAID device. Considering that this represents a fairly underpowered server, you will run into limitations when trying to do multiple concurrent backups. The available resources will likely limit you to 2–4 concurrent backups before the service console becomes too overloaded. Overloading the service console is very risky. If the service console crashes, so does the ESX server and all the VMs running on it. Use caution, test, and fall on the side of conservatism when planning how many backups to do at once.

- **Frozen Disk Files** While the REDO log is being applied to the VMDK file, the disk is frozen, meaning I/O is halted. If the REDO is small, application of the REDO log is relatively quick. If you have been running with a REDO for some time, this frozen state may cause problems. The suggested way to approach this situation is to use a second REDO log on the VMDK, while the first is being applied. The method for applying this strategy is covered next.

Layered REDO Logs

As mentioned, while the REDO log is being applied (committed), I/O to the VMDK is frozen. If your REDO file is large enough, users and applications will experience some problems due to the amount of time this takes. A common technique used to mitigate the risk of the commit taking too long is to use two REDO files. The freeze is only necessary while applying the last REDO log. As we pick up the previous walk-though of a backup, we will replace the final commit step with a slightly different process.

First, we add a second REDO log right after our export is completed. The syntax to add this second REDO is exactly like the first (see Figure 7.5):

```
vmware-cmd /home/vmware/vm/vm.vmx addredo scsi0:1
```

Figure 7.5 Second REDO Created

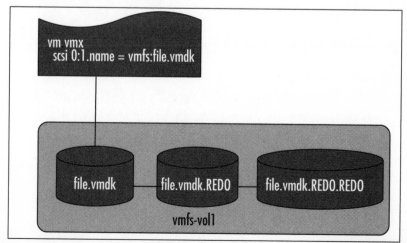

At this point, all transactions are written to the REDO.REDO file. We can commit the first REDO log to the VMDK using the following command.

```
vmware-cmd /home/vmware/vm/vm.vmx commit scsi0:1 1 0 1
```

We give the commit command the following options:

- **<level> = 1** This tells ESX to only commit one of the two REDO logs.

- **<freeze> = 0** We will not freeze I/O to the VMDK while the commit is running.

- **<wait> = 1** Wait for the commit to complete before returning.

As seen in Figure 7.6, we are now in a familiar state with one REDO on the VMDK, except this one is hopefully smaller than the first.

Figure 7.6 First REDO Has Been Applied

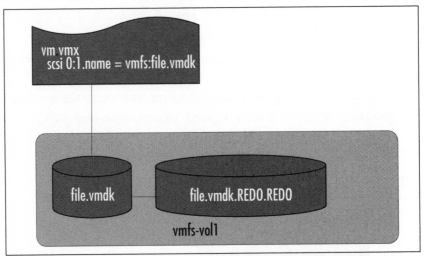

Finally, we will commit the remaining REDO file. Regardless of the freeze option chosen, we are now going to freeze the VMDK.

```
vmware-cmd /home/vmware/vm/vm.vmx commit scsi0:1 0 0 1
```

When complete, this command will leave you as you started. One VMDK and no REDO files (see Figure 7.7).

Figure 7.7 Backup Is Complete; Back to the Normal Operating State

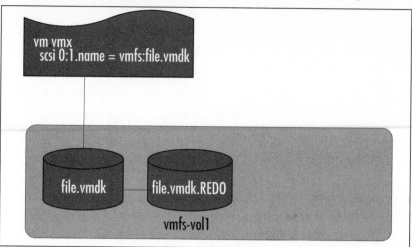

Master Craftsman…

Detecting the Current Mode for a VM Disk

Before you start adding and committing REDO log files to running virtual machines, you need to know what state the current disk file is in. You want to be sure a disk file is in Persistent mode before going to work on starting a hot backup. We've included some code as part of this Master Craftsman tip that you can use to determine the current mode of your disk file.

```perl
#!/usr/bin/perl -w
#
# This script is an example only
# Usage: detectDiskMode.pl <vmxConfigFile> <scsiDisk>
#
# Example: detectDiskMode.pl /home/vmware/vm/vm.vmx scsi0:1

use VMware::VmPerl;
use VMware::VmPerl::ConnectParams;
use VMware::VmPerl::VM;
```

Continued

```
use strict;

# User variables
my ($cfg, $disk) = @ARGV;

# Connect to the virtual machine
my $params = VMware::VmPerl::ConnectParams::new();
my $vm = VMware::VmPerl::VM::new();
$vm->connect($params, $cfg);

# Retrieve the mode of the disk in question
my $mode = $vm->get_config("$disk.mode");

if ($mode ne "persistent") {
  print "Warning: $mode\n";
} else {
  print "$mode\n";
} # End if not persistent

$vm->disconnect();
```

Hot VM Backup Sample Script

Using the preceding information, you could put together a quick shell script
to run a hot backup. Now, we can pull together all of the concepts shown
earlier, except we'll use Perl as the scripting language this time. The following
script does exactly what was discussed previously, but processes all disk files
for the VM in order. This script has the following objectives:

- The only command-line option is to provide the path to the virtual
  machine VMX file (required).

- Script will find all VMDK files attached to the virtual machine.

- Process each VMDK, one at a time.

- Apply a REDO log to the VMDK.

- Vmkfstools export on the VMDK.

- Apply a second REDO log.

- Commit the first REDO log.

- Commit the final REDO log.

This script shown in Code Listing 7.1 is an example only and should not be used in a production environment. It lacks user feedback and error checking/reporting.

Code Listing 7.1 Perl Script for Running a Hot Backup of a VM

```perl
#!/usr/bin/perl -w
#
# This script is an example only
# Usage: simpleBackup.pl <vmxPath>

use VMware::VmPerl;
use VMware::VmPerl::Server;
use VMware::VmPerl::ConnectParams;
use VMware::VmPerl::VM;
use strict;

# User variables
my $target="/vmimages";
my $cfg=$ARGV[0];
print "$cfg\n";

# Set up a connection to a virtual machine
my $params = VMware::VmPerl::ConnectParams::new();
my $vm = VMware::VmPerl::VM::new();
$vm->connect($params, $cfg);

# No smooth way to return the number of scsi controllers
# We will cycle through all possibilities checking if it is present
for (my $scsiController=0; $scsiController<=3; $scsiController++) {
  my $presentScsiController = $vm->get_config("scsi$scsiController.present");

  # If it is there, we will continue processing
```

```
    if ($presentScsiController eq "true") {

        # Again, cycle through all possible scsi IDs
        for (my $scsiID=0; $scsiID<=15; $scsiID++) {
          my $presentScsiID = $vm-
>get_config("scsi$scsiController:$scsiID.present");
            if ($presentScsiID eq "true") {
              # Get the path to the vmdk
              my $vmdk = $vm->get_config("scsi$scsiController:$scsiID.name");

              # $vmdk format is now vmfsvol:vmdk
              # Let's break this up into 2 variables
              my ($vmfsvol,$vmdkname) = split (':',$vmdk);
              my $vmdkPath = "/vmfs/$vmfsvol/$vmdkname";

              # Add the first redo
              $vm->add_redo("scsi$scsiController:$scsiID");

              # Do a backup
              `/usr/sbin/vmkfstools -e /$target/$vmdkname $vmdkPath`;

              # Add a second redo
              $vm->add_redo("scsi$scsiController:$scsiID");

              # Wait a second for the redo to be created
              sleep(1);

              # First commit with same options as vmware-cmd
              $vm->commit("scsi$scsiController:$scsiID", 1, 0, 1);

              # Commit final redo
              $vm->commit("scsi$scsiController:$scsiID", 0, 0, 1);
            } # End If SCSI ID is present
        } # End for SCSI ID Cycle
    } # End If SCSI Controller is present
} # End for SCSI Controller Cycle

# Cleanup
$vm->disconnect();
```

Master Craftsman...

Answer VM Questions from a Script

After some events occur, VMware ESX Server won't continue until you answer a question. ESX requires your answer to the question before the process can resume. For example, if you accidentally try to add a third REDO log, a question is generated. This question has only one answer, OK. Once you answer the question, the process resumes.

The problem here is that your scripts need to be able to answer these questions as they come up. Otherwise, your script will pause indefinitely. The following code can be used in your scripts to answer single option questions. You could also easily modify the script to answer more difficult questions.

```perl
#!/usr/bin/perl -w
#
# This script is an example only
# Usage: detectQuestion.pl <vmxConfigFile>
#


use VMware::VmPerl;
use VMware::VmPerl::ConnectParams;
use VMware::VmPerl::VM;
use VMware::VmPerl::Question;
use strict;


# User variables
my ($cfg) = @ARGV;


# Connect to the virtual machine
my $params = VMware::VmPerl::ConnectParams::new();
my $vm = VMware::VmPerl::VM::new();
$vm->connect($params, $cfg);
```

Continued

```perl
# Check for a question. Will return undef if
# no questions.
my $question = $vm->get_pending_question();


# If $question is defined, there is an outstanding question
if (defined $question) {
  my $text = $question->get_text();
  my @choices = $question->get_choices();
  if ($#choices == 0) {
    # There is only one choice, easy to answer it
    $vm->answer_question($question,0);
    print "Question answered: $text\n";
  } else {
    print "More than one choice.\n";
    print "Choices: @choices\n";
  } # End if only one choice
} else {
  print "No Questions\n";
} # Endif


# Cleanup
$vm->disconnect();
```

Choosing the Target for VM Backups

At some point, when writing your backup script, you'll need to decide where
your backups will go. You'll also need to decide how to get them there. In
most cases, you'll choose some type of mass storage device, like a file server, a
NAS device, or a SAN array as the target to store your backups. How you get
those backups to the chosen target can vary greatly. Considering that the
VMware ESX service console is running a modified version of Red Hat
Linux, there are a plethora of options available as to where you may target
your VM backups. Some protocols copy faster data than others. Some are
simpler to use in scripting. Some integrate better with your chosen storage

target. We'll cover some of the available options and provide some recommendations on when to use each.

In this section, we'll address the transports available for backups and discuss where the data will be stored. We won't address specific storage types, such as specific SAN arrays or NAS providers. We'll talk about these in more general terms. Since we're more concerned here about the transport protocols used to get your backups from ESX to your target storage.

Some of the more common and popular ways of moving backup data are NFS, CIFS, FTP, and copies to VMFS. We'll define each of them here, and then discuss the benefits of each in turn. Each of the following methods is listed in our order of preference. Consider these options when deciding what will be best for your scripting needs.

NFS

Network File System (NFS) is a common file sharing protocol used mainly in UNIX and Linux environments. It could be considered the standard file sharing protocol for *NIX systems. NFS works by exporting a file system from one machine and making it available to the network. Other systems use an NFS client to mount the exported file system at a mount point on their local file system. The exported file system is then accessible from the mount point as if it were part of the local file system.

NFS is a fairly simple way to share, or export, a file system from one machine and access it from another. Generally, we like NFS for facilitating all file sharing from the ESX service console, especially for VM backups. NFS is fast, native to the service console, and simple to use in scripts.

Attributes of NFS for VM Backups

In this section, we'll discuss the pros and cons of using NFS for VM backups.

Pros

The pros of using NFS for backups include:

- NFS doesn't require authentication, so you don't have to code in usernames and passwords.
- NFS is very fast over Gigabit Ethernet networks.

- NFS is usually an available option on a NAS device.

- NFS exports mounts directly into the file system on mount points. Very easy to copy data back and forth using native copy commands like *cp* and *vmkfstools*.

Cons

The cons of using NFS for backups include:

- NFS does not have any native support in Windows. Requires Services for UNIX. Not recommended.

- NFS is not as secure as other options, due to lack of authentication and data encryption.

CIFS

Common Internet File System (CIFS) is a standard implementation of the SMB (Server Message Block) protocol largely developed by Microsoft. It is essentially the base protocol that Windows uses to copy data between systems. Windows file servers and many NAS devices use CIFS as the protocol to authenticate and transfer data.

Linux uses an open-source implementation called SAMBA to interact with CIFS servers. In order to copy data to a Windows share, you'll need to install the SAMBA client on your ESX service console. CIFS is second on our list of transports because it is a more complicated implementation than NFS. It needs authentication and sometimes requires a two-step process to copy a VM.

Attributes of CIFS for VM Backups

Now we'll discuss the pros and cons of using CIFS for VM backups.

Pros

The pros of using CIFS for VM backups include:

- CIFS is easy to integrate into a Windows sharing environment.

- CIFS is commonly the preferred, or only, protocol supported on an NAS device.

- CIFS can be mounted, via SAMBA, to a local mount point.

Cons

The cons of using CIFS for VM backups include:

- CIFS is more difficult to configure in the service console.

- CIFS requires SAMBA installation and configuration.

- SAMBA has been less stable than NFS in our experience.

- CIFS is not as fast as NFS over GigE.

- CIFS is a very chatty protocol, which decreases performance over latent connections.

FTP

File Transport Protocol (FTP) is a very common protocol for copying data over a network. It is a standards-based protocol that is supported on nearly every modern computing platform. FTP is useful for copying backups to a file server. It is natively supported on the ESX service console. It is pretty easily scripted and has a substantial amount of reference resources available on the Internet.

Attributes of FTP for VM Backups

In this section we'll weigh the pros and cons of using FTP for VM backups.

Pros

The pros of using FTP for VM backups include:

- FTP servers are common and supported natively on most servers.

- FTP copies data quickly over a noncongested network.

Cons

The cons of using FTP for VM backups include:

- FTP often requires a server platform as a target since many NAS devices do not support it natively.

- FTP takes all available bandwidth it can for copying. It may step on other network traffic.

- FTP does not have the capability to mount on the local file system.

- FTP generally requires authentication, but without certificates it sends usernames and passwords in clear text.

- FTP passwords must be coded into your scripts. This is insecure and will break the script if accounts and passwords change.

VMFS

VMware File System (VMFS) is the file system used for virtual machine disk file storage in VMware ESX server. It is a distributed file system, which means it can be accessed by multiple ESX servers at the same time and not corrupt any data. VMFS locks individual files rather than entire volumes. This means many ESX servers can access files from the same VMFS volumes without any trouble.

The nature of VMFS makes it an attractive target for VM backups. A VMFS volume can be designated as a backup target and shared across all of your ESX servers. This way, backups can be directed straight from the source VMFS to the target backup VMFS volume. Since the .vmdk file format doesn't need to change when moving from VMFS to VMFS, you can copy the .vmdk files directly. This simplifies the scripting required to move data around.

Don't be too easily lulled into using VMFS as your backup target. Generally, we prefer to use non-VMFS targets for VM backups. VMFS isn't a good file system for sharing files (for example, there is no support for directories), it only supports a maximum of 192 files, and it has SCSI reservation issues when copying large amounts of data. You're better off using one of the methods discussed earlier for a permanent solution for backup targets.

Attributes of Copies to VMFS for VM Backups

Now we'll discuss the pros and cons of using copies to VMFS for VM backups.

Pros

The pros of using copies to VMFS for VM backups include

- Sharing VMFS volumes between ESX servers is easy.

- Scripting syntax is fairly simple and doesn't require additional mounts or connection syntax as FTP or CIFS might.

- VMFS is often stored on SAN LUNs, which can help facilitate a larger backup strategy. (For example, back up to VMFS, then take a snapshot and/or replicate the SAN LUN.)

Cons

The cons of using copies to VMFS for VM backups include:

- VMFS doesn't scale well in large environments. It's not practical to attach a VMFS to more than 16 ESX servers. You can run into contention issues and SCSI reservation problems when performing a large number of simultaneous backups to a single VMFS.

- VMFS was designed to host large VM disk files, not be a file server.

- VMFS has no support for a directory structure. Organizing backup files in a sensible way is difficult.

- There are limits to the number of files that can be stored in a VMFS volume. Each VMFS extent can hold 192 files. Most often you'll only have one extent, and are therefore limited to 192 total files in the VMFS. This is a big inhibitor for doing a large-scale backup solution with a VMFS target.

TIP

Never use the *cp* command when copying .vmdk files. Always use *vmkfs-tools*. An undocumented, but useful switch for *vmkfstools* copies a .vmdk in one command and is very fast. This method exports and imports the VMFS in one step. The syntax is as follows:

```
vmkfstools -e /vmfs/vmfsname/target.vmdk -d vmfs /vmfs/vmfs-
name/source.vmdk
```

If you're going to use VMFS for backup storage, dedicate an LUN to it. Don't combine active VMs on the same VMFS that you're using for backups. You could run into major performance problems due to the large amount of SCSI reservations that can occur on the VMFS volume during copies. These locks, if frequent enough, will be noticed by your VMs and can cause undesirable results.

Existing VM Backup Tools

Now that you know the basics of a hot backup, we hope that you do not set out to write your own backup application without checking out some existing applications. There are many options, both free and commercial, that cover the full spectrum of price and support. Before you sit down and reinvent the wheel, check out some of the wheels that have been created before. We'll go into detail about some affordable (free) options and provide guidance on where to look for commercial solutions.

vmsnap.pl, *vmsnap_all*, and *vmres.pl*

VMware ESX 2.x ships with three scripts that work together to create a backup system. *vmsnap.pl* will back up a single virtual machine, while *vmsnap_all.pl* will call *vmsnap.pl* for all virtual machines on the host. *vmres.pl* is the restore portion. The three tools are fully supported by VMware with no additional charges other than the original ESX licensing.

vmsnap.pl has basically the same logic as the simple sample we went through in the beginning of the chapter. It will manage the REDO log process for you and copies VMDK files using a *vmkfstools* export. It will also back up your VMX, nvram, and virtual machine log files. The script also handles logging, local or remote. The output destination options include local filesystem and ssh. VMware refers to the ssh destination as an archive server in the documentation.

vmsnap_all.pl is essentially identical to *vmsnap.pl* in functionality, except that it will back up all VMs on an ESX server.

This application has some downsides, however. It does not natively support keeping multiple versions, and will even overwrite files by default. If you have a requirement to keep more than one version of a backup, you need to apply additional scripting and sweep up the output files using a different backup system on a regular basis. Also, *vmsnap.pl* is missing file compression capabilities.

> **TIP**
>
> The three native scripts, *vmsnap.pl*, *vmsnap_all*, and *vmres.pl*, are a good place to start for ideas to apply towards your own scripts. They expose many ESX functions that are useful for other purposes.

vmbk.pl

We have to make mention of *vmbk.pl* in this text. Considering that this Perl script is made freely available by Massimiliano Daneri, and it has a broad range of fantastic features and functionality, we feel obliged to promote his efforts and provide a link to his Web site. You can find the scripts and information at www.vmts.net/.

Basically, *vmbk.pl* employs many of the functions we've described in this chapter. It uses Perl as the scripting engine (our personal favorite). Its main function is to perform hot VM backups. It adds .REDO logs to running VMs and exports the .vmdk files using *vmkfstools*. It grabs the VM config files, .VMX and CMOS files, then facilitates the transfer of the backup files via NFS, CIFS, FTP, or through Veritas NetBackup to a backup target—for example, NAS, SAN, or tape. At that point, it commits the .REDO log files back to the running VM.

vmbk.pl is a good option to consider as a script, given that you can immediately start using it for backups. It also provides a great place to start if you're looking to incorporate some of these features we've discussed into scripts of your own.

Commercial Options

Many commercial options are available that perform VM backups in various ways. Thus, the following reasons should be considered when deciding whether to use a commercial product versus writing your own scripts:

- You don't have to write your own application. This can save a tremendous amount of time and/or money.

- They carry support contracts. If things break, you have a professional to call. It also helps you keep your job if you have a real disaster.

- The vendors are generally continuing to add features and functions that will make your life easier.

- Scripted solutions generally require significant knowledge of the Linux shell. If your staff is not comfortable here, a Windows GUI option, provided commercially, will make life easier for your admins.

If you're interested in looking at a few options, consider some that we have worked with and feel have good approaches and appropriate pricing models:

- Vizioncore esxRanger
  www.vizioncore.com/esxrangerPro.html

- esXpress
  www.esxpress.com/

Swiss Army Knife...

Using Backup Technologies for Other Purposes

In the new world of virtualization, users are continuing to come up with unique uses for the technology. One idea discovered in the field is using backup technologies as version control tools for the support and development of software products. This is a rather simple but useful technique for the software development community.

The idea is that as your software goes through its various versions, an archive backup is written to a file system and stored with the version number referenced in the description. This can be simply one VM, or a complicated multitier environment. When a customer calls looking for help with an old version of your software, you can restore the complete environment to an alternate virtual infrastructure. Use this duplicate version to facilitate re-creating and solving the problem. In the physical world, this would be a large and possibly expensive task due to the amount of hardware required. In the virtual world, you can do this entirely from your desk or couch with a minimal amount of hardware.

VMX File Backups

Thus far, our focus for backup has been on VMDK files. While VMDK files are critical because they contain your actual data, VMX files are also important. They tend to sit on the local disk of an ESX host, and a copy of the configuration is not located in the VirtualCenter database. Oftentimes, the local copy of the VMX file is your only record of the configuration of each virtual machine. It would be a disaster to lose the local disk and need to figure out each virtual machine's configuration when the heat is on.

TIP

Maintain an inventory of your virtual machines outside of ESX or VirtualCenter. We recommend creating a spreadsheet that has the configuration details for all of your virtual machines. Include every option listed in the VM configuration. With the VMX files stored on the local file system of ESX server, this document will prove invaluable in a disaster.

Things you should document:

- The virtual machine name
- Which ESX host it resides on
- The path to the config files
- The number of CPUs
- The amount of RAM
- Each virtual disk, its SCSI ID, and its path to the VMDK file
- The virtual disk mode settings—for example, Persistent versus Undoable, and so on
- Any other peripherals and their config information
- The startup order in relation to other VMs on the ESX host
- The performance policy settings—for instance, the CPU and RAM shares and Min/Max settings

Many of the products listed in the existing VM backup tools section of this chapter cover VMX backups, but you may be looking outside of the existing tools for your VMX backups. An option would be to install a local backup agent in the service console and configure it to back up the /home directory on a regular basis. If you don't want to shell out for the agent costs just to back up a couple MB of data, then you can easily put together a script to copy the VMX files once a day.

The script shown in Code Listing 7.2 is an example of how to copy VMX files using Perl. This is intended to be a starting point. By default, it will copy to a locally mounted directory on the ESX host. Also included is an example line to copy to another host via SSH.

The script does not do many things that you may wish to cover. You could add /etc/vmware/ to store your ESX configuration files. You could add /var/log to cover the log files in case of system crash or security incident.

Also, you may want some versioning on the files to store older VMX files to find out what has changed.

Code Listing 7.2 Perl Script for Copying VMX Files

```perl
#!/usr/bin/perl -w
#
# This script is an example only
# Usage: vmxBackup.pl


use VMware::VmPerl;
use VMware::VmPerl::Server;
use VMware::VmPerl::ConnectParams;
use VMware::VmPerl::VM;
use strict;

# User variables
my $target="/vmimages/vmxBackup";

# Setup a connection to the local ESX host
my $params = VMware::VmPerl::ConnectParams::new();
my $host = VMware::VmPerl::Server::new();
$host->connect($params);

# List of registered virtual machines
my @vmlist = $host->registered_vm_names();

foreach my $vm (@vmlist){
  # Get the displayName of the vm
  # We will use the displayName to title the backup output file
  my $vmo = VMware::VmPerl::VM::new();
  $vmo->connect($params, $vm);
  my $displayName = $vmo->get_config("displayName");

  # Finally, you may have some problems with special characters
  # I recommend removing them to prevent hassles.
  # This line will remove ( and ) and spaces.
  $displayName =~ s/[\() ]//g;
```

```
# This will tell us what directory the vmx is in.
my @path = split("/",$vm);
my $dir;
my $cnt=0;
until ($cnt == $#path) { $dir = $dir . "$path[$cnt]/"; $cnt++; }

# Here is the actual backup command
my $cmd = `tar cvzpf \"$target/$displayName.tgz\" \"$dir\"`;

# To go remote via ssh, use this command instead
# Remember to set up ssh key auth first
#my $cmd = `tar cvzpf - \"$dir\" | ssh user\@host \"dd
of=\"$target/$displayName.tgz\"\"`;

# Cleanup
$vmo->disconnect();
} # End foreach vm

# Cleanup
$host->disconnect();
```

This script will copy all registered VMX files to the location specified. It will cover all files in the directory with the VMX, such as nvram and log files. Be aware, in its current form, the files will be overwritten each time the script is run. The output is tar gzip format with the filename of the configured display name .tgz.

Swiss Army Knife...

Scripting the Synchronization of VMX Files to Another ESX Host

You may have a need to store VMX files on another ESX host, preregistered. This may be due to a couple of reasons. First, you are replicating the SAN-based VMFS volumes and have warm servers waiting to be used at the DR site. Second, you have a need to recover a failed ESX host very fast—fast enough to warrant the additional complication of managing a

Continued

sync process. The preceding sample VMX backup script could be slightly modified to cover this situation. Only a couple of simple changes need be made.

1. The tar statement must use SSH, and needs to explode the tar-ball on the remote side. An example is shown next. Note the capital P options on both sides. This will preserve file paths.

```
my $cmd = `tar cvzPpf - \"$dir\" | ssh user\@host \"tar zxPf -"\"`;
```

2. Following the tar command, the VMX needs to be registered. We recommend using *vmware-cmd* to accomplish this.

Incorporating Hot VM Backups into Your Recovery Plan

Up to this point, we have discussed the essential knowledge needed to perform backups and restores with scripts. We also covered a few very useful scripts packaged into applications, some free and some commercial. Where do you go from here? Well, you've now got to assimilate all this technical information and merge it into your backup/restore/disaster recovery strategy. This section is where the rubber meets the road. We're going to dive into why and how you would use hot VM backups as part of your total recovery strategy.

Before we dig in, let's pause and face reality for a moment. Have you ever had an end user give you a high-five after a standard nightly backup job? I didn't think so. No one really cares about backups. No one was ever considered a hero after their backups successfully completed. What does matter, what people love, and what will get you much praise and many free lunches are successful restores. When you restore the sales forecast spreadsheet an end user lost after a week of work, you become the instant hero. Backups are important, restores are critical. The time it takes to restore data matters. The data integrity of restores matters. The amount of data your business can afford to lose and keep on running matters.

With the perspective that restores are what matters most, let's discuss how to incorporate hot VM backups (and restores) into your recovery strategy.

When talking about a backup strategy and disaster recovery, it's critically important to start with the end result in mind. You should know now what you need to have happen after a disaster occurs. Without getting into a full out discussion of DR planning topics, let's cover a few basic DR planning topics.

Some key information you need to know about every application or set of data in your environment is its RTO and RPO. Let's define these acronyms.

- **RTO (Recovery Time Objective)** This is the amount of time that may elapse after a disaster until the application or data needs to be operational. In other words, the RTO is your deadline for recovery.

- **RPO (Recovery Point Objective)** This is the largest amount of time that may exist between the present and the last recoverable point in time for the application or data. In other words, the RPO is how much data, measured in time, you can afford to lose.

Before you can determine your backup strategy, you should go through and inventory your systems, group them into applications and data sets, and then determine the RTO and RPO for each one. Done correctly, this process isn't really completed by the IT staff. It's a process that is highly dependent on the opinion of those that run your business. If the business says that the CRM database has an RTO of 12 hours and an RPO of five minutes, then your job is now defined. At this point, you can apply strategy and tools to accomplish those objectives. Without those guidelines, it's impossible to create a recovery strategy that is valid to your business.

Often, as you take the guidelines from your business and translate that into tools, human resources, and ultimately expenses, you may get a different answer regarding what the RTOs and RPOs are. Money talks, loud. A few rules of thumb when it comes to determining how redundant to make your systems based on recovery requirements:

- The lower the recovery requirements (RTO and RPO times), the more expensive and difficult the solution to achieve them will be. Zero downtime and zero data loss, for example, generally require completely redundant systems with expensive replication software and high availability clustering. Whereas a slightly less resilient system can be implemented that is good enough with much less investment and generally highly satisfactory results.

- The more complicated your redundancy systems are, the more prone you are to failures. We've often seen "highly available" systems end up with more downtime than less redundant systems. In most cases, it happens because the system became so complex in an effort to be redundant that the human factor mismanaged it.

- The K.I.S.S. factor most often works better than over engineering. K.I.S.S. = Keep It Simple Stupid. A simple system, compared to a complex system with many moving parts, generally has less chance of failing. Simply put, fewer components equates to fewer failures.

Once you and the business come to agreement on what needs to be protected, you'll get the opportunity to dig through the myriad tools and techniques to determine the best way to get it done. You'll then be armed with the data you need to determine what tools, scripts, agents, applications, libraries, arrays, replication, and so on to use for backup and recovery.

Now, the scope of this work is not to teach you how to do disaster recovery planning. However, we thought it very important to frame the concepts of hot VM backups within the discussion about disaster recovery planning. There seem to be misconceptions in the community about what hot VM backups can do. Often, they are given more credit than they deserve. Rarely have we found an enterprise implementation of VMware that can be fully protected by a standalone hot VM backup tool. Now that you've been through this chapter and understand what hot VM backups can do, you can start to figure out where it fits in your plan.

Let's simply state the functionality of hot VM backups by listing what they can and cannot do in the two lists shown in Table 7.1. In this table, the plus column stands for functions that hot backups can do; the minus column stands for functions they cannot do.

Table 7.1 Capabilities of Hot Virtual Machine Backups

Plus	Minus
Perform zero downtime backups of VMs without a performance hit	Perform file level backups and restore
Capture the entire state of the VM, including boot, sector, OS, and applications.	Create detailed catalogs of backed-up files.
Back up virtual machines without guest OS agents.	Close files and databases before taking a backup. State of backed-up VM is crash consistent.
Be written to disk, tape, or network shares.	

Crash Consistent State

Let's define crash consistent and explain why it matters to you. Have you ever pulled the power from a server while the OS is running? How about hold the power button down for 15 seconds or so? Or, have you ever pulled the fiber cable from a server that boots from SAN? The state that your server is in after it reboots is a crash consistent state. Crash consistent state usually follows an abrupt and immediate power off or freeze of the operating system. The OS and applications were not made aware of the shutdown, so consequently they didn't do any of the things they normally do before powering off. Some of these activities are quite important, such as committing transactions to a database and closing files, writing uncommitted data from memory to files, committing outstanding I/Os to disk, and other items of this sort. When the server comes back up, it has to deal with the sometimes unpleasant and often very messy situation of cleaning up after the crash.

The good news is that most operating systems and applications are aware that crashes occur once in a while. They have mechanisms built into them to recover from this type of disaster. Databases write uncommitted data to transaction logs before it is written to the database. File systems have journaling features that log any changes to a temporary journal before committing them to the main file system. These transaction logs and journals are used to replay data that wasn't committed before the crash back into the main data set.

Keep in mind, however, that crash consistent means that there is a chance that you may have corrupted data, broken file systems, uncommitted transactions, or untold other failures after a crash. We need to throw this warning out there even though in the vast majority of instances with standard applications there are no problems coming out of crash consistent states.

When you perform a hot backup of a virtual machine, you are essentially freezing the disk and taking a snapshot of it. At the exact moment you add a .REDO log to a .vmdk file, the state of the data is frozen, whether or not files are open or closed and databases are running or quiesced. The good news is that VMware takes care to commit any transactions that are in flight to the .vmdk file when the .REDO log is added. In 99+ percent of the cases, you'll have no problem recovering the data in the .vmdk file.

WARNING

We said 99+ percent of the time you'll be able to recover the data in the .vmdk file. That doesn't mean it will meet your usability expectations. If you have an application that doesn't like to be frozen in the middle of a transaction, then you may have a situation where your data is recovered, but useless. The disclaimer is this: test test test this functionality out before you rely on it as part of your disaster recovery plan. That should go without saying, but we've been consulting long enough to know that there isn't much that we leave unsaid and unchecked.

Replication

If you can't afford to lose any data, then hot VM backups are not for you. Neither are file-level backups. You just graduated to an advanced level of backups, called replication. Data replication can be performed at the file system level or at the storage array level. High-end solutions require a lot of bandwidth and can provide synchronous replications of all data. Synchronous replication ensures no data is lost. For situations with less bandwidth, asynchronous solutions queue up replications and trickle them over connections at set times. These can be five minutes behind or 24 hours behind. It's adjustable based on your configuration.

Real-time replication is currently the best solution for zero data loss environments. It's the only way to guarantee that you don't lose a single transaction during a disaster. Replication is reliable and it works, but it comes with a price. Replication solutions are generally many times more expensive than traditional backup methods. However, if you need it, you need it, and you'll be willing to pay for it. If not, then it's time to compromise.

Hot VM Backups as Part of the Recovery Plan

Now, you've taken the earlier advice and considered where this type of backup/restore procedure will fit into your disaster recovery plan. You've considered which of your applications recover well from crash consistent states and which absolutely do not. You've decided that you'll enable journaling on your ext3 and reiser file systems and you'll use transaction logs with your Exchange and SQL servers. Good. Now let's discuss a common approach for using hot VM backups in your plan.

To begin with, it's important to understand that one of the major limitations of a hot VM backup is it has absolutely no knowledge of the files inside the .vmdk file. If you need to recover that sales forecast spreadsheet that is backed up inside a .vmdk file, you're going to have to find it yourself. There is no catalog of files contained inside the guest OS file system that you can refer to. To achieve file-level restores, you'll need to use a file-level backup tool in addition to your hot VM backup tool.

Let's walk through the steps to determine the correct recovery strategy for your applications and data sets. The five-step process shown in Figure 7.8 will help you establish the correct policy for each application.

Step One: Take an Inventory of Your Virtual Machines

You can't plan for recovery unless you know what you have. A wise Electronic Janitor once told me, the majority of IT is inventory. To begin, create a simple spreadsheet that contains a detailed inventory of your virtual machines and the applications running within them. You'll need to record at least:

Figure 7.8 Process to Determine Backup Strategy

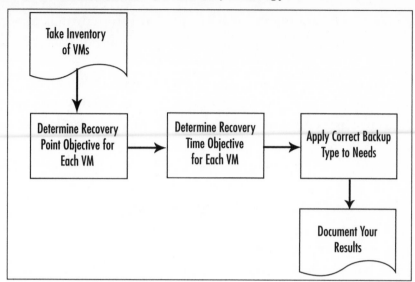

- The operating system

- Which applications run on each OS

- The location where data is stored

Especially note if some data for your VM is not stored in VMFS volumes. This data will need to be addressed individually.

Now that you've begun this document, you'll be able to use it as a foundation for building out the rest of the recovery plan. Expand the spreadsheet during the next few steps to include RTO and RPO requirements for each virtual machine.

Step Two: Determine the Recovery Point Objective for Each VM

The recovery point will tell you how often you need to perform a backup of your VM. Answer the following question for each VM:

How much data can I afford to lose?

Once you know how much data you can afford to lose, you can decide the frequency of your backup jobs. If you can afford to lose seven days work, then only back up once a week. If you can afford to lose up to 24 hours of work, then a daily backup is perfect.

Step Three: Determine the Recovery Time Objective for Each VM

Earlier, we discussed planning for recovery first. At this step, think about the type of recovery that will be required for this application or data set.

Answer the following question for each VM:

How fast does it have to be recovered after a disaster? (RTO)

The time required to recover a VM is often overlooked when applying a blanket backup strategy to systems. If you only have a tape backup of an application, the recovery time will include the process of installing a new operating system, setting up a backup agent, and restoring the application data from tape. This process at a minimum will be several hours. If your RTO is less than those several hours, rethink your tool selection.

Hot VM backups take about as much time to restore as they do to back up. If you're using compression on the backups, then the recovery time will go faster. The compression calculations are not as intense on a recovery as they are on a backup.

Step Four: Apply the Right Backup Job to the Need

Once you have the business requirement for how fast you need to recover, and how much data you can afford to lose, you can use this information to decide on the right backup tool. The tool must back up frequently enough to meet the RPO and be able to provide recovery quick enough to meet the RTO.

At this point, you have gathered enough information to decide which type of backup tool will meet your recovery requirements.

Table 7.2 shows a general comparison between the different backup/recovery tools we've discussed in this chapter. You can use this as a starting point to help decide which tool fits your recovery requirements best, and, ultimately, to determine whether hot VM backups are for you.

Table 7.2 A Comparison of Backup Tools

Backup Type	Min RTO*	Min RPO**	Cost	Complexity
VM hot backup	< one hour	24 hours	Low	Low
Tape backup agent	1–24 hours	24 hours	Medium	Medium
Storage replication	< five minutes	Real time	High	High

* Minimum Recovery Time Objective is an estimate based on experience of the time required to recover typical data using the specified tool. Your situation may vary greatly depending largely on the amount of data to be backed up and recovered.

** Minimum RPO depends on the frequency of backups. For example, daily backups provide a < 24-hour RPO, while weekly backups provide a < seven-day RPO.

Decide here whether a crash consistent copy of the VM will meet your requirements, or whether you need file-level protection and restore capability as well. Your application may require a special agent to perform a proper backup and restore—examples are open file agents, exchange agents, and SQL database agents.

If crash consistent is good enough and the recovery time is acceptable, then a hot VM backup is perfect for you. If you need file-level recovery, then you need file-level backups as well. If your requirements say that you need zero downtime, and your budget supports the need, explore highly available solutions with storage replication.

At this point, you need to prioritize which VMs (applications) are more important than others. The importance of the VM determines its priority in a recovery. You probably can't do all your restores at the same time, and you're more likely to perform recoveries in a serial manner. So, decide which VMs are the most important and categorize them as your top-tier systems. These will be the systems that get restored first after a disaster. Other VMs will be categorized as a lower tier, and will therefore be recovered after the top-tier VMs. Make sure to set expectations with your end users that top-tier systems will be restored first. To change the priority will either cost more money or require a reprioritization of the order in which systems will be recovered.

Step Five: Document Your Results

It is critical to document your plan. Although there seems to be a general aversion to documentation in the IT community, it is nevertheless of utmost importance. If your plan is not documented, you will have a difficult time explaining it to others. If the plan is not documented, you may find yourself in trouble during a disaster. For that matter, make sure your documented plan is stored outside of the system it is protecting. If the plan is stored on the file server, and the file server goes down, you won't have much luck reviewing the plan. Keep a digital and printed copy of the plan at all times. Copies of the plan should be kept in multiple locations in the event a location is inaccessible as part of the disaster.

Hybrid Backup Strategy

For systems that have file-level restore needs, the hybrid approach generally is best. The hybrid backup strategy combines the best attributes of the hot VM backup with the best attributes of the file-level backup. The advantage of the hot VM backup is that the restore is fairly quick and requires little user intervention. Once the server is restored, the last file-level backup can be applied to bring the data back to as current as possible. This approach eliminates the need to reinstall an operating system and tape backup agent. Helping you avoid having to search for OS CD-ROMs, drivers, and agent install disks during a disaster. These are small issues that can waste precious minutes and hours during a disaster.

Let's review a common hybrid backup strategy.

Backup method:

- Take a hot VM backup regularly, such as once per week.

Take a file-level backup using an agent in the guest OS every day.

Restore method:

To recover the entire server:

1. Perform a restore of the entire VM from the last hot VM backup.
2. Apply the latest file-level restore to that VM.

The advantage here is that you can recover the entire VM very quickly using the hot VM backup, and then bring its files up-to-date with the last file-level restore. This will bring your server up to a state where the OS is fully configured, the backup agent is already loaded and working, and data is current to the last hot backup. This entire effort is achieved with a minimal amount of human intervention. All that is left at this point is restoring data from the last incremental backup. You didn't have to build an OS from scratch, load the backup agent, and then perform a full system restore. You saved yourself hours of work, eliminated countless opportunities for human error, and in the end recovered your data much faster.

Table 7.3 shows an example of what a hybrid backup schedule may look like. It combines the file-level backup agent with hot VM backups, called Full VM Server images. To sum up the following schedule, a full image of the VM is captured once a week with the hot VM backup script—in this case, esxRanger. Then a daily file-level backup is taken using the CommVault agent. (CommVault is a backup software ISV.) Once a week, the repository of VM images is also copied to tape. The retention times listed here are subject to change based on your specific requirements. The times shown in Table 7.3 are merely examples to get you started on your plan.

Table 7.3 Example Backup Schedule

Backup Type	Tool	Media	Schedule	Retention
File-level backup	Example, CommVault	Tape (CommVault Media Server)	Daily	One month
Full VM server image	Example, Hot VM backup script	Disk (Linux NFS export on SAN LUN)	Weekly	One week
Tape backup of full server image files	Example, CommVault	Tape (CommVault Media Server)	Weekly	Two months

This backup schedule is also represented in Figure 7.9.

Figure 7.9 Virtual Machine Backup Process

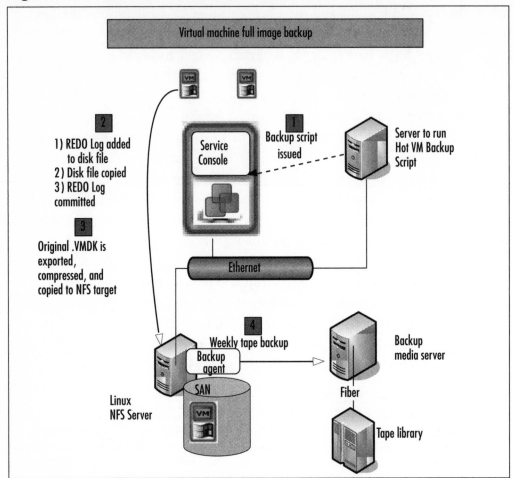

Summary

If you've mastered the topics in this section, you are well on your way to a complete backup solution for your VMware virtual infrastructure. You should be able to confidently script hot backups of your virtual machines and their related config files. You are now armed with information about alternative commercial solutions, and have the knowledge to apply what you've learned to your overall recovery strategy.

## Chapter 8

Other Cool Tools and Tricks

Topics in this chapter:

- Configuring PowerChute Network Shutdown in ESX

- Centralized User Management for ESX Server

- Extending a Cloned (Deployed) Windows VM's Root Partition

Introduction

In this chapter, I'll explain how to do a couple of cool things to VMware ESX Server to make your life as an administrator easier. First, I'll show you how to install APC PowerChute Network Shutdown, also known as PCNS, on VMware ESX Server.

Servers nowadays come with more than one power supply. In some remote offices where I once installed VMware ESX, there was a separate UPS for each power supply—and yet there's only one way for VMware ESX Server to be controlled by one UPS.

Centralized user management for VMware ESX Server has always been a big thing for me. This was even more so before VirtualCenter came into play. I'll later share with you a script that lets you query a directory for members of a given group, and from that you can add the users, assign permissions to the users, and do just about anything else a little creative thought might engender.

Configuring PowerChute Network Shutdown in ESX

Basically, because the ESX service console has no GUI, and because PowerChute has a Java GUI Installer, the only way to install APC PowerChute Network Shutdown for Linux is to use a helper Red Hat Linux virtual machine to install PCNS into, then tar up the resulting binaries and transport them into ESX.

This solution has been tested on ESX 2.5.0, 2.5.1, 2.5.2, 2.5.3, 3.0.0, and 3.0.1 and is theoretically okay on all ESX 2.x versions. I worked with Kim Wisniewski (aka, kimono) from the VMware Community forums and came up with the following method to accomplish this.

Creating the PowerChute Package

1. Create a Red Hat Linux 7.3 virtual machine, or use an existing Red Hat workstation if you have access to one. (Red Hat Linux 9.0 and Red Hat Enterprise Linux 3 were tested and worked okay, also.)

2. Download APC PowerChute Network Shutdown 2.2.1 and place it in your root directory. You can download this file from www.apc.com—the filename to look for is **pcns221lnx.bin**. This document cannot link directly to the file since registration is required to download.

3. Install PCNS 2.2.1 into the VM by entering **./pcns221lnx.bin** from a terminal window (see Figure 8.1).

Figure 8.1 PowerChute Install

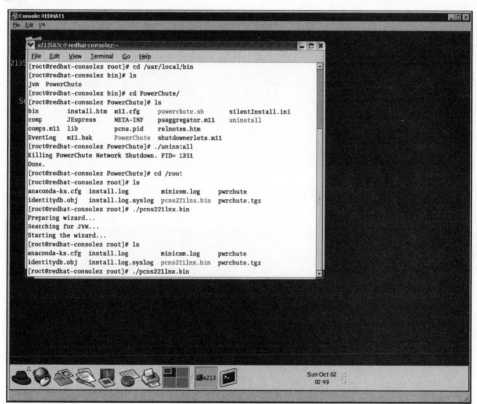

4. For the installation, use the default installation location **/usr/local/bin/PowerChute** and **Install to Single UPS Device**.

5. For the management card IP, enter the IP address of the UPS that the target ESX server will eventually be installing PCNS onto. It does not matter if the Management Card is not contactable due to firewall

restrictions. It is only important to enter these details so the configuration file for the PCNS (a file called /usr/local/bin/PowerChute/
m11.cfg) file is correct. Figure 8.2 shows a screenshot of the installer
finishing the PowerChute registration process.

Figure 8.2 PowerChute Registration

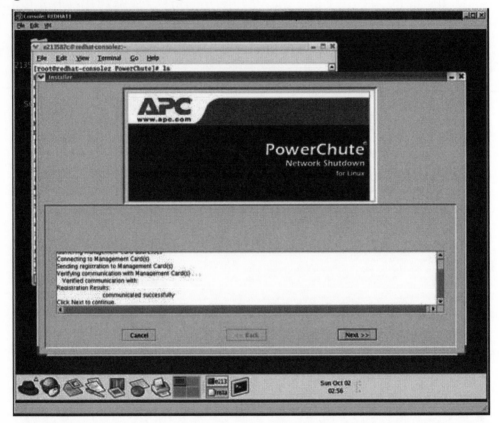

6. Tar up the installation from your helper virtual machine using the
    following command from a terminal window on your helper VM.

```
tar -pzvcf /root/pwrchute.tar.gz /usr/local/bin/jvm/usr/local/bin/PowerChute
```

7. Copy the tar ball either directly to your target ESX host or to your
    software repository location.

```
scp root@helpermachine:/pwrchute.tar.gz c:\pwrchute.tar.gz
```

NOTE

Some of the SCP commands in this document presume you already have downloaded and installed an SCP utility like Putty or OpenSSH in a Cygwin environment. There are several free and commercially available SSH clients available on the Web to perform SCP operations. In my example, I'm using Putty. By using Putty, the executable for the program is "PSCP.EXE" in Windows, which you can rename to SCP.EXE and put in your system path! This is a very handy thing to do for your Windows workstation when working with ESX and other UNIX systems.

8. Also it is wise to copy the **/usr/local/bin/PowerChute/m11.cfg** file from your helper VM and store it somewhere convenient as this (binary and unreadable) file contains the IP address of the UPS. This way you only need to install PCNS into your helper VM once per target UPS, then it is trivial to replace m11.cfg file on each ESX host to connect to the right UPS. You can maintain a repository of m11.cfg's for each UPS you connect to. If you only have one, or if you have a central management card in an enterprise-class UPS (such as the APC Symmetra), then you do not need to do this. For example, to copy the m11.cfg somewhere on your Windows host, use the following:

```
scp root@<IP OF YOUR HELPER VM>:/usr/local/bin/PowerChute/m11.cfg c:\m11.cfg
```

To install the TAR package onto your ESX host, perform the following steps:

1. Copy the TAR ball to the root directory of your ESX host:

```
scp pwrchute.tar.gz root@your-host.where.com:
```

Make sure **pwrchute.tar.gz** ends up at the root directory on the ESX host, to ensure when you extract that it all goes to the correct locations

2. Extract it by typing the following at your ESX host's console:

```
cd /
```

```
tar -zxvf pwrchute.tar.gz
```

This will re-create the same directory structure and files when PCNS is installed into your helper VM.

3. Add the symbolic links to allow PCNS to start up.*

```
ln -s /etc/rc.d/init.d/PowerChute /etc/rc.d/rc0.d/S99PowerChute
ln -s /etc/rc.d/init.d/PowerChute /etc/rc.d/rc1.d/S99PowerChute
ln -s /etc/rc.d/init.d/PowerChute /etc/rc.d/rc2.d/S99PowerChute
ln -s /etc/rc.d/init.d/PowerChute /etc/rc.d/rc3.d/S99PowerChute
ln -s /etc/rc.d/init.d/PowerChute /etc/rc.d/rc4.d/S99PowerChute
ln -s /etc/rc.d/init.d/PowerChute /etc/rc.d/rc5.d/S99PowerChute
cp /usr/local/bin/PowerChute/PowerChute /etc/init.d/PowerChute
```

NOTE

I had to create the symbolic links manually because using *chkconfig* to install the service did not work.

* These commands make an ideal shell script!

4. Copy M11.CFG, if necessary, to your ESX host by typing

```
scp c:\m11-UPS1.cfg root@your-host:/usr/local/bin/PowerChute
```

5. Start and stop PCNS (and see what happens…) using the following (note the syntax):

```
/etc/rc.d/init.d/PowerChute
            Usage PowerChute [start|stop]
```

6. Start PCNS by typing

```
/etc/rc.d/init.d/PowerChute start
```

At this stage, PowerChute is installed and running on your ESX host and is talking to (1) whichever UPS management card you configured when you installed it into your helper VM, or (2) the one you specified in the m11.cfg file you chose to copy over earlier.

That's great news! But how do I configure it?!

Configuring Your ESX Host's PowerChute

Now we'll show you how to configure your ESX host's PowerChute.

1. Log on to the PCNS Web interface using **HTTP://YOUR-HOST.WHERE.COM:3052**.

2. From the **Configure Shutdown** option, untick **Turn Off UPS**. *This is very important* for enterprise environments.

3. From the **Configure Events** option, set up the **UPS: On Battery** event to shut down the system after 600 seconds. (This is for the sake of this example only. The real setting will depend on your environment and requirements...) Figure 8.3 shows an example of configuring PowerChute for a network shutdown.

Figure 8.3 PowerChute Configuration

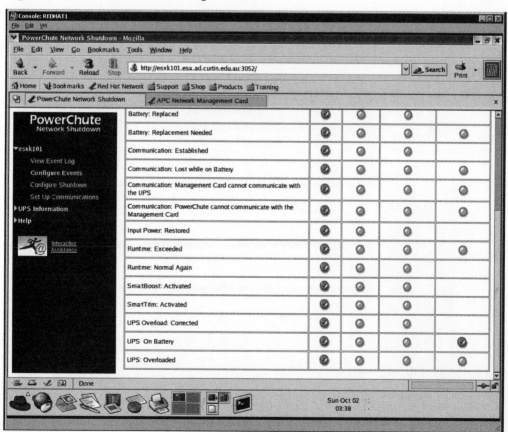

> **NOTE**
>
> *When configuring PCNS, it's best to* **Ctrl + Refresh** *the application's frames after each item you change since the application is buggy and sometimes looks like your changes haven't stuck. You may even have to do this multiple times (in Firefox) as well as right-click and* refresh *the right-hand frame so it updates with your new configuration. This is a noted bug with APC, and they do not seem to want to fix it.*

Configure PCNS Shutdown Settings on the UPS

These additional steps may be required, depending on your UPS and whether or not ESX host to UPS communications were successful. It is highly recommended you check the UPS anyway after configuring your new hosts.

1. Log on to your UPS's management cards Web interface with **HTTP://YOUR-MANAGEMENT-CARD.WHERE.COM**. (This may be https if your management card is equipped.)

Figure 8.4 Remove Helper Addresses

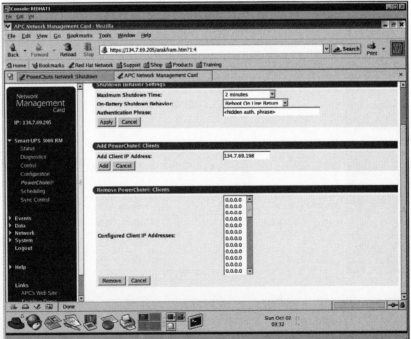

2. Remove any of your virtual machine helper IP addresses from the management card. They're unnecessary (see Figure 8.4).

3. *Check and add the IP addresses of all of the ESX hosts you're connecting to this UPS.*

Master Craftsman...

How to Uninstall PowerChute

It's easy to uninstall PowerChute from your helper virtual machine. Just enter the following from the terminal window:

```
cd /usr/local/bin/PowerChute
./uninstall
```

To uninstall from ESX is a little trickier. You need to first remove the symbolic links:

```
rm /etc/rc.d/rc0.d/S99PowerChute
rm /etc/rc.d/rc1.d/S99PowerChute
rm /etc/rc.d/rc2.d/S99PowerChute
rm /etc/rc.d/rc3.d/S99PowerChute
rm /etc/rc.d/rc4.d/S99PowerChute
rm /etc/rc.d/rc5.d/S99PowerChute
rm /etc/init.d/PowerChute
```

Then, finally remove the files and folders. Be sure you're not using the Java folder for anything else before you do this! On a default ESX 2.x server system, there is no jvm directory anyway, so unless you have installed some other third-party jvm-based product, PowerChute should be the only thing using it.

```
rm -rf /usr/local/bin/jvm
rm -rf /usr/local/bin/PowerChute
```

Continued

Centralized User Management for ESX Server

When I first started building VMware ESX Server systems, VirtualCenter was not yet out, which left a problem of centralized user management. Basically, at that time there was none. I knew that this was going to be a big issue with each and every VMware ESX Server that I added to the infrastructure. Some basic documentation at that time existed letting VMware ESX Server authenticate to Active Directory and some other Lightweight Directory Access Protocol or LDAP-driven directories, but that only covered authentication. I needed a way to get the users added to the local host server.

As a refresher, Lightweight Directory Access Protocol is an Internet protocol that e-mail and other programs use to look up directory information from a server. Because LDAP is an open protocol, applications need not worry about the type of server hosting the directory.

The LDAP search script was created to answer this need. This is part of my ESX server build and configuration to this day. In ESX 2.X, I needed to add a couple of RPM to be installed. These Open LDAP packages are what the service console uses to search remote directories.

```
rpm -ivh openldap-2.0.11-13.i386.rpm
rpm -ivh openldap-clients-2.0.11-13.i386.rpm
```

To have the ability to authenticate using LDAP, you would also need this package:

```
rpm ivh nss_ldap-185-1.i386.rpm
```

NOTE

In ESX 3.0, LDAP is configured using a different method to accomplish this. The packages are already in place and just need to be configured. The commands for ESX 3.0 to configure the server for LDAP searches is

```
esxcfg-auth --enableldapauth --ldapserver=domain.com --
ldapbasedn=DC=domain,DC=com
```

To enable Active Directory Authentication in ESX 3.x, the command is as follows

```
esxcfg-auth --enablead --addomain domain.com --addc domain.com--
enablekrb5 --krb5realm=domain.com --krb5kdc=domain.com
```

Once these packages are installed, you will need to configure them for your environment with a list of directory servers to use. When the RPMs are installed, they create a new folder /etc/openldap/. The file ldap.conf in that folder is the one we need to edit and match the environment you are working in. Figure 8.5 shows an example of the /etc/openldap/ldap.conf file. Code Listing 8.1 shows an example of /etc/ldap.conf. The relative sections you would edit are shown. Several more options can be configured, but these are outside the scope of this book. To learn more, check out the OpenLDAP project at www.openldap.org/.

Figure 8.5 /etc/openldap/ldap.conf

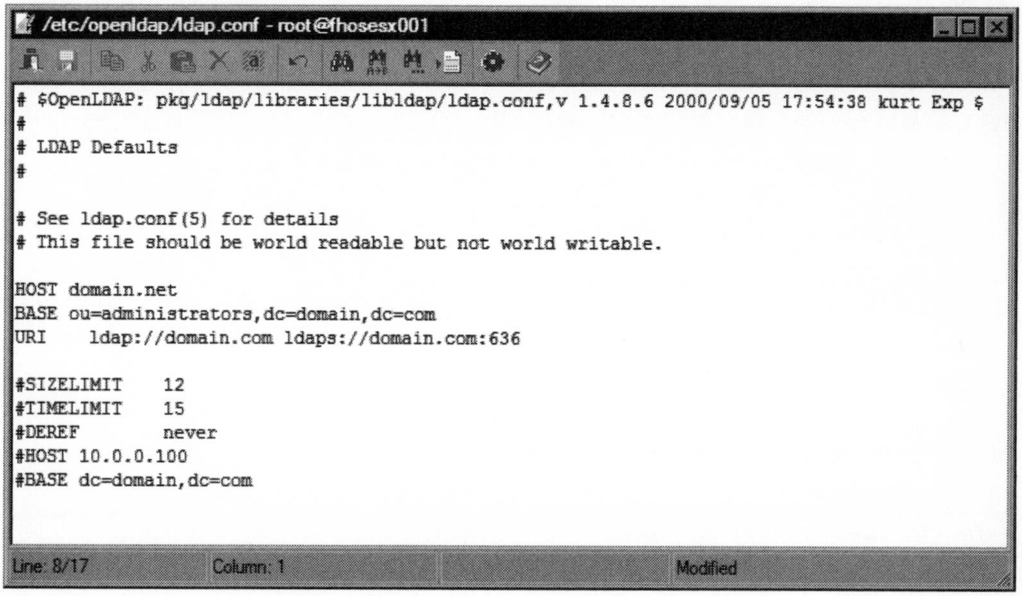

```
/etc/openldap/ldap.conf - root@fhosesx001                              _ □ ✕

# $OpenLDAP: pkg/ldap/libraries/libldap/ldap.conf,v 1.4.8.6 2000/09/05 17:54:38 kurt Exp $
#
# LDAP Defaults
#


# See ldap.conf(5) for details
# This file should be world readable but not world writable.

HOST domain.net
BASE ou=administrators,dc=domain,dc=com
URI     ldap://domain.com ldaps://domain.com:636

#SIZELIMIT    12
#TIMELIMIT    15
#DEREF        never
#HOST 10.0.0.100
#BASE dc=domain,dc=com



Line: 8/17              Column: 1                              Modified
```

Code Listing 8.1 /etc/ldap.conf

```
# @(#)$Id: ldap.conf,v 1.24 2001/09/20 14:12:26 lukeh Exp $
#
# This is the configuration file for the LDAP nameservice
# switch library and the LDAP PAM module.
#
```

```
# PADL Software
# http://www.padl.com
#

# Your LDAP server. Must be resolvable without using LDAP.
host domain.com

# The distinguished name of the search base.
# base dc=example,dc=com
base ou=administrators,dc=domain,dc=com

# Another way to specify your LDAP server is to provide a
# uri with the server name. This allows you to use
# Unix Domain Sockets to connect to a local LDAP Server.
#uri ldap://127.0.0.1/
#uri ldaps://127.0.0.1/
uri ldap://domain.com
#uri ldaps://domain.com
#uri ldapi://%2fvar%2frun%2fldapi_sock/
# Note: %2f encodes the '/' used as directory separator

# The LDAP version to use (defaults to 3
# if supported by client library)
ldap_version 3

# The distinguished name to bind to the server with.
# Optional: default is to bind anonymously.
binddn cn=proxyuser,dc=example,dc=com

# The credentials to bind with.
# Optional: default is no credential.
bindpw secret

# The distinguished name to bind to the server with
# if the effective user ID is root. Password is
# stored in /etc/ldap.secret (mode 600)
#rootbinddn cn=manager,dc=example,dc=com

# The port.
```

```
# Optional: default is 389.
#port 389

# The search scope.
scope sub
#scope one
#scope base

# Search timelimit
#timelimit 30

# Bind timelimit
#bind_timelimit 30

# OpenLDAP SSL mechanism
# start_tls mechanism uses the normal LDAP port, LDAPS typically 636
#ssl start_tls
#ssl on
```

NOTE

On all client machines, both /etc/ldap.conf and /etc/openldap/ldap.conf need to contain the proper server and search base information for your organization.

The simplest way to do this is to run the **authconfig** application and select **Use LDAP** on the **User Information Configuration** screen. In ESX 3.0, use the *esxcfg-auth* command from the shell.

You can also edit these files by hand, and in my case I have precon-figured files that I can just copy and paste into place for speedy deploy-ment.

The most important thing in these configuration files are the names and locations of the LDAP servers and the port to use to connect, as well as the account to bind with and the password to use. I do not have this configured here, and the script includes that information as part of the command.

Now that we have things configured, we can set up the LDAP search script to add and remove users for us. The script presented next will do three searches of the LDAP directory and add or remove the members of the groups that the script is searching. In this specific case, the three different groups represent three different security levels for the users on the VMware ESX Server.

The first group that's searched will just add the user and not add that user to any groups. My original thought for this was that if members of the help desk needed to log on to ESX, they would be able to see the status of the different virtual machines and the status of the host itself. I like to consider this as the "read only" search.

The second group that's searched adds the users the script finds, but also adds those users to a flagship group that I have already created on the host. Rights would be given to the virtual machines so that the flagship group could control or administer the virtual machines. I like to call this the "operator" mode. These could easily be broken down so that the script could search for a Linux group as well as a windows group and assign the correct group depending on the virtual machines those users would control.

The third and last group for this script is what I call the ESX admin group. The users that are in this group would get added to the VMware ESX Server as a user with uid=0. This is basically equal to the root account.

In most cases, now that VirtualCenter is a big part of managing the virtualization hosts, one search or group may be all that's needed to have ESX host access. The limit of how far you can take things with this script is just your imagination.

When this scripts runs, it creates the file and folders it needs automatically. The default location is /usr/LDAP, but you can easily change it to match your needs. If something should go haywire, just delete the working directory and let the script re-create from scratch. Also, if needed, remove any users before starting from scratch. I have not had any issues except for an error message stating that the account already existed. Other than that, there were no problems. I have this script set up as a cron job in /etc/cron.hourly/, which runs every hour on the hour.

Code Listing 8.2 shows an example of the LDAP search script. You should only need to make changes in the "User Edit Area"; nothing else should require edits.

Code Listing 8.2 The LDAP Search Script

```
################
#!/bin/bash
# LDAP Search Script to add and remove users based on AD Group Membership
# Steve Beaver

######## Start User Edit Area ########
#  This first part sets up the variables for the member search
#  If there is an error doing the search, the script will move on to the
next group search
base="-b DC=domain,DC=com"
# Replace with your domain name
#user="-D CN=LDAPUSER,OU=VMWare,DC=domain,DC=com"
user="-D LDAPUSER@DOMAIN.COM"
# Notice you can use LDAP DN or you can use the AD Full Account
pass="-w password"
# The AD user password
ADgroup1="ESX_VIEW"
# The 1st AD group -- Read Only Privilege
ADgroup2="ESX_OP"
# The 2nd AD group -- VM Admin Privilege
ADgroup3="ESX_ADMIN"
# The 3rd AD group -- Root Privilege
esxgroup="ESXFlagGroup"
# The ESX group you would like the users to be a member off
programdir="/usr/LDAP"
# The directory this script will use to run
#####  End User Edit Area #####
    ##################################################
# More variables that do not need to be edited
cmd="ldapsearch -x -LLL"
pipe="-u -tt -T ${programdir}"
pipe2="-u -tt -T ${programdir}/Member"
filter1="CN=${ADgroup1} member"
filter2="CN=${ADgroup2} member"
```

```
filter3="CN=${ADgroup3} member"
filtersam="samAccountName"
###############################################

# Sanity Check to make sure all the files and folders needed are in place or
create them

if test ! -x "$programdir" ; then
        mkdir $programdir
        mkdir $programdir/Member
        mkdir $programdir/Member/New
        mkdir $programdir/Member/Old
        echo > $programdir/Member/New/$ADgroup1.txt
        echo > $programdir/Member/Old/$ADgroup1.txt
        echo > $programdir/Member/New/$ADgroup2.txt
        echo > $programdir/Member/Old/$ADgroup2.txt
        echo > $programdir/Member/New/$ADgroup3.txt
        echo > $programdir/Member/Old/$ADgroup3.txt
fi
###############            NEW SEARCH            ###############
# The first search to find the group and see who, if any, are members
VIEW_search ()
{
        ${cmd} ${base} ${user} ${pass} ${pipe} ${filter1}
        if [ "$?" -ne "0" ]; then
                printf "ERROR running LDAP Search script exiting"
                return
        fi
        VIEW_search_member
}

# Now that I have a temp file for each user, I need to collect and list them
in a file to read from
# If I find no users in the group, then there's no need to continue. Return
and move on

VIEW_search_member ()
{
        cd $programdir
```

```
        ls -1 $programdir/ldapsearch-member-* > $programdir/filelist.txt
        if [ "$?" -ne "0" ]; then
                printf "No Members moving on...  "
                return
        fi
        declare LINE
        declare MEMBER
        cat $programdir/filelist.txt |
                while read abc
                        do case $abc in
                        Member) echo $abc ;;
                        *) awk '{print $0}' $abc >> $programdir/ulist.txt ;;
                        esac
                done
        sed 's/,OU=.*//g' $programdir/ulist.txt > $programdir/mlist.txt
        VIEW_search_sam
}


# Now I have a list in a usable format.
# Time to search again to get the samAccountName or userid
# of each user in the group.

VIEW_search_sam ()
{
        infile="$programdir/mlist.txt"
        cat $infile |
                while read def
                        do ${cmd} ${base} ${user} ${pass} ${pipe2} "$def"
${filtersam}
                done
        rm -R $programdir/ldapsearch*
        rm -R $programdir/filelist.txt
        rm -R $programdir/ulist.txt
        rm -R $programdir/mlist.txt
        mv -f $programdir/Member/New/$ADgroup1.txt
$programdir/Member/Old/$ADgroup1.txt
        VIEW_search_create
}
```

```
# Now that I have a temp file for each user, I need to collect and list them
in a file to read from
# Sort the list and compare the old one with the new to see if I need to add
or remove users
# The useradd command below gives the user the READ ONLY privilege


VIEW_search_create ()
{
        cd $programdir/Member
        ls -1 $programdir/Member/ldapsearch-* >
$programdir/Member/filelist.txt
        cat $programdir/Member/filelist.txt |
                while read xyz
                        do awk '{print $0}' $xyz | tr [:upper:] [:lower:] >>
$programdir/Member/$ADgroup1.txt
                done
        rm -R $programdir/Member/ldapsearch*
        rm -R $programdir/Member/filelist.txt
        mv -f $programdir/Member/$ADgroup1.txt
$programdir/Member/New/$ADgroup1.txt
        sort -f -o $programdir/Member/New/$ADgroup1.txt
$programdir/Member/New/$ADgroup1.txt
                comm -1 -3 $programdir/Member/New/$ADgroup1.txt
$programdir/Member/Old/$ADgroup1.txt > $programdir/remuser.txt
                comm -2 -3 $programdir/Member/New/$ADgroup1.txt
$programdir/Member/Old/$ADgroup1.txt > $programdir/adduser.txt
        cat $programdir/remuser.txt |
                while read oldlist
                        do userdel -r $oldlist
                done
        rm -R $programdir/remuser.txt
        cat $programdir/adduser.txt |
                while read newlist
                        do useradd -M $newlist
                done
        rm -R $programdir/adduser.txt
}
################        NEW SEARCH        #################


# The first search to find the group and see who if any are members
OP_search ()
```

```
{
        ${cmd} ${base} ${user} ${pass} ${pipe} ${filter2}
        if [ "$?" -ne "0" ]; then
                printf "ERROR running LDAP Search script exiting"
                return
        fi
        OP_search_member
}
```

```
# Now that I have a temp file for each user, I need to collect and list them
in a file to read from
# If I find no users in the group, then there's no need to continue. Return
and move on
```

```
OP_search_member ()
{
        cd $programdir
        ls -1 $programdir/ldapsearch-member-* > $programdir/filelist.txt
        if [ "$?" -ne "0" ]; then
                printf "No Members moving on...  "
                return
        fi
        declare LINE
        declare MEMBER
        cat $programdir/filelist.txt |
                while read abc
                        do case $abc in
                        Member) echo $abc ;;
                        *) awk '{print $0}' $abc >> $programdir/ulist.txt ;;
                        esac
                done
        sed 's/,OU=.*//g' $programdir/ulist.txt > $programdir/mlist.txt
        OP_search_sam
}
```

```
# Now I have a list in a usable format.
# Time to search again to get the samAccountName or userid
# of each user in the group.
```

```
OP_search_sam ()
{
        infile="$programdir/mlist.txt"
        cat $infile |
                while read def
                        do ${cmd} ${base} ${user} ${pass} ${pipe2} "$def"
${filtersam}
                done
        rm -R $programdir/ldapsearch*
        rm -R $programdir/filelist.txt
        rm -R $programdir/ulist.txt
        rm -R $programdir/mlist.txt
        mv -f $programdir/Member/New/$ADgroup2.txt
$programdir/Member/Old/$ADgroup2.txt
        OP_search_create
}


# Now that I have a temp file for each user, I need to collect and list them
in a file to read from
# Sort the list and compare the old with the new to see if I need to add or
remove users
# The useradd command below gives the user ESX VM Admin privilege


OP_search_create ()
{
        cd $programdir/Member
        ls -1 $programdir/Member/ldapsearch-* >
$programdir/Member/filelist.txt
        cat $programdir/Member/filelist.txt |
                while read xyz
                        do awk '{print $0}' $xyz | tr [:upper:] [:lower:] >>
$programdir/Member/$ADgroup2.txt
                done
        rm -R $programdir/Member/ldapsearch*
        rm -R $programdir/Member/filelist.txt
        mv -f $programdir/Member/$ADgroup2.txt
$programdir/Member/New/$ADgroup2.txt
        sort -f -o $programdir/Member/New/$ADgroup2.txt
$programdir/Member/New/$ADgroup2.txt
                comm -1 -3 $programdir/Member/New/$ADgroup2.txt
$programdir/Member/Old/$ADgroup2.txt > $programdir/remuser.txt
```

```
        comm -2 -3 $programdir/Member/New/$ADgroup2.txt
$programdir/Member/Old/$ADgroup2.txt > $programdir/adduser.txt
        cat $programdir/remuser.txt |
            while read oldlist
                do userdel -r $oldlist
            done
        rm -R $programdir/remuser.txt
        cat $programdir/adduser.txt |
            while read newlist
                do useradd -M -g $esxgroup $newlist
            done
        rm -R $programdir/adduser.txt
}
################          NEW SEARCH          #################
# The first search to find the group and see who if any are members
ADMIN_search ()
{
        ${cmd} ${base} ${user} ${pass} ${pipe} ${filter3}
        if [ "$?" -ne "0" ]; then
            printf "ERROR running LDAP Search script exiting"
            return
        fi
        ADMIN_search_member
}


# Now that I have a temp file for each user, I need to collect and list them
in a file to read from
# If I find no users in the group, then there's no need to continue. Return
and move on

ADMIN_search_member ()
{
        cd $programdir
        ls -1 $programdir/ldapsearch-member-* > $programdir/filelist.txt
        if [ "$?" -ne "0" ]; then
            printf "No Members moving on...   "
            return
        fi
        declare LINE
```

```
        declare MEMBER
        cat $programdir/filelist.txt |
                while read abc
                        do case $abc in
                        Member) echo $abc ;;
                        *) awk '{print $0}' $abc >> $programdir/ulist.txt ;;
                        esac
                done
        sed 's/,OU=.*//g' $programdir/ulist.txt > $programdir/mlist.txt
        ADMIN_search_sam
}


# Now I have a list in a usable format.
# Time to search again to get the samAccountName or userid
# of each user in the group.

ADMIN_search_sam ()
{
        infile="$programdir/mlist.txt"
        cat $infile |
                while read def
                        do ${cmd} ${base} ${user} ${pass} ${pipe2} "$def"
${filtersam}
                done
        rm -R $programdir/ldapsearch*
        rm -R $programdir/filelist.txt
        rm -R $programdir/ulist.txt
        rm -R $programdir/mlist.txt
        mv -f $programdir/Member/New/$ADgroup3.txt
$programdir/Member/Old/$ADgroup3.txt
        ADMIN_search_create
}


# Now that I have a temp file for each user, I need to collect and list them
in a file to read from
# Sort the list and compare the old with the new to see if I need to add or
remove users
# The useradd command below gives the user root privilege


ADMIN_search_create ()
```

```
{
        cd $programdir/Member
        ls -1 $programdir/Member/ldapsearch-* >
$programdir/Member/filelist.txt
        cat $programdir/Member/filelist.txt |
                while read xyz
                        do awk '{print $0}' $xyz | tr [:upper:] [:lower:] >>
$programdir/Member/$ADgroup3.txt
                done
        rm -R $programdir/Member/ldapsearch*
        rm -R $programdir/Member/filelist.txt
        mv -f $programdir/Member/$ADgroup3.txt
$programdir/Member/New/$ADgroup3.txt
        sort -f -o $programdir/Member/New/$ADgroup3.txt
$programdir/Member/New/$ADgroup3.txt
                comm -1 -3 $programdir/Member/New/$ADgroup3.txt
$programdir/Member/Old/$ADgroup3.txt > $programdir/remuser.txt
                comm -2 -3 $programdir/Member/New/$ADgroup3.txt
$programdir/Member/Old/$ADgroup3.txt > $programdir/adduser.txt
        cat $programdir/remuser.txt |
                while read oldlist
                        do userdel -r $oldlist
                done
        rm -R $programdir/remuser.txt
        cat $programdir/adduser.txt |
                while read newlist
                        do useradd -o -u 0 -g $esxgroup $newlist
                done
        rm -R $programdir/adduser.txt
}


######### This section is the main body which calls all the functions
listed above
VIEW_search
OP_search
ADMIN_search
exit
# Done
```

Now that you've had a chance to look over the script, let's break the script down and see what's really happening behind the scenes. The script will first look for the working directory—in this case, /usr/LDAP—to see if it exists. If the script finds the directory and folders are not created, it will create them. Once the structure is there, the script will start its first search. The search will get the members of a group and write those members to temporary files, as shown in Figure 8.6.

Figure 8.6 Temporary Search Files

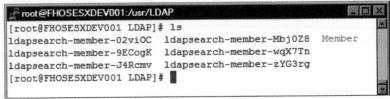

If we look at the content of the temporary files, we see something like the following:

```
CN=User3,OU=Administrators,DC=DOMAIN,DC=COM
```

The next step the script performs is to create a file called filelist.txt that lists all the temp files (as shown in Figure 8.7).

Figure 8.7 Search File List

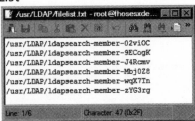

From that list of all the temporary files, the script then reads the content of each of these temporary files and creates another text file called ulist.txt. That file lists all of the users, as shown in Figure 8.8.

Figure 8.8 Search User List

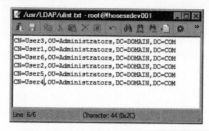

Using the sed tool, the script then edits the file ulist.txt to strip everything but the "CN=User", and then adds this to another file called mlist.txt, as shown in Figure 8.9.

Figure 8.9 Edited Search List

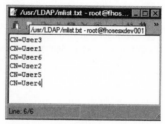

Once the script has just the username, it then does another LDAP search to find the SamAccountName or login identification of the user and puts the results of that search into temp files in a new location: /usr/LDAP/Member/ (as shown in Figure 8.10).

Figure 8.10 Second Search Output

Taking a look at the content of the temporary files, we see the sAMAccountName or Sam Account Name of the users, as shown in Figure 8.11.

Figure 8.11 sAMAccountName List

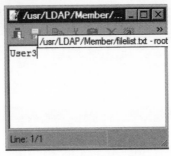

The script will then remove any and all temporary files, as well as move the last master list of users from /usr/LDAP/Member/New/ADGroup.txt to /usr/LDAP/Member/Old/ADGroup.txt.

The same steps as that shown earlier will continue, but the script will use /usr/LDAP/Member/ to work out of instead of /usr/LDAP. The script then makes a list of all the sAMAccountName temporary files and pipes that list to a new text file called /usr/LDAP/Member/filelist.txt (as shown in Figure 8.12).

Figure 8.12 The New Member File List

The script will then read each of those temporary files and make sure everything is in lower case format, as well as create the master user list for that group in another file called ADGroup.txt, which is shown in Figure 8.13.

Figure 8.13 The Edited Member File List

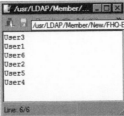

You may have noticed that in some of the searches the users were listed in a random format. This can make any comparison to the old or last search list impossible. The script's next function is to take the ADGroup.txt and sort everything alphabetically (see Figure 8.14).

Figure 8.14 Sorted Member File List

The script then moves this new master user list to /usr/LDAP/Member/New/ADGroup.txt. The script will then do a comparison of the old and new user list.

```
/usr/LDAP/Member/New/ADGroup.txt
/usr/LDAP/Member/Old/ADGroup.txt
```

If there are any users that are in the new ADGroup.txt file that are not in the old ADGroup.txt file, the script then adds those users to the ESX server using the *useradd* command. The same is true for the reverse. If the script finds users in the old.ADGroup.txt file that are not in the new ADGroup.txt file, it will remove those users from the ESX server.

NOTE

There are a couple of things to take note of. In this search and example, the Common Name (CN=) is the same as the SamAccountName. This may not always be the case and is why the multiple searches are done.

The big difference in each section is the way the users are added to the ESX server.

In the first search, the goal was for a user to have "read only" access rights. To accomplish this, the user would not be added to any groups by using –M switch.

The home directory for that user would not be created as well.

```
do useradd -M $newlist
```

For the VM Admin or regular user, the only difference is that I assign those users to be a member of a group that will give those users permissions to the virtual machines needed.

```
do useradd -M -g $esxgroup $newlist
```

Lastly for the ESX server administrators, I use the –o switch which allows the account to be created with a non-unique or duplicate UID (Uniform Identification). The –u switch lets me specify the numerical value of the user's ID. In this case, the users are created with a UID of 0 giving those accounts the root equivalent.

```
do useradd -o -u 0 -g $esxgroup $newlist
```

Extending a Cloned (Deployed) Windows VM's Root Partition

I will show you how to leverage the additional power of Microsoft's Sysprep utility to extend a newly cloned, or deployed, Windows virtual machine's root partition from the original clone size to a size greater than the originally deployed root partition.

> **WARNING**
>
> Make any modifications to your VirtualCenter installation only if you are comfortable with making these changes. I strenuously recommend you make backups of the files you modify before making any modifications.

Jase McCarty (a.k.a., Jasemccarty) from the VMware Community forums came up with the ability to take a standard Clone, or Template, and deploy it with a root partition size greater than the original Clone, or Template, without using any third-party tools.

This becomes very useful in the virtualization world by giving the administrators the ability to deploy Windows VM's with variable sizes, which in turn means less templates will be necessary, while being more flexible with regards to virtual disk space.

Well that sounds great but how does it work. Microsoft's Sysprep, which is utilized by VMware VirtualCenter, has a minimal Sysprep configuration that is used to customize Windows Virtual Machines.

When VMware VirtualCenter clones/deploys a Windows VM, an opportunity is given to customize the guest OS. This process "drops off" a generic sysprep.inf (and other necessary files) to have Windows perform this task.

The additional setting we need to add to the generated sysprep.inf is the ExtendOEMPartition setting in the Unattended section.

The ExtendOEMPartition setting contains the options shown in Table 8.1.

Table 8.1 ExtendOEMPartition Options

Setting	Value	Result
ExtendOEMPartition	0	Do not extend
	1	Extend to the end of the disk
	X	Extend the volume X megabytes

Source: http://support.microsoft.com/kb/240126/

If we modify the process of creating the generic sysprep.inf, then we can grow our partition to the full size of an expanded virtual disk file before it is powered on the first time.

For the initial setup, you will need to modify two files that VMware has provided that generate the sysprep.inf file:

- **Gensysprepinf.vbs** The actual script that generates the sysprep.inf file

- **Autoprep.wsf** The script handling some duties in the deployment of a VM

They are typically located in (as of this writing) **C:\Program Files\VMware\VMware VirtualCenter\scripts** for VC 1.x, and **C:\Program Files\VMware\VMware VirtualCenter 2.0\scripts** for VC 2.x.

These files are encoded using the Microsoft Script Encoder, which you can find here:

`www.microsoft.com/downloads/details.aspx?FamilyId=E7877F67-C447-4873-B1B0-21F0626A6329&displaylang=en` (as of this writing).

You will need to decode these files to be able to work with them. I will not cover the process of decoding these files here, but for more information, check out the Windows Script Decoder which can be found at the this address: www.virtualconspiracy.com/index.php?page=scrdec/intro.

When the files have been decoded, you will need to edit gensysprepinf.vbs to include the ExtendOEMPartition setting.

Look for the [Unattended] section:

```
outStr = "[Unattended]" & vbCrLf _
        & "   OemSkipEula=Yes" & vbCrLf _
        & "   InstallFilesPath=\sysprep\i386" & vbCrLf _
        & vbCrLf _
        & "[GuiUnattended]" & vbCrLf _
        & "   AdminPassword=" & mAdminPassword & vbCrLf _
        & "   OEMSkipRegional=1" & vbCrLf _
        & "   TimeZone=" & mTimeZone & vbCrLf _
        & "   OemSkipWelcome=1" & vbCrLf
```

And change it to:

```
outStr = "[Unattended]" & vbCrLf _
        & "   OemSkipEula=Yes" & vbCrLf _
        & "   ExtendOemPartition=1" & vbCrLf _
        & "   InstallFilesPath=\sysprep\i386" & vbCrLf _
        & vbCrLf _
        & "[GuiUnattended]" & vbCrLf _
        & "   AdminPassword=" & mAdminPassword & vbCrLf _
        & "   OEMSkipRegional=1" & vbCrLf _
        & "   TimeZone=" & mTimeZone & vbCrLf _
        & "   OemSkipWelcome=1" & vbCrLf
```

Then save gensysprepinf.vbs. Because Gensysprepinf.vbs is no longer encoded, autoprep.wsf will need to be modified also. Decode autoprep.wsf, and look for the following line:

```
<script language="VBScript.Encode" src="gensysprepinf.vbs"/>
```

Then change it to:

```
<script language="VBScript" src="gensysprepinf.vbs"/>
```

Then save autoprep.wsf.

The configuration changes are complete.

If you work with clones, you also have the ability to add the ExtendOEMPartition to the sysprep.inf file, which you can create using the setupmgr.exe that comes with Microsoft Sysprep Utility. Once you have created the sysprep.inf file, you can add the ExtendOEMPartition value to the Unattended section of the file:

```
;SetupMgrTag
[Unattended]
    oemSkipEula=Yes
    InstallFilesPath=C:\sysprep\i386
    ExtendOEMPartition=1
```

Deploying a Windows VM with an Expanded Root Partition

Now let's deploy a Windows VM with an expanded root partition.

1. Clone/Deploy a Windows VM and leave the **Automatically Power On** option in the **Clone Virtual Machine Wizard** unchecked, as in Figure 8.15 for VirtualCenter 1.4, or leave the Power On The New Virtual Machine After Creation option unchecked in VirtualCenter 2.0, as shown in Figure 8.16.

Figure 8.15 In VC 1.4: Uncheck "Automatically Power On"

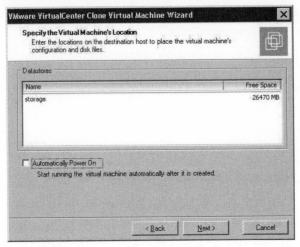

Figure 8.16 In VC 2.0: Uncheck "Power on the New Virtual Machine after Creation"

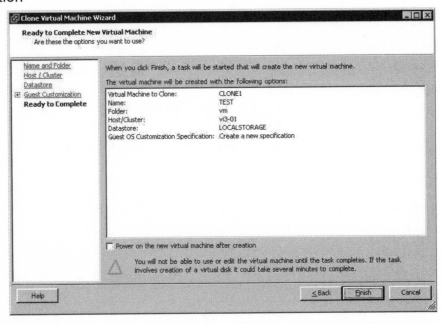

This will give you the opportunity to resize the disk before it runs Sysprep.

2. Use Putty to SSH to an ESX server that has access to the LUN that has the .vmdk on it. (This can be a SAN LUN or on local storage.)

3. Use **vmkfstools –X Size[gGmMkK]** and the full path of the .vmdk. For example, if using a 2GB .vmdk, the following command would resize the .vmdk to 10GB:

```
[root@esxserver ~]# vmkfstools -X 10G /vmfs/storage/winvm.vmdk
```

And with that, you're done. When the Windows VM powers on, the root partition (C:\) will automatically extend to the new .vmdk size of 10GB, rather than having a 2GB partition and an 8GB empty partition.

Summary

So let's review what we have done so far in this chapter. First, we installed APC's Network Shutdown, which is also called PCNS. We used a helper Linux virtual machine that has a graphical interface or GUI to help with the installation and do the configuration to point to the correct UPS. We also learned how to set up Kerberos authentication with ESX and how to search Active Directory or another kind of LDAP server with a script allowing centralized users management for all the ESX servers. Finally, we made a change to the Sysprep scripts to be able to make a template that can have the boot drive grow to fill up an expanded disk, and what to add to the sysprep.inf files on clones to accomplish the same thing.

Appendix A

All Scripts and Program Source

In this appendix, we've compiled the key scripts cited in this book. You can use this appendix as a quick reference point to review these scripts.

Scripts from Chapter 3

The following demonstrates the instantiation of the *VmConnectParams* object in VBScript and how to set the properties listed earlier.

```
Set objConnParams = CreateObject("VmCOM.VmConnectParams")
objConnParams.hostname = "esxserver1"
objConnParams.username = "adminuser1"
objConnParams.password = "password1"
```

The following continues from the previous code example, adding the instantiation of the *VmServerCtl* object and connecting to the host using the previously defined *VmConnectParams* object.

```
Set objVMServer = CreateObject("VmCOM.VmServerCtl")
objVMServer.Connect objConnParams
objVMList = objVMServer.RegisteredVmNames
for vmIndex = 1 to objVMList.Count
     WScript.Echo VM.objVMList(vmCounter)
     vmCounter = vmCounter + 1
next
```

The following demonstrates how you can ensure that no floppy drives are left connected to the VM. After connecting to the ESX host and retrieving a *VmCollection* of all registered VMs, the script connects to each VM individually, checks the connection status of the floppy device, and disconnects it accordingly.

```
' Set parameters used to connect to the ESX Server.
Set objConnParams = CreateObject("VmCOM.VmConnectParams")
objConnParams.hostname = "esxserver1 "
objConnParams.username = "adminuser1"
objConnParams.password = "password1"

' Establish connection with ESX host
Set objVMServer = CreateObject("VmCOM.VmServerCtl")
objVMServer.Connect objConnParams

' Obtain list of registered VMs on host
Set objVMList = objVMServer.RegisteredVmNames

' Step through list of VMs and connect to each one
' individually. Disconnect floppy drive, if connected
For each ConfigFile in objVMList
     Set objVM = CreateObject("VmCOM.VmCtl")
     objVM.Connect objConnParams, ConfigFile
     vmDevice = "floppy0"
     if objVM.DeviceIsConnected(vmDevice) Then
          objVM.DisconnectDevice(vmDevice)
          vmDeviceStatus = "Now Disconnected"
     Else
          vmDeviceStatus = "Was already disconnected"
```

```
        End If
        WScript.Echo "Floppy for VM " & ConfigFile & ":"
        WScript.Echo vbTab & "Status: " & vmDeviceStatus
        WScript.Echo
Next

objVM = Nothing
objVMServer = Nothing
objConnParams = Nothing
```

To pass information to or from the running virtual machine, you must set the *GuestInfo* class of variable using the *VmCtl* object. You can define any number of key names and assign any string value to them. The following example assumes that you have already established a connection to a specific VM using the *VmCtl* object. Here we pass specific values to be retrieved later inside the Guest OS.

```
Set objVM = CreateObject("VmCOM.VmCtl")
objVM.Connect objConnParams, "/home/vmware/server1/server1.vmx"

objVM.GuestInfo("Department") = "Accounting"
objVM.GuestInfo("CostCenter") = "5008620"
objVM.GuestInfo("Priority") = "Low"
```

The following demonstrates the instantiation of the *VMware::VmPerl::ConnectParams* object:

```
use VMware::VmPerl;
use VMware::VmPerl::ConnectParams;
use strict;

my $sName = "esxserver1";
my $port = 902;
my $user = "adminuser1";
my $passwd = "password1";

my $connectParams =
VMware::VmPerl::ConnectParams::new($sName,$port,$user,$passwd);
```

It is always a good practice to code error handling each time you invoke a method. The most basic way to handle any exception is to simply stop the execution of the script with the die directive.

```
# Create a Connect_Params object; no params to new() connects to local machine
my $sName = "esxserver1";
my $port = 902;
my $user = "adminuser1";
my $passwd = "password1";

my $connectParams =
 VMware::VmPerl::ConnectParams::new($sName,$port,$user,$passwd);

# Create a Server object
my $server = VMware::VmPerl::Server::new();
```

```
# Connect to the server using the connect_params
if(!$server->connect($connect_params)) {
        die "Could not connect to local server\n";
}
```

Next, we enumerate the VMs registered with the VMware host and attempt to disconnect the floppy drive and CD-ROM drive from each VM. In this example, we are assuming that only one floppy drive exists as floppy0 and that only one CD/DVD-ROM exists on the IDE bus as ide1:0.

```
# Get a list of registered vmxs
my @list=$server->registered_vm_names();
foreach my $vmx (@list) {
        my $vm = VMware::VmPerl::VM::new();
        if($vm->connect($connect_params, $vmx)) {
                print "\n" . $vm->get_config("displayName");
                if($vm->disconnect_device("floppy0")) {
                        print "\n\tFloppy disconnected.";
                } else {
                        print "\n\tFloppy not disconnected.";
                }
                if($vm->disconnect_device("ide1:0")) {
                        print "\n\tCD-ROM disconnected.";
                } else {
                        print "\n\tCD-ROM not disconnected.";
                }
        } else {
                print "\nCould not connect to VM.";
        }
}
```

The *btnConnect* control is then used to pass this data to *frmVMList*. This is accomplished by creating a new instance of *frmVMList* and assigning the *ConnectToHost* method to the click event of the control, as shown in the following code fragment.

```
Public Class frmConnect
    Private Sub btnConnect_Click(ByVal sender As Object, ByVal e As _
    System.EventArgs) Handles btnConnect.Click
        Dim VMListForm As New frmVMList
        VMListForm.ConnectToHost(vHostName.Text, vUserName.Text, _
          vPassword.Text)
        VMListForm.Show()
    End Sub
End Class
```

The logic in *frmVMList* captures the value for the host name, username, and password to build to connection parameters. After establishing the connection to the host, we then enumerate all of the VMs registered with the Vmware host and retrieve the configuration file for each one, afterward adding that string value to a *listbox* control visible in the form. The following code shows how this is done.

```
Public Class frmVMList
    Dim objConnParams As New VMCOMLib.VmConnectParams
    Dim objVMServer As New VMCOMLib.VmServerCtl
    Dim objVMList As New VMCOMLib.VmCollection
    Dim ConfigFile As String

    Friend Sub ConnectToHost(ByVal HostName As String, ByVal UserName As _
      String, ByVal Password As String)
        objConnParams.Hostname = HostName
        objConnParams.Username = UserName
        objConnParams.Password = Password
        objVMServer.Connect(objConnParams)
        objVMList = objVMServer.RegisteredVmNames
        For Each ConfigFile In objVMList
            lbxVMs.Items.Add(ConfigFile)
        Next
    End Sub

    Private Sub btnClose_Click(ByVal sender As Object, ByVal e As _
      System.EventArgs) Handles btnClose.Click
        Me.Close()
    End Sub

End Class
```

Code Listing 3.1 A vmaConfig.xml File

```
<vma>
    <service>
        <wsdl>vma.wsdl</wsdl>
        <eventlog rollover="true" file="vma" level="info"
    console="true"/>
        <sslport>8443</sslport>
        <externalSchemas>
            <schema>autoprep-types.xsd</schema>
        </externalSchemas>
        <sslCert>C:\Documents and Settings\All Users\Application
    Data\VMware\VMware VirtualCenter\VMA\server.pem</sslCert>
        <sslCAChain>C:\Documents and Settings\All Users\Application
    Data\VMware\VMware VirtualCenter\VMA\root.pem</sslCAChain>
    </service>

    <subjects>
        <subject>
            <implementation>VCenter 1.1</implementation>
            <path>/vcenter</path>
            <hostname>localhost</hostname>
            <port>905</port>
            <eventlog level="info"/>
            <ssl>true</ssl>
            <preload>true</preload>
```

```
      <index>
          <defaultFarm>Default Farm</defaultFarm>
      </index>
    </subject>
  </subjects>
</vma>
```

Code Listing 3.2 C# Script for Connecting to VI Web Service

```csharp
using System;
using VMware.vma;

protected vmaService vma_;

string url = "https://esx1.sample.com:8443";
string username = "adminuser1";
string password = "password1";

public void Connect(string url, string username, string password) {
    vma_ = new vmaService();
    vma_.Url = url;
    vma_.CookieContainer = new System.Net.CookieContainer();
    vma_.Login(username, password);
}
```

Code Listing 3.3 VB.NET Script for Connecting to VI Web Service

```vbnet
Imports System
Imports VMware.vma

Protected vma As VMware.vma.vmaService

Dim url As String = "https://esx1.sample.com:8443"
Dim username As String = "adminuser1"
Dim password As String = "password1"

Public Function Connect(url As string, username As string, password As _
  string)
    vma = New vmaService
    vma.Url = url
    vma.CookieContainer = New System.Net.CookieContainer
    vma.Login(username, password)
End Function
```

Code Listing 3.4 C# Script for Implementing ICerfificatePolicy

```csharp
using System.Net;
using System.Security.Cryptography.X509Certificates;

public class CertPolicy : ICertificatePolicy {
```

```
    public bool CheckValidationResult(
        ServicePoint svcPnt
      , X509Certificate cert
      , WebRequest req
      , int certProblem) {
        return true;
    } // end CheckValidationResult
} // class CertPolicy
```

Code Listing 3.5 VB.NET Script for Implementing ICerfificatePolicy

```
Imports System.Net
Imports System.Security.Cryptography.X509Certificates
Public Class CertPolicy Implements ICertificatePolicy
  Public Function CheckValidationResult(ByVal _
    svcPnt As ServicePoint, ByVal cert As X509Certificate, _
    ByVal req As WebRequest, ByVal certProblem As Integer) _
     As Boolean Implements ICertificatePolicy.CheckValidationResult
    Return True
  End Function
End Class
```

Code Listing 3.6 C# Script for Obtaining Information with *ResolvePath* and *GetContents*

```
string path = "/vm";
string handle = vma_.ResolvePath(path);
ViewContents contentsXML = vma_.GetContents(handle);
Container objContainer = (Container) contentsXML.body;
```

Code Listing 3.7 VB.NET Script for Obtaining Information with *ResolvePath* and *GetContents*

```
Dim contentsXML As VMware.vma.ViewContents
Dim objContainer As VMware.vma.Container

Dim path As String = "/vm"
Dim handle As String = vma.ResolvePath(path)
contentsXML = = vma.GetContents(handle)
objContainer = CType(contentsXML.body, VMware.vma.Container)
```

In this example, we target /vm of the VI Web service hierarchy. We obtain its handle by invoking *ResolvePath* and passing it the string value of the path as set by vPath. The returned XML document from invoking *ResolvePath* is similar to Code Listing 3.8.

Code Listing 3.8 XML Document Returned by Invoking *ResolvePath*

```
<?xml version="1.0" encoding="UTF-8"?>
<env:Envelope xmlns:xsd="http://www.w3.org/2001/XMLSchema"
xmlns:env="http://schemas.xmlsoap.org/soap/envelope/"
xmlns:xsi="http://www.w3.org/2001/XMLSchema-instance">
```

Continued

```
<env:Body>
  <GetContentsResponse xmlns="urn:vma1">
    <returnval>
      <handle>vma-0000-0000-0008</handle>
      <vHandle>vma-0000-0000-0008@c2f53ca4e000003</vHandle>
      <body xsi:type="Container">
        <item>
          <key>vma-vm-00000000011</key>
          <name>564d0f8b-3bde-1003-fe19-0f77cc31a3dc</name>
          <type>VirtualMachine</type>
        </item>
        <item>
          <key>vma-vm-00000000012</key>
          <name>564d71c5-d04d-b62e-748a-9020f0ee481e</name>
          <type>VirtualMachine</type>
        </item>
        <item>
          <key>vma-vm-00000000014</key>
          <name>564d63db-9aaf-97af-4c47-8562e1dc65e0</name>
          <type>VirtualMachine</type>
        </item>
        <item>
          <key>vma-vm-00000000015</key>
          <name>564d71b4-d1fc-fdb9-9c4b-125b3ba0b32a</name>
          <type>VirtualMachine</type>
        </item>
      </body>
    </returnval>
  </GetContentsResponse>
</env:Body>
</env:Envelope>
```

Code Listing 3.9 C# Script for Using vHandles

```
while (
    myTask.currentState.Equals(TaskRunState.running) ||
    myTask.currentState.Equals(TaskRunState.scheduled) ||
    myTask.currentState.Equals(TaskRunState.starting)
    ) {
        VMware.vma.VHandleList vhlist = new VHandleList();
        vhlist.vHandle = new string[] { vc.vHandle };
        UpdateList ul = vma_.GetUpdates(vhlist, true);

        for (int u = 0; u < ul.update.Length; u++) {
            for (int c = 0; c < ul.update[u].change.Length; c++) {
                if (ul.update[u].change[c].target == "currentState") {
                    myTask.currentState =
                        (TaskRunState)ul.update[u].change[c].val;
                } else if (ul.update[u].change[c].target ==
```

```
                    "percentCompleted") {
            myTask.percentCompleted =
                (Single)ul.update[u].change[c].val;
            Console.Write("..." +
                myTask.percentCompleted.ToString());
        }
    }
  }
}
```

Code Listing 3.10 VB.NET Script for Using VHandles

```
While migrateTask.currentState = VMware.vma.TaskRunState.running Or _
 migrateTask.currentState = VMware.vma.TaskRunState.scheduled Or _
 migrateTask.currentState = VMware.vma.TaskRunState.starting
    Dim vhlist As VMware.vma.VHandleList = New VMware.vma.VHandleList
    vhlist.vHandle = New String() {vc.vHandle}
    Dim ul As VMware.vma.UpdateList = vma.GetUpdates(vhlist, True)
    For u = 0 To ul.update.Length - 1
      For c = 0 To ul.update(u).change.Length - 1
        If (ul.update(u).change(c).target = "currentState") Then
          migrateTask.currentState = ul.update(u).change(c).val
        ElseIf (ul.update(u).change(c).target = "percentCompleted") Then
          migrateTask.percentCompleted = ul.update(u).change(c).val
          Console.Write("..." + migrateTask.percentCompleted.ToString())
        End If
      Next c
    Next u
End While
```

Code Listing 3.11 C# Script for Enumerating VMs in a Particular Group

```
string path = "/vcenter/ESXFarm1/ProductionVMs-Fin";
string handle = vma_.ResolvePath(path);
ViewContents contentsXML = vma_.GetContents(handle);
Container objContainer = (Container) contentsXML.body;
Item[] listVMs = objContainer.item;

for (int i = 1; i <= listVMs.Length-1; i++)
{
    contentsXML = vma_.GetContents(listVMs(i).key);
    VirtualMachine vm = contentsXML.body;
    string Name = vm.info.name
    int cfgNumCPU = vm.hardware.cpu.count
    string cfgCPUShares = vm.hardware.cpu.controls.shares
    int cfgSizeMem = vm.hardware.memory.sizeMb
    string CfgMemShares = vm.hardware.memory.controls.shares
    string msg = vmName + "\t"+ cfgNumCPU + "\t" + cfgCPUShares +
      "\t" + cfgSizeMem + "\t" + CfgMemShares;
    System.Console.WriteLine(msg);
}
```

Code Listing 3.12 VB.NET Script for Enumerating VMs in a Particular Group

```
Dim path, handle, vmName, cfgCPUShares, CfgMemShares, msg As String
Dim i, cfgNumCPU, cfgSizeMem As Integer
Dim contentsXML As VMware.vma.ViewContents
Dim objContainer As VMware.vma.Container
Dim listVMs() As VMware.vma.Item
Dim vm As VMware.vma.VirtualMachine

path = "/vcenter/ESXFarm1/ProductionVMs-Fin"
handle = vma.ResolvePath(path)
contentsXML = vma.GetContents(handle)
objContainer = CType(contentsXML.body, VMware.vma.Container)
listVMs = objContainer.item

For i = 0 To listVMs.Length - 1
    contentsXML = vma.GetContents(listVMs(i).key)
    vm = contentsXML.body
    vmName = vm.info.name
    cfgNumCPU = vm.hardware.cpu.count
    cfgCPUShares = vm.hardware.cpu.controls.shares
    cfgSizeMem = vm.hardware.memory.sizeMb
    CfgMemShares = vm.hardware.memory.controls.shares
    msg = vmName & vbTab & cfgNumCPU & vbTab & cfgCPUShares & _
       vbTab & cfgSizeMem & vbTab & CfgMemShares
    System.Console.WriteLine(msg)
Next i
```

Code Listing 3.13 C# Script for Migrating a VM via VMotion

```
string handleHost = vma_.ResolvePath(pathHost);
string handleVM = vma_.ResolvePath(pathVM);
ViewContents contentsXML = vma_.MigrateVM(handleVM, handleHost,
  Level.normal);
```

Code Listing 3.14 VB.NET Script for Migrating a VM via VMotion

```
Dim handleHost, handleVM As String
Dim contentsXML As VMware.vma.ViewContents

handleHost = vma.ResolvePath(pathHost)
handleVM = vma.ResolvePath(pathVM)
contentsXML = vma.MigrateVM(vm, host, VMware.vma.Level.normal)
```

This particular operation, like many others, can be monitored by using the returned vHandle to retrieve updates on the task's progress. For example, Code Listing 3.15 is a sample result from a *StopVM* operation.

Code Listing 3.15 Results for a *StopVM* Operation

```
<?xml version="1.0" encoding="UTF-8"?>
```

```
<env:Envelope xmlns:xsd="http://www.w3.org/2001/XMLSchema"
xmlns:env="http://schemas.xmlsoap.org/soap/envelope/"
xmlns:xsi="http://www.w3.org/2001/XMLSchema-instance">
  <env:Body>
    <StopVMResponse xmlns="urn:vma1">
      <returnval>
        <handle>vma-task-active-0a810</handle>
        <vHandle>vma-task-active-0a810@c2f53ca4e000001</vHandle>
        <body xsi:type="Task">
          <cause>user</cause>
          <entity>vma-vm-00000000012</entity>
          <eventCollector>vma-0000-0000-009b</eventCollector>
          <operationName>Power off VM</operationName>
          <queueTime>2006-07-12T00:56:10-05:00</queueTime>
          <allowCancel>false</allowCancel>
          <currentState>starting</currentState>
        </body>
      </returnval>
    </StopVMResponse>
  </env:Body>
</env:Envelope>
```

Code Listings 3.16 and 3.17 demonstrate how to change the priority of a virtual machine by adjusting the shares allocated to its vCPUs.

Code Listing 3.16 C# Script for Changing the Priority of a VM

```
ViewContents vc = vma_.GetContents(vm);
Change change = new Change();
change.target = "hardware/cpu/controls/shares";
change.val = "high";
change.op = ChangeOp.edit;
change.valSpecified = true;

ChangeReqList changeList = new ChangeReqList();
ChangeReq changeReq = new ChangeReq();
changeReq.handle = vc.handle;
changeReq.change = new Change[] { change };
ChangeReq[] changeReqs = new ChangeReq[] { changeReq };
changeList.req = changeReqs;
UpdateList updateList = vma_.PutUpdates(changeList);
```

Code Listing 3.17 VB.NET Script for Changing the Priority of a VM

```
Dim vc As VMware.vma.ViewContents = vma.GetContents(vm)
Dim change As New VMware.vma.Change
change.target = "hardware/cpu/controls/shares"
change.val = "high"
change.op = VMware.vma.ChangeOp.edit
change.valSpecified = True

Dim changeList As New VMware.vma.ChangeReqList
```

```
Dim changeReq As New VMware.vma.ChangeReq
changeReq.handle = vc.handle
changeReq.change = New VMware.vma.Change() {change}
Dim changeReqs() As VMware.vma.ChangeReq = {changeReq}
changeList.req = changeReqs
Dim updateList As VMware.vma.UpdateList = vma.PutUpdates(changeList)
```

Code Listing 3.18 Port Configuration for the HTTP/HTTPS Proxy

```
<proxyDatabase>
    <server id="0">
        <namespace> / </namespace>
        <host> localhost </host>
        <port> -1 </port>
    </server>
    <server id="1">
        <namespace> /sdk </namespace>
        <host> localhost </host>
        <port> -2 </port>
    </server>
    <redirect id="2">/ui</redirect>
    <server id="3">
        <namespace> /mob </namespace>
        <host> localhost </host>
        <port> 8087 </port>
    </server>
</proxyDatabase>
```

The following example shows the portion of the build batch files for Visual Studio 2005 included in the SDK package that generates the .CS stubs and compiles them as VimService2005.dll.

```
wsdl /n:VimApi /out:stage\VimObjects.cs ..\..\vimService.wsdl ..\..\vim.wsdl
csc /t:library /out:VimService2005.dll stage\*.cs
```

Code Listing 3.19 C# Script for Logging on to the Web Service

```
using System;
using VimApi;

protected VimService _service;
protected ServiceContent _sic;
protected ManagedObjectReference _svcRef;

public void Connect(string url, string username, string password) {
    _service = new VimService();
    _service.Url = url;
    _service.CookieContainer = new System.Net.CookieContainer();

    _svcRef = new ManagedObjectReference();
    _svcRef.type = "ServiceInstance";
```

```
    _svcRef.Value = "ServiceInstance";

    _sic = _service.RetrieveServiceContent(_svcRef);

    if (_sic.sessionManager != null) {
        _service.Login(_sic.sessionManager, username, password, null);
    }
}
```

Code Listing 3.20 VB.NET Script for Logging on to the Web Service

```
Imports System
Imports VimApi

protected _service As VimService
protected _sic As ServiceContent
protected _svcRef as ManagedObjectReference

Public Function connect(url As string, username as String, password As _
  String)
    _service = New VimService
    _service.Url = url
    _service.CookieContainer = New System.Net.CookieContainer

    _svcRef = New ManagedObjectReference
    _svcRef.type = "ServiceInstance"
    _svcRef.Value = "ServiceInstance"

    _sic = _service.RetrieveServiceContent(_svcRef)

    if (_sic.sessionManager != null)
        _service.Login(_sic.sessionManager, username, password, null)
    End if
End Function
```

In addition to using the *CertPolicy* distributed in the SDK package, you can create you own *CertPolicy* that will validate, for example, all certificates. The following sample code implements *ICertificatePolicy* and then accepts every request under SSL:

```
using System.Net;
using System.Security.Cryptography.X509Certificates;

public class CertPolicy : ICertificatePolicy {
    public bool CheckValidationResult(
            ServicePoint svcPnt
          , X509Certificate cert
          , WebRequest req
          , int certProblem) {
        return true;
    } // end CheckValidationResult
} // class CertPolicy
```

Next, we invoke the *retrieveProperties* operation, passing it the *PropertyCollector* managed object reference and the *PropertyFilterSpec* that we constructed. The resulting *ObjectContent* is then used alongside a *DynamicProperty* array to store the values retrieved, which we then write to the console. Note that the variable *_service* was declared and defined upon establishing a connection with the Web service.

```
ObjectContent[] ocary = vimService.retrieveProperties(pCollector,
  new PropertyFilterSpec[] { pfSpec });

if (ocary != null) {
  ObjectContent oc = null;
  ManagedObjectReference mor = null;
  DynamicProperty[] pcary = null;
  DynamicProperty pc = null;
  oc = ocary[0];
  mor = oc.obj;
  pcary = oc.propSet;

  Console.WriteLine("Object Type : " + mor.type);
  Console.WriteLine("Reference Value : " + mor.Value);

  if (pcary != null) {
    pc = pcary[0];
    Console.WriteLine("    Property Name : " + pc.name);
    Console.WriteLine("    Property Value : " + pc.val);
  }
}
```

We begin by creating a new *PropertySpec* instance, followed by a single *ObjectSpec* property:

```
PropertySpec pSpec = new PropertySpec();
pSpec.Type = "VirtualMachine";
pSpec.all = false; pSpec.allSpecified = true;
pSpec.pathSet = new String[] { "guest.hostName", "guest.guestFullName" };

ObjectSpec oSpec = new ObjectSpec();
oSpec.Obj = refDataCenter;
oSpec.Skip = FALSE;
```

Code Listing 3.21 Defining TraversalSpec Objects

```
TraversalSpec dc2HostTSpec = new TraversalSpec();
dc2HostTSpec.Type = "Datacenter";
dc2HostTSpec.Path = "hostFolder";
dc2HostTSpec.SelectSet = new SelectionSpec[]{recursiveSpec};

TraversalSpec dc2VmTSpec = new TraversalSpec();
dc2VmTSpec.Type = "Datacenter";
dc2VmTSpec.Path = "vmFolder";
dc2VmTSpec.SelectSet = new SelectionSpec[]{recursiveSpec};
```

```
TraversalSpec cr2RpTSpec = new TraversalSpec();
cr2RpTSpec.Type = "ComputeResource";
cr2RpTSpec.Path = "resourcePool";

TraversalSpec cr2HostTSpec = new TraversalSpec();
cr2HostTSpec.Type = "ComputeResource";
cr2HostTSpec.Path = "host";

TraversalSpec rp2rpTSpec = new TraversalSpec();
rp2rpTSpec.Type = "ResourcePool";
rp2rpTSpec.Path = "resourcePool";

TraversalSpec folderTSpec = new TraversalSpec();
folderTSpec.Type = "Folder";
folderTSpec.Path = "childEntity";
folderTSpec.SelectSet = new SelectionSpec[]{recursiveSpec,
                                            dc2VmTSpec,
                                            dc2HostTSpec,
                                            cr2RpTSpec,
                                            cr2HostTSpec,
                                            rp2rpTSpec};
```

At that point, we can construct the *PropertyFilterSpec*, as shown Code Listing 3.22.

Code Listing 3.22 *PropertyFilterSpec*

```
oSpec.SelectSet = new SelectionSpec[]{folderTSpec};

PropertyFilterSpec pfSpec = new PropertyFilterSpec();
pfSpec.PropSet = new PropertySpec[] {pSpec};
pfSpec.ObjectSet = new ObjectSpec[] {ospec};
```

Code Listing 3.23 demonstrates the PowerOffVM_Task operation.

Code Listing 3.23 *PowerOffVM_Task*

```
ManagedObjectReference MgdObjRef_VM =
    _service.findByInventoryPath(_sic.SearchIndex(), pathVM);
ManagedObjectReference MgdObjRef_Host =
    _service.findByInventoryPath(_sic.SearchIndex(), pathHost);
ManagedObjectReference MgdObjRef_Task =
    _service.PowerOffVM(MgdObjRef_VM, MgdObjRef_Host);
```

Code Listing 3.24 *MigrateVM_Task*

```
ManagedObjectReference MgdObjRef_VM =
    _service.findByInventoryPath(_sic.SearchIndex(), pathVM);
ManagedObjectReference MgdObjRef_Host =
    _service.findByInventoryPath(_sic.SearchIndex(), pathHost);
ManagedObjectReference MgdObjRef_RPool =
    _service.findByInventoryPath(_sic.SearchIndex(), pathResourcePool);
ManagedObjectReference MgdObjRef_Task =
    _service.MigrateVM(MgdObjRef_VM, MgdObjRef_RPool, MgdObjRef_Host
```

```
        VirtualMachineMovePriority.highPriority,
        VirtualMachinePowerState.poweredOn);
```

Code Listing 3.25 *CreateSnapshot_Task*

```
ManagedObjectReference MgdObjRef_VM =
      _service.findByInventoryPath(_sic.SearchIndex(), pathVM);
boolean memoryDump = false;
boolean quiesceFileSys = true;
string snapName = "Pre-SP1 Snapshot #3";
string snapDescription = "Pre-SP1 Snapshot #3 Created on 2006/08/20";
ManagedObjectReference MgdObjRef_Task =
      _service.CreateSnapshot_Task(MgdObjRef_VM, snapName, snapDescription,
      memoryDump, quiesceFileSys);
```

Code Listing 3.26 *CreateScheduledTask*

```
ManagedObjectReference MgdObjRef_VM =
      _service.FindByInventoryPath(_sic.SearchIndex(), pathVM);

MethodActionArgument[] mActArgumnt = new MethodActionArgument();
MethodAction mAction = new MethodAction();
mActArgumnt.Value = MgdObjRef_VM;
ma.Argument = mActArgumnt;
ma.Name = "MigrateVM";

DailyTaskScheduler dtScheduler = new DailyTaskScheduler();
dtScheduler.Hour = 12;
dtScheduler.Minute = 0;

ScheduledTaskSpec tSpec = new ScheduledTaskSpec();
tSpec.Action = mAction;
tSpec.Scheduler = dtScheduler;
tSpec.Enabled = true;
tSpec.Name = "Migrate virtual machine";
tSpec.Description = "Migrate virtual machine at noon");
tSpec.Notification = "VMAdmin@syngress.com";

_service.createScheduledTask(_sic.ScheduledTaskManager,MgdObjRef_VM,tSpec);
```

Scripts from Chapter 4

Code Listing 4.1 ESX 2.x VMX Code

```
guestOS = "winnetenterprise"
config.version = "6"
virtualHW.version = "3"
scsi0.present = "true"
scsi0.sharedBus = "none"
scsi0.virtualDev = "lsilogic"
```

```
memsize = "512"
scsi0:0.present = "true"
scsi0:0.fileName = "ESX Created VM.vmdk"
scsi0:0.deviceType = "scsi-hardDisk"
ethernet0.present = "true"
ethernet0.allowGuestConnectionControl = "false"
ethernet0.networkName = "VM Network"
ethernet0.addressType = "vpx"
```

Code Listing 4.2 ESX 3.x VMX Code

```
guestOS = "winnetenterprise"
config.version = "8"
virtualHW.version = "4"
scsi0.present = "true"
scsi0.sharedBus = "none"
scsi0.virtualDev = "lsilogic"
memsize = "512"
scsi0:0.present = "true"
scsi0:0.fileName = "ESX Created VM.vmdk"
scsi0:0.deviceType = "scsi-hardDisk"
ethernet0.present = "true"
ethernet0.allowGuestConnectionControl = "false"
ethernet0.networkName = "VM Network"
ethernet0.addressType = "vpx"
```

Once you start a VM using a VMX configuration file like the ones shown in Code Listings 4.1 and 4.2, VMware will generate additional entries in the VMX. These entries identify the virtual machine and set default values for the virtual machine. Examples of these types of entries are shown in Code Listing 4.3

Code Listing 4.3 VMWare Auto Generated VMX Entry Examples

```
uuid.bios = "56 4d ee 3c 52 06 a3 de-be 4a 73 9c cc 79 25 2b "
ethernet0.generatedAddress = "00:50:56:a7:42:e2"
powerType.powerOff = "default"
powerType.powerOn = "default"
powerType.suspend = "default"
powerType.reset = "default"
```

Code Listing 4.4 Example Virtual Machine Configuration File

```
config.version = "6"
virtualHW.version = "3"
memsize = "256"
floppy0.present = "false"
displayName = "newVM"
guestOS = "winNetStandard"
ide0:0.present = "TRUE"
ide0:0.deviceType = "cdrom-raw"
ide:0.startConnected = "false"
floppy0.startConnected = "FALSE"
floppy0.fileName = "/dev/fd0"
Ethernet0.present = "TRUE"
```

```
Ethernet0.connectionType = "monitor_dev"
Ethernet0.networkName = "VM Network"
Ethernet0.addressType = "vpx"
scsi0.present = "true"
scsi0.sharedBus = "none"
scsi0.virtualDev = "lsilogic"
scsi0:0.present = "true"
scsi0:0.fileName = "newvm.vmdk"
scsi0:0.deviceType = "scsi-hardDisk"
```

Code Listing 4.5 vmkfstools Command Options for Virtual Disks

```
vmkfstools
OPTIONS FOR VIRTUAL DISKS:
vmkfstools -c --createvirtualdisk #[gGmMkK]
               -d --diskformat [zeroedthick|
                                eagerzeroedthick|
                                thick|
                                thin]
               -a --adapterType [buslogic|lsilogic]
           -w --writezeros
           -j --inflatedisk
           -U --deletevirtualdisk
           -E --renamevirtualdisk srcDisk
           -i --clonevirtualdisk srcDisk
               -d --diskformat [rdm:<device>|rdmp:<device>|
                                raw:<device>|thin|2gbsparse]
           -X --extendvirtualdisk #[gGmMkK]
           -M --migratevirtualdisk
           -r --createrdm /vmfs/devices/disks/...
           -q --queryrdm
           -z --createrdmpassthru /vmfs/devices/disks/...
           -Q --createrawdevice /vmfs/devices/generic/...
           -v --verbose #
           -g --geometry
    vmfsPath
```

Code Listing 4.6 Scripted VM Creation

```
##### VM Creation Script ###################################
#Script Version 1.1
#Author David E. Hart
#Date 10-05-06
#
#--------+
# Purpose|
#--------+-------------------------------------------------
# This script will create a VM with the following attributes;
# Virtual Machine Name = ScriptedVM
# Location of Virtual Machine = /VMFS/volumes/storage1/ScriptedVM
# Virtual Machine Type = "Microsoft Windows 2003 Standard"
# Virtual Machine Memory Allocation = 256 meg
```

```
#
#----------------------------------------+
#Custom Variable Section for Modification|
#----------------------------------------+--------------------
#NVM is name of virtual machine(NVM). No Spaces allowed in name
#NVMDIR is the directory which holds all the VM files
#NVMOS specifies VM Operating System
#NVMSIZE is the size of the virtual disk to be created
#------------------------------------------------------------
############################################################

### Default Variable settings - change this to your preferences
NVM="ScriptedVM"          # Name of Virtual Machine
NVMDIR="ScriptedVM"       # Specify only the folder name to be created; NOT the
complete path
NVMOS="winnetstandard" # Type of OS for Virtual Machine
NVMSIZE="4g"              # Size of Virtual Machine Disk
VMMEMSIZE="256"           # Default Memory Size

### End Variable Declaration

mkdir /vmfs/volumes/storage1/$NVMDIR # Creates directory
exec 6>&1                              # Sets up write to file
exec 1>/vmfs/volumes/storage1/$NVMDIR/$NVM.vmx # Open file
# write the configuration
echo config.version = '"'6'"'        # For ESX 3.x the value is 8
echo virtualHW.version = '"'3'"'  # For ESX 3.x the value is 4
echo memsize = '"'$VMMEMSIZE'"'
echo floppy0.present = '"'TRUE'"' # setup VM with floppy
echo displayName = '"'$NVM'"'        # name of virtual machine
echo guestOS = '"'$NVMOS'"'
echo
echo ide0:0.present = '"'TRUE'"'
echo ide0:0.deviceType = '"'cdrom-raw'"'
echo ide:0.startConnected = '"'false'"'   # CDROM enabled
echo floppy0.startConnected = '"'FALSE'"'
echo floppy0.fileName = '"'/dev/fd0'"'
echo Ethernet0.present = '"'TRUE'"'
echo Ethernet0.networkName = '"'VM Network'"' # Default network
echo Ethernet0.addressType = '"'vpx'"'
echo
echo scsi0.present = '"'true'"'
echo scsi0.sharedBus = '"'none'"'
echo scsi0.virtualDev = '"'lsilogic'"'
echo scsi0:0.present = '"'true'"'    # Virtual Disk Settings
echo scsi0:0.fileName = '"'$NVM.vmdk'"'
echo scsi0:0.deviceType = '"'scsi-hardDisk'"'


echo
# close file
```

```
exec 1>&-

# make stdout a copy of FD 6 (reset stdout), and close FD6
exec 1>&6
exec 6>&-

# Change permissions on the file so it can be executed by anyone
chmod 755 /vmfs/volumes/storage1/$NVMDIR/$NVM.vmx

#Creates 4gb Virtual disk
cd /vmfs/volumes/storage1/$NVMDIR    #change to the VM dir
vmkfstools -c $NVMSIZE $NVM.vmdk -a lsilogic

#Register VM
vmware-cmd -s register /vmfs/volumes/storage1/$NVMDIR/$NVM.vmx
```

Code Listing 4.7 Scripted VM Creation with PERL

```
#!/usr/bin/perl -w

use VMware::VmPerl;
use VMware::VmPerl::Server;
use VMware::VmPerl::ConnectParams;
#use strict;

##### VM Menu Driven Creation Script ############
#Script Version 1.8
#Author David E. Hart
#Date 10-05-06
#
#----------+
#Purpose   |
#----------
# This script present a menu for automatically building
# Virtual Machine config files (VMX) and Dis files (VMDK)
# This script demonstrates how to could automate the setup
# of a virtual environments
#-------------------------+
#Custom Variables Section  |
#-------------------------+
#vmname = virtual machine name, will be used for disk as well
#vmmem = amount of memory assigned to VM
#vmos = OS that VM is configured for
#vmdisk = size of VM disk
#################################################

main:      # main menu

system("clear");
print "                       MAIN MENU \n";
print "------------------- Virtual Machine Creation --------- \n";
print "\n";
```

```perl
print "\n";
print "\n";
print "                      1) Create a Custom VM \n";
print "\n";
print "                      2) Create VM's from Defined Templates \n";
print "\n";
print "                      3) View ESX's registered VM's \n";
print "\n";
print "                      4) Exit \n";
print "\n";
print "        Your Selection - ";
$menuopt = <>; chomp $menuopt;        # Get user selection
if ($menuopt == 1) {    # Get input for custom VM
        system("clear");
        print "What do you Want to Name your VM? ";
        $vmname = <>; chomp $vmname;    # use chomp to remove carriage return
        print "How much memory do you want to assign? ";
        $vmmem = <>;chomp $vmmem;
        print "Do you want to Run Windows 2003STD as the OS? (y/n) ";
        $vmos = <>;chomp $vmos;
        if ($vmos eq "y") {
            $vmos = "winNetStandard";
            }            # Only 2 options for this example
        else {
            print "Do you want to Run Windows 2003Ent as the OS? (y/n) ";
            $vmos2 = <>;chomp $vmos2;
            if ($vmos2 eq "y") {
                $vmos = "winnetenterprise";
            }
            }
        print "What size hard disk do you want to setup (gb)? ";
        $vmdisk = <>;chomp $vmdisk;
        print "\n";
        $x = writevmx();    # Subrouting for creating VMX file
        if ($x == 1) {
            print "VMX File written successfully \n";
            }
        $w = setper();      # Subroutine to set permissions so anyone can use
VM
        if ($w == 1) {
            print "Permisions set successfully \n";
            }
        $y = createdisk();  # subrouting to create VMDK disk file
        if ($y == 1) {
            print "Virtual Disk Created successfully \n";
            }
        $z = registervm();  # subroutine to register VM with ESX
        if ($z == 1) {
            print "VM registered successfully \n";
            }
        print "Press the ENTER key to continue ...";
```

```
            $pause = <STDIN>;
            goto main


                }
if ($menuopt == 2) {    # option to displays the templates
menu1:
            system("clear");
            print "                        Defined Templates \n";
            print "                        ----------------- \n";
            print "\n";
            print "\n";
            print "         1) Windows 2003std VM with 256m, 4gb drive \n";
            print "\n";
            print "         2) Windows 2003ent VM with 1gig, 8gb drive \n";
            print "\n";
            print "\n";
            print "\n";
            print "\n";
            print "   Your Selection - ";
            $menu1opt = <>; chomp $menu1opt;
            if ($menu1opt == 1) {
                $vmname = "2003std25m4gb";
                $vmmem = "256";   # change and add on similar sections
                $vmdisk = "4";  , # to create templates for your environment
                $vmos = "winnetstandard";
                $x = writevmx();
                  if ($x == 1) {
                  print "VMX File written successfully \na";
                  }
                $w = setper();
                  if ($w == 1) {
                  print "Permisions set successfully \na";
                  }
                $y = createdisk();           # Call subroutines to create VM's
                  if ($y == 1) {
                  print "Virtual Disk Created successfully \na";
                  }
                $z = registervm();
                  if ($z == 1) {
                  print "VM registered successfully \na";
                  }
                 print "Press the ENTER key to continue ...";
                 $pause = <STDIN>;
                 goto main
                }
            if ($menu1opt == 2) {
                $vmname = "2003Ent1gb8gb";
                $vmmem = "1024";
                $vmdisk = "8";
                $vmos = "winnetenterprise";
                $x = writevmx();
```

```
            if ($x == 1) {
            print "VMX File written successfully \na";
            }
        $w = setper();
            if ($w == 1) {
            print "Permisions set successfully \na";
            }
        $y = createdisk();
            if ($y == 1) {
            print "Virtual Disk Created successfully \na";
            }
        $z = registervm();
            if ($z == 1) {
            print "VM registered successfully \na";
            }
        print "Press the ENTER key to continue ...";
        $pause = <STDIN>;
        goto main
        }
    else {
        goto menu1;
        }


    }
if ($menuopt == 3) {      # Use a function of VMPERL to display registered VM's
        system("clear");
        my ($server_name, $user, $passwd) = @ARGV;  # Assume running in ESX
server
        my $port = 902;                              # with appropriate
rights
        VMware::VmPerl::ConnectParams::new($server_name,$port,$user,$passwd);
        VMware::VmPerl::ConnectParams::new(undef,$port,$user,$passwd);
        my $connect_params = VMware::VmPerl::ConnectParams::new();


        # Establish a persistent connection with server
        my $server = VMware::VmPerl::Server::new();
        if (!$server->connect($connect_params)) {
            my ($error_number, $error_string) = $server->get_last_error();
            die "Could not connect to server: Error $error_number:
$error_string\n";
        }

        print "\nThe following virtual machines are registered:\n";

        # Obtain a list containing every config file path registered with the
server.
        my @list = $server->registered_vm_names();
        if (!defined($list[0])) {
            my ($error_number, $error_string) = $server->get_last_error();
            die "Could not get list of VMs from server: Error $error_number: ".
```

```
                      "$error_string\n";
            }

        print "$_\n" foreach (@list);

        # Destroys the server object, thus disconnecting from the server.
        undef $server;
        print "Press the ENTER key to continue ...";
        $pause = <STDIN>;
        goto main


}
if ($menuopt == 4) {
    goto end1
  }


sub writevmx {        # Subroutine to Create VM's VMX config file

#        $file = '/vmfs/volumes/storage1/perlvm/perlvm.vmx';          # Name
the file
        $file = "/vmfs/volumes/storage1/perlvm/" . $vmname . ".vmx";
        open(INFO, ">$file");    # Open for output
        print INFO 'config.version = "6" ' . "\n";
        print INFO 'virtualHW.version = "3" ' . "\n";
        print INFO 'memsize = "' . $vmmem . '" ' . "\n";
        print INFO 'floppy0.present = "TRUE" ' . "\n";
        print INFO 'displayName = "' . $vmname . '" ' . "\n";
        print INFO 'guestOS = "' . $vmos . '" ' . "\n";
        print INFO 'ide0:0.present = "TRUE" ' . "\n";
        print INFO 'ide0:0.deviceType = "cdrom-raw" ' . "\n";
        print INFO 'ide:0.startConnected = "false" ' . "\n";
        print INFO 'floppy0.startConnected = "FALSE" ' . "\n";
        print INFO 'floppy0.fileName = "/dev/fd0" ' . "\n";
        print INFO 'Ethernet0.present = "TRUE" ' . "\n";
        print INFO 'Ethernet0.connectionType = "monitor_dev" ' . "\n";
        print INFO 'Ethernet0.networkName = "VM Network" ' . "\n";
        print INFO 'Ethernet0.addressType = "vpx" ' . "\n";
        print INFO 'scsi0.present = "true" ' . "\n";
        print INFO 'scsi0.sharedBus = "none" ' . "\n";
        print INFO 'scsi0.virtualDev = "lsilogic" ' . "\n";
        print INFO 'scsi0:0.present = "true" ' . "\n";
        print INFO 'scsi0:0.fileName = "' . $vmname . '.vmdk" ' . "\n";
        print INFO 'scsi0:0.deviceType = "scsi-hardDisk" ' . "\n";

        close(INFO);                          # Close the file
}

sub createdisk {    # Subroutine to Create Virtual Disk
        $cr = "vmkfstools -c " . $vmdisk . "g " . "
/vmfs/volumes/storage1/perlvm/". $vmname . ".vmdk -a lsilogic";
```

```
                        system("$cr");
                };



sub registervm {       # Subroutine to Register VM with ESX server
                $rg = "vmware-cmd -s register /vmfs/volumes/storage1/perlvm/" .
$vmname . ".vmx";
                system("$rg");
        }


sub setper{            # Subroutine to set permission on VMX file
                $pm = "chmod 755 /vmfs/volumes/storage1/perlvm/" . $vmname . ".vmx";
                system("$pm");
        }


end1:
```

Code Listing 4.8 Scripted Creation of VM with Perl Key Variables

```
$vmname = virtual machine name, will be used for disk as well
$vmmem = amount of memory assigned to VM
$vmos = OS that VM is configured for
$vmdisk = size of VM disk
```

Code Listing 4.9 Perl Script Static Variables for Template VM Creation

```
if ($menu1opt == 1) {
                $vmname = "2003std25m4gb";
                $vmmem = "256";
                $vmdisk = "4";
                $vmos = "winnetstandard";
```

Once you have your source Template virtual disk ready, go ahead and edit the code to support cloning (see Code Listing 4.10)

Code Listing 4.10 ESX Shell Script VM Creation Utilizing Cloning

```
##### VM Creation Script Utilizing Cloning ###################
#Script Version 1.2
#Author David E. Hart
#Date 10-05-06
#
#--------+
# Purpose|
#--------+--------------------------------------------------------
# This script will create a VM utilizing the cloning option of # vmkfstools
command tool;
# The New Virtual Machine Configuration will be set as follows
# Virtual Machine Name = ScriptedCloneVM
# Location of Virtual Machine = /VMFS/volumes/storage1/ScriptedVM
# Virtual Machine Type = "Microsoft Windows 2003 Standard"
# Virtual Machine Memory Allocation = 256 meg
#
```

```
#----------------------------------------+
#Custom Variable Section for Modification|
#----------------------------------------+--------------------
#NVM is name of virtual machine(NVM). No Spaces allowed in name
#NVMDIR is the directory which holds all the VM files
#NVMOS specifies VM Operating System
#-------------------------------------------------------------
###############################################################

### Default Variable settings - change this to your preferences
NVM="ScriptedCloneVM"        # Name of Virtual Machine
NVMDIR="ScriptedCloneVM"     # Specify only the folder name to be created; NOT
the complete path
NVMOS="winnetstandard" # Type of OS for Virtual Machine
VMMEMSIZE="256"             # Default Memory Size

### End Variable Declaration

mkdir /vmfs/volumes/storage1/$NVMDIR # Creates directory
exec 6>&1                            # Sets up write to file
exec 1>/vmfs/volumes/storage1/$NVMDIR/$NVM.vmx # Open file
# write the configuration
echo config.version = '"'6'"'      # For ESX 3.x the value is 8
echo virtualHW.version = '"'3'"'   # For ESX 3.x the value is 4
echo memsize = '"'$VMMEMSIZE'"'
echo floppy0.present = '"'TRUE'"' # setup VM with floppy
echo displayName = '"'$NVM'"'       # name of virtual machine
echo guestOS = '"'$NVMOS'"'
echo
echo ide0:0.present = '"'TRUE'"'
echo ide0:0.deviceType = '"'cdrom-raw'"'
echo ide:0.startConnected = '"'false'"'  # CDROM enabled
echo floppy0.startConnected = '"'FALSE'"'
echo floppy0.fileName = '"'/dev/fd0'"'
echo Ethernet0.present = '"'TRUE'"'
echo Ethernet0.networkName = '"'VM Network'"' # Default network
echo Ethernet0.addressType = '"'vpx'"'
echo
echo scsi0.present = '"'true'"'
echo scsi0.sharedBus = '"'none'"'
echo scsi0.virtualDev = '"'lsilogic'"'
echo scsi0:0.present = '"'true'"'    # Virtual Disk Settings
echo scsi0:0.fileName = '"'$NVM.vmdk'"'
echo scsi0:0.deviceType = '"'scsi-hardDisk'"'


echo
# close file
exec 1>&-
```

```
# make stdout a copy of FD 6 (reset stdout), and close FD6
exec 1>&6
exec 6>&-

# Change permissions on the file so it can be executed by anyone
chmod 755 /vmfs/volumes/storage1/$NVMDIR/$NVM.vmx

#Clone existing Template VM's VMDK into current directory
cd /vmfs/volumes/storage1/$NVMDIR    #change to the VM dir
vmkfstools -i /vmfs/volumes/storage1/ScriptedVM/ScriptedVM.vmdk $NVM.vmdk

#Register VM
vmware-cmd -s register /vmfs/volumes/storage1/$NVMDIR/$NVM.vmx
```

Code Listing 4.11 Scripted VM Creation with Perl Utilizing Cloning

```perl
#!/usr/bin/perl -w

use VMware::VmPerl;
use VMware::VmPerl::Server;
use VMware::VmPerl::ConnectParams;
#use strict;

##### VM Menu Driven Creation Script with Cloning ############
#Script Version 1.3
#Author David E. Hart
#Date 10-05-06
#
#----------+
#Purpose   |
#----------
# This script present a menu for automatically building
# Virtual Machine config files (VMX) and Disk files (VMDK)
# This script demonstrates how to could automate the setup
# of a virtual environments and includes Cloning of VM.s
#-------------------------+
#Custom Variables Section  |
#-------------------------+
#vmname = virtual machine name, will be used for disk as well
#vmmem = amount of memory assigned to VM
#vmos = OS that VM is configured for
#vmdisk = size of VM disk
###################################################

main:      # main menu

system("clear");
print "                     MAIN MENU \n";
print "------------------ Virtual Machine Creation --------- \n";
print "\n";
```

```perl
print "\n";
print "\n";
print "                    1) Create a Custom VM \n";
print "\n";
print "                    2) Create VM's from Defined Templates \n";
print "\n";
print "                    3) View ESX's registered VM's \n";
print "\n";
print "                    4) Clone an Existing VM \n";
print "\n";
print "                    5) Exit \n";
print "\n";
print "      Your Selection - ";
$menuopt = <>; chomp $menuopt;        # Get user selection
if ($menuopt == 1) {    # Get input for custom VM
        system("clear");
        print "What do you Want to Name your VM? ";
        $vmname = <>; chomp $vmname;    # use chomp to remove carriage return
        print "How much memory do you want to assign? ";
        $vmmem = <>;chomp $vmmem;
        print "Do you want to Run Windows 2003STD as the OS? (y/n) ";
        $vmos = <>;chomp $vmos;
        if ($vmos eq "y") {
            $vmos = "winNetStandard";
            }            # Only 2 options for this example
        else {
            print "Do you want to Run Windows 2003Ent as the OS? (y/n) ";
            $vmos2 = <>;chomp $vmos2;
            if ($vmos2 eq "y") {
                $vmos = "winnetenterprise";
            }
        }
        print "What size hard disk do you want to setup (gb)? ";
        $vmdisk = <>;chomp $vmdisk;
        print "\n";
        $x = writevmx();    # Subrouting for creating VMX file
        if ($x == 1) {
            print "VMX File written successfully \n";
            }
        $w = setper();        # Subroutine to set permissions so anyone can use
VM
        if ($w == 1) {
            print "Permisions set successfully \n";
            }
        $y = createdisk();  # subrouting to create VMDK disk file
        if ($y == 1) {
            print "Virtual Disk Created successfully \n";
            }
        $z = registervm();  # subroutine to register VM with ESX
        if ($z == 1) {
            print "VM registered successfully \n";
```

```
            }
        print "Press the ENTER key to continue ...";
        $pause = <STDIN>;
        goto main


            }
if ($menuopt == 2) {    # option to displays the templates
menu1:
        system("clear");
        print "                    Defined Templates \n";
        print "                    ---------------- \n";
        print "\n";
        print "\n";
        print "          1) Windows 2003std VM with 256m, 4gb drive \n";
        print "\n";
        print "          2) Windows 2003ent VM with 1gig, 8gb drive \n";
        print "\n";
        print "\n";
        print "\n";
        print "\n";
        print "   Your Selection - ";
        $menu1opt = <>; chomp $menu1opt;
        if ($menu1opt == 1) {
            $vmname = "2003std25m4gb";
            $vmmem = "256";   # change and add on similar sections
            $vmdisk = "4";    # to create templates for your environment
            $vmos = "winnetstandard";
            $x = writevmx();
              if ($x == 1) {
              print "VMX File written successfully \na";
              }
            $w = setper();
              if ($w == 1) {
              print "Permisions set successfully \na";
              }
            $y = createdisk();           # Call subroutines to create VM's
              if ($y == 1) {
              print "Virtual Disk Created successfully \na";
              }
            $z = registervm();
              if ($z == 1) {
              print "VM registered successfully \na";
              }
             print "Press the ENTER key to continue ...";
             $pause = <STDIN>;
             goto main
            }
        if ($menu1opt == 2) {
            $vmname = "2003Ent1gb8gb";
            $vmmem = "1024";
            $vmdisk = "8";
```

```perl
                $vmos = "winnetenterprise";
                $x = writevmx();
                    if ($x == 1) {
                    print "VMX File written successfully \na";
                    }
                $w = setper();
                    if ($w == 1) {
                    print "Permisions set successfully \na";
                    }
                $y = createdisk();
                    if ($y == 1) {
                    print "Virtual Disk Created successfully \na";
                    }
                $z = registervm();
                    if ($z == 1) {
                    print "VM registered successfully \na";
                    }
            print "Press the ENTER key to continue ...";
            $pause = <STDIN>;
            goto main
               }
         else {
               goto menu1;
             }


         }
if ($menuopt == 3) {      # Use a function of VMPERL to display registered VM's
        system("clear");
        my ($server_name, $user, $passwd) = @ARGV;   # Assume running in ESX
server
        my $port = 902;                              # with appropriate
rights
        VMware::VmPerl::ConnectParams::new($server_name,$port,$user,$passwd);
        VMware::VmPerl::ConnectParams::new(undef,$port,$user,$passwd);
        my $connect_params = VMware::VmPerl::ConnectParams::new();


        # Establish a persistent connection with server
        my $server = VMware::VmPerl::Server::new();
        if (!$server->connect($connect_params)) {
            my ($error_number, $error_string) = $server->get_last_error();
            die "Could not connect to server: Error $error_number:
$error_string\n";
            }

        print "\nThe following virtual machines are registered:\n";

        # Obtain a list containing every config file path registered with the
server.
        my @list = $server->registered_vm_names();
        if (!defined($list[0])) {
```

```
          my ($error_number, $error_string) = $server->get_last_error();
          die "Could not get list of VMs from server: Error $error_number: ".
             "$error_string\n";
       }

       print "$_\n" foreach (@list);

       # Destroys the server object, thus disconnecting from the server.
       undef $server;
       print "Press the ENTER key to continue ...";
       $pause = <STDIN>;
       goto main


}
if ($menuopt == 4) {
       system("clear");
       print "                        Clone Existing VM.s \n";
       print "                        ------------------- \n";
       print "\n";
       print "\n";
       print "          1) Clone ScriptedVM \n";
       print "\n";
       print "          2) Clone ScriptedPerlVM \n";
       print "\n";
       print "\n";
       print "\n";
       print "\n";
       print "   Your Selection - ";
       $menu4opt = <>; chomp $menu4opt;
       if ($menu4opt == 1) {
          $vmname = "ScriptedPerlCloneVM";
          $vmmem = "256";  # change and add on similar sections
          $vmdisk = "4";   # to create templates for your environment
          $vmos = "winnetstandard";
          $vmpath ="/vmfs/volumes/storage1/ScriptedVM/ScriptedVM.vmdk";
          $x = writevmx();
            if ($x == 1) {
            print "VMX File written successfully \na";
            }
          $w = setper();
            if ($w == 1) {
            print "Permisions set successfully \na";
            }
          $y = clonedisk();          # Call subroutines to create VM's
            if ($y == 1) {
            print "Virtual Disk Cloned successfully \na";
            }
          $z = registervm();
            if ($z == 1) {
            print "VM registered successfully \na";
            }
```

```perl
                        print "Press the ENTER key to continue ...";
                        $pause = <STDIN>;
                        goto main
                        }
                if ($menu4opt == 2) {
                        $vmname = "ScriptedPerlVMClone";
                        $vmmem = "1024";
                        $vmdisk = "8";
                        $vmos = "winnetenterprise";
                        $vmpath ="/vmfs/volumes/storage1/perlvm/ScriptedPerlVM";

                        $x = writevmx();
                          if ($x == 1) {
                          print "VMX File written successfully \na";
                          }
                        $w = setper();
                          if ($w == 1) {
                          print "Permisions set successfully \na";
                          }
                        $y = clonedisk();
                          if ($y == 1) {
                          print "Virtual Disk Cloned successfully \na";
                          }
                        $z = registervm();
                          if ($z == 1) {
                          print "VM registered successfully \na";
                          }
                        print "Press the ENTER key to continue ...";
                        $pause = <STDIN>;
                        goto main
                          }
                else {
                          goto menu1;
                          }

        }


if ($menuopt == 5) {
    goto end1
    }

sub writevmx {          # Subroutine to Create VM's VMX config file

#          $file = '/vmfs/volumes/storage1/perlvm/perlvm.vmx';          # Name
the file
          $file = "/vmfs/volumes/storage1/perlvm/" . $vmname . ".vmx";
          open(INFO, ">$file");    # Open for output
          print INFO 'config.version = "6" ' . "\n";
          print INFO 'virtualHW.version = "3" ' . "\n";
          print INFO 'memsize = "' . $vmmem . '" ' . "\n";
```

```perl
        print INFO 'floppy0.present = "TRUE" ' . "\n";
        print INFO 'displayName = "' . $vmname . '" ' . "\n";
        print INFO 'guestOS = "' . $vmos . '" ' . "\n";
        print INFO 'ide0:0.present = "TRUE" ' . "\n";
        print INFO 'ide0:0.deviceType = "cdrom-raw" ' . "\n";
        print INFO 'ide:0.startConnected = "false" ' . "\n";
        print INFO 'floppy0.startConnected = "FALSE" ' . "\n";
        print INFO 'floppy0.fileName = "/dev/fd0" ' . "\n";
        print INFO 'Ethernet0.present = "TRUE" ' . "\n";
        print INFO 'Ethernet0.connectionType = "monitor_dev" ' . "\n";
        print INFO 'Ethernet0.networkName = "VM Network" ' . "\n";
        print INFO 'Ethernet0.addressType = "vpx" ' . "\n";
        print INFO 'scsi0.present = "true" ' . "\n";
        print INFO 'scsi0.sharedBus = "none" ' . "\n";
        print INFO 'scsi0.virtualDev = "lsilogic" ' . "\n";
        print INFO 'scsi0:0.present = "true" ' . "\n";
        print INFO 'scsi0:0.fileName = "' . $vmname . '.vmdk" ' . "\n";
        print INFO 'scsi0:0.deviceType = "scsi-hardDisk" ' . "\n";

        close(INFO);                            # Close the file
}

sub createdisk {    # Subroutine to Create Virtual Disk
        $cr = "vmkfstools -c " . $vmdisk . "g " . "
/vmfs/volumes/storage1/perlvm/". $vmname . ".vmdk -a lsilogic";
        system("$cr");
        };

sub clonedisk {    # Subroutine to Create Virtual Disk
        $cr = "vmkfstools -i " . $vmpath . " " . "
/vmfs/volumes/storage1/perlvm/" . $vmname . "vmdk";
        system("$cr");
        };

sub registervm {    # Subroutine to Register VM with ESX server
        $rg = "vmware-cmd -s register /vmfs/volumes/storage1/perlvm/" .
$vmname . ".vmx";
        system("$rg");
        }

sub setper{         # Subroutine to set permission on VMX file
        $pm = "chmod 755 /vmfs/volumes/storage1/perlvm/" . $vmname . ".vmx";
        system("$pm");
        }

end1:
```

Scripts from Chapter 5

Code Listing 5.1 A Disk Descriptor File

```
# Disk DescriptorFile
version=1
CID=2af6d34d
parentCID=ffffffff
createType="twoGbMaxExtentSparse"

# Extent description
RW 4192256 SPARSE "Windows-s001.vmdk"
RW 4192256 SPARSE "Windows-s002.vmdk"
RW 4096 SPARSE "Windows-s003.vmdk"

# The Disk Data Base
#DDB

ddb.adapterType = "ide"
ddb.geometry.sectors = "63"
ddb.geometry.heads = "16"
ddb.geometry.cylinders = "8322"
ddb.virtualHWVersion = "4"
ddb.toolsVersion =
```

If you need to change the type of file, use the tool vmware-vdiskmanager to change the type.

```
# Extent description
RW 4192256 SPARSE "Windows-s001.vmdk"
RW 4192256 SPARSE "Windows-s002.vmdk"
RW 4096 SPARSE "Windows-s003.vmdk"
```

Code Listing 5.2 A Disk Descriptor for an IDE Virtual Disk

```
# The Disk Data Base
#DDB

ddb.adapterType = "ide"
ddb.geometry.sectors = "63"
ddb.geometry.heads = "16"
ddb.geometry.cylinders = "8322"
ddb.virtualHWVersion = "4"
ddb.toolsVersion = "6404"
```

Code Listing 5.3 A vmx File

```
#!/usr/bin/vmware
config.version = "6"
scsi0:0.present = "TRUE"
scsi0:0.name = "ESX_SAN4:2K900.vmdk"
scsi0:0.mode = "persistent"
```

```
scsi0.present = "true"
scsi0.virtualDev = "vmxbuslogic"
memSize = "512"
displayName = "2K900"
guestOS = "win2000Serv"
ethernet0.present = "true"
ethernet0.connectionType = "monitor_dev"
ethernet0.devName = "bond0"
ethernet0.networkName = "FH_Network"
Ethernet0.addressType = "vpx"
Ethernet0.generatedAddress = "00:50:56:9d:4d:10"
Ethernet0.virtualDev = "vmxnet"
floppy0.present = "true"
floppy0.startConnected = "false"
ide1:0.present = "true"
ide1:0.fileName = "/dev/cdrom"
ide1:0.deviceType = "atapi-cdrom"
ide1:0.startConnected = "FALSE"

draw = "gdi"
uuid.bios = "50 1d 07 5c a9 f3 2b dd-8b 3e 83 10 b2 ea 89 0b"
uuid.location = "56 4d b5 45 28 5a b0 20-29 52 da f8 22 74 60 1d"
uuid.action = "keep"
priority.grabbed = "normal"
priority.ungrabbed = "normal"

isolation.tools.dnd.disable = "TRUE"

suspend.Directory = "/vmfs/vmhba1:0:83:1"

autostart = "true"
autostop = "softpoweroff"

tools.syncTime = "FALSE"
```

The following parameter is the configuration of the floppy and CD-ROM for the virtual machine. Notice that I have startConnected set to "false" for these devices. As a rule of thumb, I recommend leaving these disconnected until you need them.

```
floppy0.present = "true"
floppy0.startConnected = "false"
ide1:0.present = "true"
ide1:0.fileName = "/dev/cdrom"
ide1:0.deviceType = "atapi-cdrom"
ide1:0.startConnected = "false"
```

The following example shows autostart and autostop command scripts.

```
autostart = "true" or "false"
autostop = "softpoweroff" or "poweroff"
autostart.order = ""
autostop.order = ""
```

Code Listing 5.4 Descriptor File for a Virtual Machine Using an IDE Drive

```
# Disk DescriptorFile
version=1
CID=2af6d34d
parentCID=ffffffff
createType="twoGbMaxExtentSparse"

# Extent description
RW 4192256 SPARSE "Windows-s001.vmdk"
RW 4192256 SPARSE "Windows-s002.vmdk"
RW 4096 SPARSE "Windows-s003.vmdk"

# The Disk Data Base
#DDB

ddb.adapterType = "ide"
ddb.geometry.sectors = "63"
ddb.geometry.heads = "16"
ddb.geometry.cylinders = "8322"
ddb.virtualHWVersion = "4"
ddb.toolsVersion = "6404"
```

There is one change left to be done, however. We will need to change the ddb.virtualHWVersion. The ddb.virtualHWVersion is dependent upon which VMware platform you are using. You may need to change the version number to get the virtual machine to start in certain cases, namely moving a virtual machine in to ESX Server.

Change the ddb.virtualHWVersion = "4" and make it ddb.virtualHWVersion = "3". You now have a legacy virtual machine disk file you have converted from IDE to SCSI. You've also brought the virtual machine disk file down to legacy mode so that it can run on ESX.

```
# Disk DescriptorFile
version=1
CID=826d3b6e
parentCID=ffffffff
createType="twoGbMaxExtentSparse"

# Extent description
RW 4192256 SPARSE "Windows-s001.vmdk"
RW 4192256 SPARSE "Windows-s002.vmdk"
RW 4096 SPARSE "Windows-s003.vmdk"

# The Disk Data Base
#DDB

ddb.adapterType = "buslogic"
ddb.geometry.sectors = "63"
ddb.geometry.heads = "255"
ddb.geometry.cylinders = "522"
ddb.virtualHWVersion = "3"
ddb.toolsVersion = "6309"
```

Code Listing 5.5 Configuring a Disk to Use an IDE

```
config.version = "8"
virtualHW.version = "4"
scsi0.present = "TRUE"
memsize = "200"
ide0:0.present = "TRUE"
ide0:0.fileName = "Windows.vmdk"
ide1:0.present = "TRUE"
ide1:0.fileName = "auto detect"
ide1:0.deviceType = "cdrom-raw"
floppy0.fileName = "A:"
ethernet0.present = "TRUE"
usb.present = "TRUE"
sound.present = "TRUE"
sound.virtualDev = "es1371"
displayName = "Windows XP Professional 1"
guestOS = "winxppro"
nvram = "winxppro.nvram"

ide0:0.redo = ""
ethernet0.addressType = "generated"
uuid.location = "56 4d b7 df d7 1d 42 ca-3e 81 5d a3 5e 05 7a f7"
uuid.bios = "56 4d b7 df d7 1d 42 ca-3e 81 5d a3 5e 05 7a f7"
tools.remindInstall = "FALSE"
ethernet0.generatedAddress = "00:0c:29:05:7a:f7"
ethernet0.generatedAddressOffset = "0"

ide1:0.autodetect = "TRUE"

ide1:0.startConnected = "TRUE"
tools.syncTime = "FALSE"
```

Code Listing 5.6 Disconnecting Devices in Virtual Machines Registered on an ESX Server

```
#!/bin/bash
# IDE / Floppy Disconnect Script
# Script by: Stuart Thompson and Matt Pound
# Edit by: Steve Beaver (Added floppy drive)

vmwarelist=`vmware-cmd -l`
vmwarelist=`echo $vmwarelist | sed -e 's/ /*/g'`
vmwarelist=`echo $vmwarelist | sed -e 's/.vmx/.vmx /g'`
for vm in $vmwarelist
do
    vm=`echo $vm | sed -e 's/*/ /g'`
    vm=`echo $vm | sed -e 's/ \//*/g'`

    if [ `vmware-cmd "$vm" getstate | sed -e 's/getstate() = //'` = "on" ]
    then
```

```
    echo Looking @ $vm
    IDEBUS=`seq 0 1`
    for i in $IDEBUS;
    do
        echo BUS : $i
            IDEDEVICE=`seq 0 1`
        for j in $IDEDEVICE;
        do
                PRESENT=`vmware-cmd "$vm" getconfig ide$i:$j.present | cut -f3 -d
" "`

                if [ $PRESENT = "true" ]
                then
                        TYPE=`vmware-cmd "$vm" getconfig ide$i:$j.deviceType | cut
-f3 -d " "`

                        if [[ $TYPE == "atapi-cdrom" || $TYPE == "cdrom-image" ]]
                        then
                            echo Found CDROM on IDE$i:$j
                            vmware-cmd "$vm" disconnectdevice ide$i:$j
                        fi
                fi
        done
    done
    fi
done
```

Code Listing 5.7 Starting All Registered Virtual Machines

```
#!/bin/bash
vmwarelist=`vmware-cmd -l`
vmwarelist=`echo $vmwarelist | sed -e 's/ /*/g'`
vmwarelist=`echo $vmwarelist | sed -e 's/.vmx/.vmx /g'`
for vm in $vmwarelist
do
    vm=`echo $vm | sed -e 's/*/ /g'`
    vm=`echo $vm | sed -e 's/ \//*/g'`

    if [ `vmware-cmd "$vm" getstate | sed -e 's/getstate() = //'` = "off" ]
    then
        echo Found $vm that is off, Starting $vm
        vmware-cmd "$vm" start
    fi
done
```

Now, let's take a look at a script to stop those virtual machines that are running.

```
#!/bin/bash
vmwarelist=`vmware-cmd -l`
vmwarelist=`echo $vmwarelist | sed -e 's/ /*/g'`
vmwarelist=`echo $vmwarelist | sed -e 's/.vmx/.vmx /g'`
for vm in $vmwarelist
do
```

```
    vm=`echo $vm | sed -e 's/*/ /g'`
    vm=`echo $vm | sed -e 's/ \//*/g'`

    if [ `vmware-cmd "$vm" getstate | sed -e 's/getstate() = //'` = "on" ]
    then
        echo Found $vm that is on, Stopping $vm
        vmware-cmd "$vm" stop trysoft
    fi
done
```

Code Listing 5.8 is one more example of this script, which will reboot all of the running virtual machines. This is very handy if you have installed updates or anything else and want to delay the reboot till later.

Code Listing 5.8 Script for Rebooting All Running Virtual Machines

```
#!/bin/bash
vmwarelist=`vmware-cmd -l`
vmwarelist=`echo $vmwarelist | sed -e 's/ /*/g'`
vmwarelist=`echo $vmwarelist | sed -e 's/.vmx/.vmx /g'`
for vm in $vmwarelist
do
    vm=`echo $vm | sed -e 's/*/ /g'`
    vm=`echo $vm | sed -e 's/ \//*/g'`

    if [ `vmware-cmd "$vm" getstate | sed -e 's/getstate() = //'` = "on" ]
    then
        echo Found $vm that is on, Rebooting $vm
        vmware-cmd "$vm" reset trysoft
    fi
done
```

Code Listing 5.9 Using a Golden Image Disk File to Dynamically Create a Virtual Machine

```
#!/bin/bash
#Scripting VMware Power Tools: Automating Virtual Infrastructure Administration
#Dynamic Creation of a new Virtual Machine using a Golden Image
#Stephen Beaver
#####USER MODIFICATION################
#VMNAME is the name of the new virtual machine
#VMOS specifies which Operating System the virtual machine will have
#GLDIMAGE is the path to the "Golden Image" VMDK file
#DESTVMFS is the path to VMFS partition that the VMDK file
###################################
VMOS="winNetStandard"
VMMEMSIZE="256"
GLDIMAGE="/vmfs/FHVMFS1/Windows_2003_Standard.vmdk"
DESTVMFS="vmhba0:0:0:10"
#####END MODIFICATION#####
LOG="/var/log/$1.log"
```

```
echo "Start of Logging" > $LOG
echo "Importing Golden Image Disk File VMDK" >> $LOG
vmkfstools -i $GLDIMAGE $DESTVMFS:$1.vmdk
echo "Creating VMX Configuration File" >> $LOG
mkdir /home/vmware/$1
exec 6>&1
exec 1>/home/vmware/$1/$1.vmx
# write the configuration file
echo #!/usr/bin/vmware
echo config.version = '"'6'"'
echo virtualHW.version = '"'3'"'
echo memsize = '"'$VMMEMSIZE'"'
echo floppy0.present = '"'TRUE'"'
echo usb.present = '"'FALSE'"'
echo displayName = '"'$1'"'
echo guestOS = '"'$VMOS'"'
echo suspend.Directory = '"'/vmfs/vmhba0:0:0:10/'"'
echo checkpoint.cptConfigName = '"'$1'"'
echo priority.grabbed = '"'normal'"'
echo priority.ungrabbed = '"'normal'"'
echo ide1:0.present = '"'TRUE'"'
echo ide1:0.fileName = '"'auto detect'"'
echo ide1:0.deviceType = '"'cdrom-raw'"'
echo ide1:0.startConnected = '"'FALSE'"'
echo floppy0.startConnected = '"'FALSE'"'
echo floppy0.fileName = '"'/dev/fd0'"'
echo Ethernet0.present = '"'TRUE'"'
echo Ethernet0.connectionType = '"'monitor_dev'"'
echo Ethernet0.networkName = '"'Network0'"'
echo draw = '"'gdi'"'
echo
echo scsi0.present = '"'TRUE'"'
echo scsi0:1.present = '"'TRUE'"'
echo scsi0:1.name = '"'$DESTVMFS:$1.vmdk'"'
echo scsi0:1.writeThrough = '"'TRUE'"'
echo scsi0.virtualDev = '"'vmxlsilogic'"'
echo
# close file
exec 1>&-
# make stdout a copy of FD 6 (reset stdout), and close FD6
exec 1>&6
exec 6>&-
echo "VMX Configuration File Created Successfully" >> $LOG
#Change the file permissions
chmod 755 /home/vmware/$1/$1.vmx
#Register the new VM
echo "Registering .vmx Configuration" >> $LOG
vmware-cmd -s register /home/vmware/$1/$1.vmx
echo "VMX Initialization Completed Successfully" >> $LOG
```

Code Listing 5.10 Creating a New Virtual Machine to Use with an ESX Server Managed by Altiris

```bash
#!/bin/bash
#Scripting VMware Power Tools: Automating Virtual Infrastructure Administration
#Creates a new Virtual Machine for use with Altiris
#Stephen Beaver
#####USER MODIFICATION###############
#VMNAME is the name of the new virtual machine
#VMOS specifies which Operating System the virtual machine will have
#DESTVMFS is the path to the VMFS partition of the VMDK file
#VMDSIZE is the size of the Virtual Disk File being created ex (500mb) or (10g)
####################################
VMNAME="vm_name"
VMOS="winNetStandard"
VMMEMSIZE="256"
DESTVMFS="vmhba0:6:0:1 #Must use the vmhba path
VMDSIZE="10g"
#####END MODIFICATION#####
LOG="/opt/altiris/deployment/adlagent/bin/logevent"
$LOG -l:1 -ss:"Creating VMX Configuration File"
mkdir /home/vmware/$VMNAME
exec 6>&1
exec 1>/home/vmware/$VMNAME/$VMNAME.vmx
# write the configuration file
echo #!/usr/bin/vmware
echo config.version = '"'6'"'
echo virtualHW.version = '"'3'"'
echo memsize = '"'$VMMEMSIZE'"'
echo floppy0.present = '"'TRUE'"'
echo usb.present = '"'FALSE'"'
echo displayName = '"'$VMNAME'"'
echo guestOS = '"'$VMOS'"'
echo suspend.Directory = '"'/vmfs/vmhba0:0:0:5/'"'
echo checkpoint.cptConfigName = '"'$VMNAME'"'
echo priority.grabbed = '"'normal'"'
echo priority.ungrabbed = '"'normal'"'
echo ide1:0.present = '"'TRUE'"'
echo ide1:0.fileName = '"'auto detect'"'
echo ide1:0.deviceType = '"'cdrom-raw'"'
echo ide1:0.startConnected = '"'FALSE'"'
echo floppy0.startConnected = '"'FALSE'"'
echo floppy0.fileName = '"'/dev/fd0'"'
echo Ethernet0.present = '"'TRUE'"'
echo Ethernet0.connectionType = '"'monitor_dev'"'
echo Ethernet0.networkName = '"'Network0'"'
echo draw = '"'gdi'"'
echo
echo scsi0.present = '"'TRUE'"'
echo scsi0:1.present = '"'TRUE'"'
```

```
echo scsi0:1.name = '"'vmhba0:0:0:5:$VMNAME.vmdk'"'
echo scsi0:1.writeThrough = '"'TRUE'"'
echo scsi0.virtualDev = '"'vmxlsilogic'"'
echo
# close file
exec 1>&-
# make stdout a copy of FD 6 (reset stdout), and close FD6
exec 1>&6
exec 6>&-
$LOG -l:1 -ss:"VMX Configuration File Created Successfully"
#Change the file permissions
chmod 755 /home/vmware/$VMNAME/$VMNAME.vmx
#Create the Virtual Disk
$LOG -l:1 -ss:"Creating Virtual Disk"
vmkfstools -c $VMDSIZE vmhba0:0:0:5:$VMNAME.vmdk
$LOG -l:1 -ss:"Virtual Disk Created Successfully"
#Register the new VM
$LOG -l:1 -ss:"Registering VMX Configuration"
#Registering .vmx Configuration"
vmware-cmd -s register /home/vmware/$VMNAME/$VMNAME.vmx
$LOG -l:1 -ss:"VMX Initialization Completed Successfully"
#Starting the Virtual Machine
$LOG -l:1 -ss:"Starting the Virtual Machine"
vmware-cmd /home/vmware/$VMNAME/$VMNAME.vmx start
$LOG -l:1 -ss:"Virtual Machine Started"
$LOG -l:1 -ss:"Passing control to Altiris for PXE boot and install of VM"
```

Code Listing 5.11 Creating a New Virtual Machine That Boots to an ISO

```
#!/bin/bash
#Scripting VMware Power Tools: Automating Virtual Infrastructure Administration
#Creates a new Virtual Machine booting to an ISO
#Stephen Beaver
#####USER MODIFICATION################
#VMNAME is the name of the new virtual machine
#VMOS specifies which Operating System the virtual machine will have
#GLDIMAGE is the path to the "Golden Image" VMDK file
#DESTVMFS is the path to the VMFS partition of the VMDK file
#VMDSIZE is the size of the Virtual Disk File being created ex (500mb) or (10g)
#ISOIMAGE is the path and file name of the ISO file you are using
####################################
VMOS="winNetStandard"
VMMEMSIZE="256"
GLDIMAGE="/vmfs/FHVMFS1/Windows_2003_Standard.vmdk"
DESTVMFS="vmhba0:0:0:10"
VMDSIZE="10g"
ISOIMAGE"/vmfs/ESX_SAN/Windows2000.iso"
#####END MODIFICATION#####
LOG="/var/log/$1.log"
echo "Start of Logging" > $LOG
echo "Importing Golden Image Disk File VMDK" >> $LOG
```

```
vmkfstools -i $GLDIMAGE $DESTVMFS:$1.vmdk
echo "Creating VMX Configuration File" >> $LOG
mkdir /home/vmware/$1
exec 6>&1
exec 1>/home/vmware/$1/$1.vmx
# write the configuration file
echo #!/usr/bin/vmware
echo config.version = '"'6'"'
echo virtualHW.version = '"'3'"'
echo memsize = '"'$VMMEMSIZE'"'
echo floppy0.present = '"'TRUE'"'
echo usb.present = '"'FALSE'"'
echo displayName = '"'$1'"'
echo guestOS = '"'$VMOS'"'
echo suspend.Directory = '"'/vmfs/vmhba0:0:0:10/'"'
echo checkpoint.cptConfigName = '"'$1'"'
echo priority.grabbed = '"'normal'"'
echo priority.ungrabbed = '"'normal'"'
echo ide1:0.present = '"'TRUE'"'
echo ide0:0.present = '"'TRUE'"'
echo ide0:0.fileName = '"'$ISOIMAGE'"'
echo ide0:0.deviceType = '"'cdrom-image'"'
echo floppy0.startConnected = '"'FALSE'"'
echo floppy0.fileName = '"'/dev/fd0'"'
echo Ethernet0.present = '"'TRUE'"'
echo Ethernet0.connectionType = '"'monitor_dev'"'
echo Ethernet0.networkName = '"'Network0'"'
echo draw = '"'gdi'"'
echo
echo scsi0.present = '"'TRUE'"'
echo scsi0:1.present = '"'TRUE'"'
echo scsi0:1.name = '"'$DESTVMFS:$1.vmdk'"'
echo scsi0:1.writeThrough = '"'TRUE'"'
echo scsi0.virtualDev = '"'vmxlsilogic'"'
echo
# close file
exec 1>&-
# make stdout a copy of FD 6 (reset stdout), and close FD6
exec 1>&6
exec 6>&-
#Create the Virtual Disk
echo "Creating Virtual Disk" >> $LOG
vmkfstools -c $VMDSIZE vmhba0:0:0:5:$VMNAME.vmdk
echo "Virtual Disk Created Successfully" >> $LOG
echo "VMX Configuration File Created Successfully" >> $LOG
#Change the file permissions
chmod 755 /home/vmware/$1/$1.vmx
#Register the new VM
echo "Registering .vmx Configuration" >> $LOG
vmware-cmd -s register /home/vmware/$1/$1.vmx
echo "VMX Initialization Completed Successfully" >> $LOG
```

```
#Starting the Virtual Machine
echo "Starting the Virtual Machine" >> $LOG
vmware-cmd /home/vmware/$VMNAME/$VMNAME.vmx start
echo "Virtual Machine Started" >> $LOG
```

Scripts from Chapter 6

By typing **fdisk –l**, you should get a list of all the known hard drive devices, which should look like the following example:

```
Disk /dev/sda: 41.9 GB, 41943040000 bytes
255 heads, 63 sectors/track, 5099 Cylinders
Units = cylinders of 16065 * 512 = 8225280 bytes
Device Boot    Start   End    Blocks        Id     System
/dev/sda1      *       1      5098   40949653+      7      HPFS/NTFS
```

Starting the FTP Process
Type:
cat /dev/sda | /tmp/ncftpput –u <username> -p <password> –c <remote esx host ip> <Full /vmfs
path and new file name>

For example:
cat /dev/sda | /tmp/ncftpput –u phdbot –p "p2v" –c 10.10.10.1
/vmfs/LOCAL/newdisk.vmdk.
With phdcat: **phdcat /dev/sda | /tmp/ncftpput –u phdbot –p "p2v" –c 10.10.10.1**
/vmfs/LOCAL/newdisk.vmdk

Scripts from Chapter 7

The syntax of the *vmware-cmd* command is

```
vmware-cmd <cfg> commit <disk_device_name> <level> <freeze> <wait>
```

First, we add a second REDO log right after our export is completed. The syntax to add this second REDO is exactly like the first:

```
vmware-cmd /home/vmware/vm/vm.vmx addredo scsi0:1
```

Determining the Current Mode of Your Disk File

```
#!/usr/bin/perl -w
#
# This script is an example only
# Usage: detectDiskMode.pl <vmxConfigFile> <scsiDisk>
#
# Example: detectDiskMode.pl /home/vmware/vm/vm.vmx scsi0:1

use VMware::VmPerl;
```

```perl
use VMware::VmPerl::ConnectParams;
use VMware::VmPerl::VM;
use strict;

# User variables
my ($cfg, $disk) = @ARGV;

# Connect to the virtual machine
my $params = VMware::VmPerl::ConnectParams::new();
my $vm = VMware::VmPerl::VM::new();
$vm->connect($params, $cfg);

# Retrieve the mode of the disk in question
my $mode = $vm->get_config("$disk.mode");

if ($mode ne "persistent") {
  print "Warning: $mode\n";
} else {
  print "$mode\n";
} # End if not persistent

$vm->disconnect();
```

Code Listing 7.1 Perl Script for Running a Hot Backup of a VM

```perl
#!/usr/bin/perl -w
#
# This script is an example only
# Usage: simpleBackup.pl <vmxPath>

use VMware::VmPerl;
use VMware::VmPerl::Server;
use VMware::VmPerl::ConnectParams;
use VMware::VmPerl::VM;
use strict;

# User variables
my $target="/vmimages";
my $cfg=$ARGV[0];
print "$cfg\n";

# Set up a connection to a virtual machine
my $params = VMware::VmPerl::ConnectParams::new();
my $vm = VMware::VmPerl::VM::new();
$vm->connect($params, $cfg);

# No smooth way to return the number of scsi controllers
# We will cycle through all possibilities checking if it is present
for (my $scsiController=0; $scsiController<=3; $scsiController++) {
  my $presentScsiController = $vm->get_config("scsi$scsiController.present");
```

```perl
    # If it is there, we will continue processing
  if ($presentScsiController eq "true") {

    # Again, cycle through all possible scsi IDs
    for (my $scsiID=0; $scsiID<=15; $scsiID++) {
      my $presentScsiID = $vm->get_config("scsi$scsiController:$scsiID.present");
      if ($presentScsiID eq "true") {
        # Get the path to the vmdk
        my $vmdk = $vm->get_config("scsi$scsiController:$scsiID.name");

        # $vmdk format is now vmfsvol:vmdk
        # Let's break this up into 2 variables
        my ($vmfsvol,$vmdkname) = split (':',$vmdk);
        my $vmdkPath = "/vmfs/$vmfsvol/$vmdkname";

        # Add the first redo
        $vm->add_redo("scsi$scsiController:$scsiID");

        # Do a backup
        `/usr/sbin/vmkfstools -e /$target/$vmdkname $vmdkPath`;

        # Add a second redo
        $vm->add_redo("scsi$scsiController:$scsiID");

        # Wait a second for the redo to be created
        sleep(1);

        # First commit with same options as vmware-cmd
        $vm->commit("scsi$scsiController:$scsiID", 1, 0, 1);

        # Commit final redo
        $vm->commit("scsi$scsiController:$scsiID", 0, 0, 1);
      } # End If SCSI ID is present
    } # End for SCSI ID Cycle
  } # End If SCSI Controller is present
} # End for SCSI Controller Cycle

# Cleanup
$vm->disconnect();
```

The following code can be used in your scripts to answer single option questions. You could also easily modify the script to answer more difficult questions.

```perl
#!/usr/bin/perl -w
#
# This script is an example only
# Usage: detectQuestion.pl <vmxConfigFile>
#

use VMware::VmPerl;
use VMware::VmPerl::ConnectParams;
```

```perl
use VMware::VmPerl::VM;
use VMware::VmPerl::Question;
use strict;

# User variables
my ($cfg) = @ARGV;

# Connect to the virtual machine
my $params = VMware::VmPerl::ConnectParams::new();
my $vm = VMware::VmPerl::VM::new();
$vm->connect($params, $cfg);

# Check for a question. Will return undef if
# no questions.
my $question = $vm->get_pending_question();

# If $question is defined, there is an outstanding question
if (defined $question) {
  my $text = $question->get_text();
  my @choices = $question->get_choices();
  if ($#choices == 0) {
    # There is only one choice, easy to answer it
    $vm->answer_question($question,0);
    print "Question answered: $text\n";
  } else {
    print "More than one choice.\n";
    print "Choices: @choices\n";
  } # End if only one choice
} else {
  print "No Questions\n";
} # Endif

# Cleanup
$vm->disconnect();
```

Code Listing 7.2 Perl Script for Copying VMX Files

```perl
#!/usr/bin/perl -w
#
# This script is an example only
# Usage: vmxBackup.pl

use VMware::VmPerl;
use VMware::VmPerl::Server;
use VMware::VmPerl::ConnectParams;
use VMware::VmPerl::VM;
use strict;

# User variables
my $target="/vmimages/vmxBackup";
```

```
# Setup a connection to the local ESX host
my $params = VMware::VmPerl::ConnectParams::new();
my $host = VMware::VmPerl::Server::new();
$host->connect($params);

# List of registered virtual machines
my @vmlist = $host->registered_vm_names();

foreach my $vm (@vmlist){
  # Get the displayName of the vm
  # We will use the displayName to title the backup output file
  my $vmo = VMware::VmPerl::VM::new();
  $vmo->connect($params, $vm);
  my $displayName = $vmo->get_config("displayName");

  # Finally, you may have some problems with special characters
  # I recommend removing them to prevent hassles.
  # This line will remove ( and ) and spaces.
  $displayName =~ s/[\() ]//g;

  # This will tell us what directory the vmx is in.
  my @path = split("/",$vm);
  my $dir;
  my $cnt=0;
  until ($cnt == $#path) { $dir = $dir . "$path[$cnt]/"; $cnt++; }

  # Here is the actual backup command
  my $cmd = `tar cvzpf \"$target/$displayName.tgz\" \"$dir\"`;

  # To go remote via ssh, use this command instead
  # Remember to set up ssh key auth first
  #my $cmd = `tar cvzpf - \"$dir\" | ssh user\@host \"dd
of=\"$target/$displayName.tgz\"\"`;

  # Cleanup
  $vmo->disconnect();
} # End foreach vm

# Cleanup
$host->disconnect();
```

This script will copy all registered VMX files to the location specified. It will cover all files in the directory with the VMX, such as nvram and log files. Be aware, in its current form, the files will be overwritten each time the script is run. The output is tar gzip format with the filename of the configured display name .tgz.

Scripts from Chapter 8

Add the symbolic links to allow PCNS to start up.★

```
ln -s /etc/rc.d/init.d/PowerChute /etc/rc.d/rc0.d/S99PowerChute
ln -s /etc/rc.d/init.d/PowerChute /etc/rc.d/rc1.d/S99PowerChute
ln -s /etc/rc.d/init.d/PowerChute /etc/rc.d/rc2.d/S99PowerChute
ln -s /etc/rc.d/init.d/PowerChute /etc/rc.d/rc3.d/S99PowerChute
ln -s /etc/rc.d/init.d/PowerChute /etc/rc.d/rc4.d/S99PowerChute
ln -s /etc/rc.d/init.d/PowerChute /etc/rc.d/rc5.d/S99PowerChute
cp /usr/local/bin/PowerChute/PowerChute /etc/init.d/PowerChute
```

To uninstall from ESX is a little trickier. You need to first remove the symbolic links:

```
rm /etc/rc.d/rc0.d/S99PowerChute
rm /etc/rc.d/rc1.d/S99PowerChute
rm /etc/rc.d/rc2.d/S99PowerChute
rm /etc/rc.d/rc3.d/S99PowerChute
rm /etc/rc.d/rc4.d/S99PowerChute
rm /etc/rc.d/rc5.d/S99PowerChute
rm /etc/init.d/PowerChute
```

Code Listing 8.1 /etc/ldap.conf

```
# @(#)$Id: ldap.conf,v 1.24 2001/09/20 14:12:26 lukeh Exp $
#
# This is the configuration file for the LDAP nameservice
# switch library and the LDAP PAM module.
#
# PADL Software
# http://www.padl.com
#

# Your LDAP server. Must be resolvable without using LDAP.
host domain.com

# The distinguished name of the search base.
# base dc=example,dc=com
base ou=administrators,dc=domain,dc=com

# Another way to specify your LDAP server is to provide a
# uri with the server name. This allows you to use
# Unix Domain Sockets to connect to a local LDAP Server.
#uri ldap://127.0.0.1/
#uri ldaps://127.0.0.1/
uri ldap://domain.com
#uri ldaps://domain.com
#uri ldapi://%2fvar%2frun%2fldapi_sock/
# Note: %2f encodes the '/' used as directory separator

# The LDAP version to use (defaults to 3
# if supported by client library)
ldap_version 3

# The distinguished name to bind to the server with.
```

```
# Optional: default is to bind anonymously.
binddn cn=proxyuser,dc=example,dc=com

# The credentials to bind with.
# Optional: default is no credential.
bindpw secret

# The distinguished name to bind to the server with
# if the effective user ID is root. Password is
# stored in /etc/ldap.secret (mode 600)
#rootbinddn cn=manager,dc=example,dc=com

# The port.
# Optional: default is 389.
#port 389

# The search scope.
scope sub
#scope one
#scope base

# Search timelimit
#timelimit 30

# Bind timelimit
#bind_timelimit 30

# OpenLDAP SSL mechanism
# start_tls mechanism uses the normal LDAP port, LDAPS typically 636
#ssl start_tls
#ssl on
```

Code Listing 8.2 The LDAP Search Script

```
#################
#!/bin/bash
# LDAP Search Script to add and remove users based on AD Group Membership
# Steve Beaver

######## Start User Edit Area ########
#   This first part sets up the variables for the member search
#   If there is an error doing the search, the script will move on to the next
group search
base="-b DC=domain,DC=com"
# Replace with your domain name
#user="-D CN=LDAPUSER,OU=VMWare,DC=domain,DC=com"
user="-D LDAPUSER@DOMAIN.COM"
# Notice you can use LDAP DN or you can use the AD Full Account
pass="-w password"
# The AD user password
ADgroup1="ESX_VIEW"
```

```
# The 1st AD group -- Read Only Privilege
ADgroup2="ESX_OP"
# The 2nd AD group -- VM Admin Privilege
ADgroup3="ESX_ADMIN"
# The 3rd AD group -- Root Privilege
esxgroup="ESXFlagGroup"
# The ESX group you would like the users to be a member off
programdir="/usr/LDAP"
# The directory this script will use to run
#####  End User Edit Area #####
       ##################################################
# More variables that do not need to be edited
cmd="ldapsearch -x -LLL"
pipe="-u -tt -T ${programdir}"
pipe2="-u -tt -T ${programdir}/Member"
filter1="CN=${ADgroup1} member"
filter2="CN=${ADgroup2} member"
filter3="CN=${ADgroup3} member"
filtersam="samAccountName"
###################################################

# Sanity Check to make sure all the files and folders needed are in place or
create them

if test ! -x "$programdir" ; then
       mkdir $programdir
       mkdir $programdir/Member
       mkdir $programdir/Member/New
       mkdir $programdir/Member/Old
       echo > $programdir/Member/New/$ADgroup1.txt
       echo > $programdir/Member/Old/$ADgroup1.txt
       echo > $programdir/Member/New/$ADgroup2.txt
       echo > $programdir/Member/Old/$ADgroup2.txt
       echo > $programdir/Member/New/$ADgroup3.txt
       echo > $programdir/Member/Old/$ADgroup3.txt
fi
################     NEW SEARCH        ###############
# The first search to find the group and see who, if any, are members
VIEW_search ()
{
       ${cmd} ${base} ${user} ${pass} ${pipe} ${filter1}
       if [ "$?" -ne "0" ]; then
              printf "ERROR running LDAP Search script exiting"
              return
       fi
       VIEW_search_member
}

# Now that I have a temp file for each user, I need to collect and list them in
a file to read from
```

```
# If I find no users in the group, then there's no need to continue. Return and
move on

VIEW_search_member ()
{
        cd $programdir
        ls -1 $programdir/ldapsearch-member-* > $programdir/filelist.txt
        if [ "$?" -ne "0" ]; then
                printf "No Members moving on...   "
                return
        fi
        declare LINE
        declare MEMBER
        cat $programdir/filelist.txt |
                while read abc
                        do case $abc in
                        Member) echo $abc ;;
                        *) awk '{print $0}' $abc >> $programdir/ulist.txt ;;
                        esac
                done
        sed 's/,OU=.*//g' $programdir/ulist.txt > $programdir/mlist.txt
        VIEW_search_sam
}

# Now I have a list in a usable format.
# Time to search again to get the samAccountName or userid
# of each user in the group.

VIEW_search_sam ()
{
        infile="$programdir/mlist.txt"
        cat $infile |
                while read def
                        do ${cmd} ${base} ${user} ${pass} ${pipe2} "$def"
${filtersam}
                done
        rm -R $programdir/ldapsearch*
        rm -R $programdir/filelist.txt
        rm -R $programdir/ulist.txt
        rm -R $programdir/mlist.txt
        mv -f $programdir/Member/New/$ADgroup1.txt
$programdir/Member/Old/$ADgroup1.txt
        VIEW_search_create
}

# Now that I have a temp file for each user, I need to collect and list them in
a file to read from
# Sort the list and compare the old one with the new to see if I need to add or
remove users
# The useradd command below gives the user the READ ONLY privilege
```

```
VIEW_search_create ()
{
        cd $programdir/Member
        ls -1 $programdir/Member/ldapsearch-* > $programdir/Member/filelist.txt
        cat $programdir/Member/filelist.txt |
                while read xyz
                        do awk '{print $0}' $xyz | tr [:upper:] [:lower:] >>
$programdir/Member/$ADgroup1.txt
                done
        rm -R $programdir/Member/ldapsearch*
        rm -R $programdir/Member/filelist.txt
        mv -f $programdir/Member/$ADgroup1.txt
$programdir/Member/New/$ADgroup1.txt
        sort -f -o $programdir/Member/New/$ADgroup1.txt
$programdir/Member/New/$ADgroup1.txt
                comm -1 -3 $programdir/Member/New/$ADgroup1.txt
$programdir/Member/Old/$ADgroup1.txt > $programdir/remuser.txt
                comm -2 -3 $programdir/Member/New/$ADgroup1.txt
$programdir/Member/Old/$ADgroup1.txt > $programdir/adduser.txt
        cat $programdir/remuser.txt |
                while read oldlist
                        do userdel -r $oldlist
                done
        rm -R $programdir/remuser.txt
        cat $programdir/adduser.txt |
                while read newlist
                        do useradd -M $newlist
                done
        rm -R $programdir/adduser.txt
}
###############                 NEW SEARCH                 #################

# The first search to find the group and see who if any are members
OP_search ()
{
        ${cmd} ${base} ${user} ${pass} ${pipe} ${filter2}
        if [ "$?" -ne "0" ]; then
                printf "ERROR running LDAP Search script exiting"
                return
        fi
        OP_search_member
}

# Now that I have a temp file for each user, I need to collect and list them in
a file to read from
# If I find no users in the group, then there's no need to continue. Return and
move on

OP_search_member ()
{
        cd $programdir
```

```
        ls -1 $programdir/ldapsearch-member-* > $programdir/filelist.txt
    if [ "$?" -ne "0" ]; then
            printf "No Members moving on...   "
            return
    fi
    declare LINE
    declare MEMBER
    cat $programdir/filelist.txt |
            while read abc
                    do case $abc in
                    Member) echo $abc ;;
                    *) awk '{print $0}' $abc >> $programdir/ulist.txt ;;
                    esac
            done
    sed 's/,OU=.*//g' $programdir/ulist.txt > $programdir/mlist.txt
    OP_search_sam
}


# Now I have a list in a usable format.
# Time to search again to get the samAccountName or userid
# of each user in the group.

OP_search_sam ()
{
    infile="$programdir/mlist.txt"
    cat $infile |
            while read def
                    do ${cmd} ${base} ${user} ${pass} ${pipe2} "$def"
${filtersam}
            done
    rm -R $programdir/ldapsearch*
    rm -R $programdir/filelist.txt
    rm -R $programdir/ulist.txt
    rm -R $programdir/mlist.txt
    mv -f $programdir/Member/New/$ADgroup2.txt
$programdir/Member/Old/$ADgroup2.txt
    OP_search_create
}


# Now that I have a temp file for each user, I need to collect and list them in
a file to read from
# Sort the list and compare the old with the new to see if I need to add or
remove users
# The useradd command below gives the user ESX VM Admin privilege

OP_search_create ()
{
    cd $programdir/Member
    ls -1 $programdir/Member/ldapsearch-* > $programdir/Member/filelist.txt
    cat $programdir/Member/filelist.txt |
            while read xyz
```

```
                       do awk '{print $0}' $xyz | tr [:upper:] [:lower:] >>
$programdir/Member/$ADgroup2.txt
               done
       rm -R $programdir/Member/ldapsearch*
       rm -R $programdir/Member/filelist.txt
       mv -f $programdir/Member/$ADgroup2.txt
$programdir/Member/New/$ADgroup2.txt
       sort -f -o $programdir/Member/New/$ADgroup2.txt
$programdir/Member/New/$ADgroup2.txt
               comm -1 -3 $programdir/Member/New/$ADgroup2.txt
$programdir/Member/Old/$ADgroup2.txt > $programdir/remuser.txt
               comm -2 -3 $programdir/Member/New/$ADgroup2.txt
$programdir/Member/Old/$ADgroup2.txt > $programdir/adduser.txt
       cat $programdir/remuser.txt |
               while read oldlist
                       do userdel -r $oldlist
               done
       rm -R $programdir/remuser.txt
       cat $programdir/adduser.txt |
               while read newlist
                       do useradd -M -g $esxgroup $newlist
               done
       rm -R $programdir/adduser.txt
}
###############              NEW SEARCH              #################
# The first search to find the group and see who if any are members
ADMIN_search ()
{
       ${cmd} ${base} ${user} ${pass} ${pipe} ${filter3}
       if [ "$?" -ne "0" ]; then
               printf "ERROR running LDAP Search script exiting"
               return
       fi
       ADMIN_search_member
}


# Now that I have a temp file for each user, I need to collect and list them in
a file to read from
# If I find no users in the group, then there's no need to continue. Return and
move on

ADMIN_search_member ()
{
       cd $programdir
       ls -1 $programdir/ldapsearch-member-* > $programdir/filelist.txt
       if [ "$?" -ne "0" ]; then
               printf "No Members moving on...   "
               return
       fi
       declare LINE
       declare MEMBER
```

```
            cat $programdir/filelist.txt |
                  while read abc
                        do case $abc in
                        Member) echo $abc ;;
                        *) awk '{print $0}' $abc >> $programdir/ulist.txt ;;
                        esac
                  done
            sed 's/,OU=.*//g' $programdir/ulist.txt > $programdir/mlist.txt
            ADMIN_search_sam
}


# Now I have a list in a usable format.
# Time to search again to get the samAccountName or userid
# of each user in the group.

ADMIN_search_sam ()
{
            infile="$programdir/mlist.txt"
            cat $infile |
                  while read def
                        do ${cmd} ${base} ${user} ${pass} ${pipe2} "$def"
${filtersam}
                  done
            rm -R $programdir/ldapsearch*
            rm -R $programdir/filelist.txt
            rm -R $programdir/ulist.txt
            rm -R $programdir/mlist.txt
            mv -f $programdir/Member/New/$ADgroup3.txt
$programdir/Member/Old/$ADgroup3.txt
            ADMIN_search_create
}


# Now that I have a temp file for each user, I need to collect and list them in
a file to read from
# Sort the list and compare the old with the new to see if I need to add or
remove users
# The useradd command below gives the user root privilege

ADMIN_search_create ()
{
            cd $programdir/Member
            ls -1 $programdir/Member/ldapsearch-* > $programdir/Member/filelist.txt
            cat $programdir/Member/filelist.txt |
                  while read xyz
                        do awk '{print $0}' $xyz | tr [:upper:] [:lower:] >>
$programdir/Member/$ADgroup3.txt
                  done
            rm -R $programdir/Member/ldapsearch*
            rm -R $programdir/Member/filelist.txt
            mv -f $programdir/Member/$ADgroup3.txt
$programdir/Member/New/$ADgroup3.txt
```

```
            sort -f -o $programdir/Member/New/$ADgroup3.txt
$programdir/Member/New/$ADgroup3.txt
            comm -1 -3 $programdir/Member/New/$ADgroup3.txt
$programdir/Member/Old/$ADgroup3.txt > $programdir/remuser.txt
            comm -2 -3 $programdir/Member/New/$ADgroup3.txt
$programdir/Member/Old/$ADgroup3.txt > $programdir/adduser.txt
        cat $programdir/remuser.txt |
            while read oldlist
                    do userdel -r $oldlist
            done
        rm -R $programdir/remuser.txt
        cat $programdir/adduser.txt |
            while read newlist
                    do useradd -o -u 0 -g $esxgroup $newlist
            done
        rm -R $programdir/adduser.txt
}


######### This section is the main body which calls all the functions listed
above
VIEW_search
OP_search
ADMIN_search
exit
# Done
```

When the files have been decoded, you will need to edit gensysprepinf.vbs to include the ExtendOEMPartition setting.

Look for the [Unattended] section:

```
outStr = "[Unattended]" & vbCrLf _
        & "   OemSkipEula=Yes" & vbCrLf _
        & "   InstallFilesPath=\sysprep\i386" & vbCrLf _
        & vbCrLf _
        & "[GuiUnattended]" & vbCrLf _
        & "   AdminPassword=" & mAdminPassword & vbCrLf _
        & "   OEMSkipRegional=1" & vbCrLf _
        & "   TimeZone=" & mTimeZone & vbCrLf _
        & "   OemSkipWelcome=1" & vbCrLf
```

And change it to:

```
outStr = "[Unattended]" & vbCrLf _
        & "   OemSkipEula=Yes" & vbCrLf _
        & "   ExtendOemPartition=1" & vbCrLf _
        & "   InstallFilesPath=\sysprep\i386" & vbCrLf _
        & vbCrLf _
        & "[GuiUnattended]" & vbCrLf _
        & "   AdminPassword=" & mAdminPassword & vbCrLf _
        & "   OEMSkipRegional=1" & vbCrLf _
        & "   TimeZone=" & mTimeZone & vbCrLf _
        & "   OemSkipWelcome=1" & vbCrLf
```

Index

W

X